Malaysian Business in the New Era

We dedicate this book to Professor Ishak Shari,
whose contributions to the study of Malaysia's socio-economic
development and whose concern for the viewpoints of all ethnic
groups and all strata of society will be sorely missed.

Malaysian Business in the New Era

Edited by

Chris Nyland

Professor of Management, Monash University, Australia

Wendy Smith

Director, Centre of Malaysian Studies, Monash Asia Institute, Monash University, Australia

Russell Smyth

Senior Lecturer, Department of Economics, Monash University, Australia

Antonia Marika Vicziany

Director, National Centre for South Asian Studies; Convenor, Asian Economies Research Unit, Department of Economics/ Monash Asia Institute, Monash University, Australia

Edward Elgar
Cheltenham, UK • Northampton, MA, USA

Published by
Edward Elgar Publishing Limited
Glensanda House
Montpellier Parade
Cheltenham
Glos GL50 1UA
UK

Edward Elgar Publishing, Inc.
136 West Street
Suite 202
Northampton
Massachusetts 01060
USA

A catalogue record for this book
is available from the British Library

ISBN 978 1 84064 624 5 (Hardback)
ISBN 978 1 84376 255 3 (Paperback)

Printed and bound by CPI Group (UK) Ltd, Croydon, CR0 4YY

Contents

Figures

Tables

Contributors

Adlina Ahmad is a Lecturer in the Department of Management, Monash University, Malaysia

S. Gulay Avsar is a Research Fellow in the Department of Economics, Monash University, Australia

Ahmad Zubaidi Baharumshah is a Professor in the Department of Economics, Universiti Putra Malaysia

Mita Bhattacharya is a Lecturer in the Department of Economics, Monash University, Australia

Ergun Dogan is a Lecturer in the Department of Economics, Monash University, Malaysia

David W. Edgington is an Associate Professor in the Department of Geography, University of British Columbia, Canada

Ron Edwards is an Associate Professor in the Department of Management, Monash University, Australia

Barry A. Goss is a Reader in the Department of Economics, Monash University, Australia

Muzafar Shah Habibullah is an Associate Professor in the Department of Economics, Universiti Putra Malaysia

Lim Hong Hai is an Associate Professor in the School of Social Sciences, Universiti Sains Malaysia

Ali Haidar is a Lecturer in the Department of Management, Monash University, Australia

Sam H. Ham is a Professor in the Department of Resource Recreation and Tourism, College of Forestry, Wildlife and Range Sciences, University of Idaho, USA and an Adjunct Professor in the Department of Management, Monash University

Roger Hayter is a Professor in the Department of Geography, Simon Fraser University, Canada

Owen Hughes is a Professor in the Department of Management, Monash University, Australia

Azali Mohamed is a Lecturer in the Department of Economics, Universiti Putra Malaysia

Simon Moss is a Lecturer in the Department of Psychology, Monash University, Australia

Tan Sri Ramon Navaratnam is Corporate Advisor to the Sungei Way group of companies, Executive Director of Sunway College and a Director of the Asian Strategy & Leadership Institute

Chris Nyland is a Professor in the Department of Management, Monash University, Australia

Len Pullin is a Senior Lecturer in the Department of Management, Monash University, Australia

P. Ramasamy is a Professor in the Faculty of Political Science, Universiti Kebangsaan Malaysia

Rajah Rasiah is a Professor in the Faculty of Economics and Business, Universiti Malaysia Sarawak and Professor of Industrial Organisation, Universiti Kebangsaan Malaysia

Stanley Richardson is an Associate Professor in the Faculty of Management, Multimedia University, Malaysia

A. B. Shamsul is the Director of the Institute of Malay World and Civilisation (ATMA) and a Professor of Social Anthropology at Universiti Kebangsaan Malaysia

The late **Ishak Shari**, formerly the Director of the Institute of Malaysian and International Studies (IKMAS) and Professor of Development Studies at Universiti Kebangsaan Malaysia

Wendy A. Smith is the Director of the Centre of Malaysian Studies and a Senior Lecturer in the Department of Management, Monash University, Australia

Russell Smyth is a Senior Lecturer in the Department of Economics, Monash University, Australia

Tim Thornton is a Project Officer in the Department of Economics, Monash University, Australia

Marika Vicziany is the Director of the Monash Asia Institute and an Associate Professor in the Department of Economics, Monash University, Australia

Khong Kok Wei is a Lecturer at Sunway College, Malaysia and a Ph.D student in the Faculty of Management, Multimedia University, Malaysia

Betty Weiler is an Associate Professor in the Department of Management, Monash University, Australia

Ian Wills is an Associate Professor in the Department of Economics, Monash University, Australia

Peter Wilson is an Associate Professor in the Department of Economics, National University of Singapore

Koi Nyen Wong is a Lecturer in the Department of Economics, Monash University, Malaysia

Preface

This book has developed from an international symposium on 'Malaysian Business in the New Era', which was held at Monash University's Malaysia campus in Kuala Lumpur in February 2000. The symposium was an initiative of Monash University's Faculty of Business and Economics, and in particular of the Asian Economies Research Unit, in the Department of Economics, and the International Business Research Unit, in the Department of Management, supported by the cross-university Centre for Malaysian Studies in the Monash Asia Institute.

The symposium brought together Australian and Malaysian scholars to analyse the emerging trends in the Malaysian business environment. The title of the symposium, and of this book, was chosen to focus attention on how the Malaysian business environment today differs from that of the New Economic Policy era of 1971 to 1990 and its successor, the New Development Policy of the 1990s. The impact of the 1997–99 Asian financial crisis was naturally of special and topical concern. The chapters gathered in this volume reflect the different perspectives taken by various authors but all of them deal with some aspect of the shifting nature of Malaysia's economic, business and socio-cultural situation.

The International Symposium started with a Public Policy Forum launched by the Malaysian Minister of Foreign Affairs, The Honourable Dato' Seri Syed Hamid bin Syed Jaafar Albar and the Australian High Commissioner, His Excellency Mr Peter Varghese. Representatives from many prominent Australian and Malaysian companies attended this one-day event and provided additional insights into the Malaysian business environment. One of the highlights of this Forum was a keynote address by Mr Stephen Hess, Vice President and Senior Analyst from Moody's Investors Service in New York. The Public Policy Forum was organised by Monash University in partnership with the Asian Strategy and Leadership Institute (ASLI) in Kuala Lumpur, a prominent think tank in Southeast Asia. The expertise of ASLI, together with the contributions of our colleagues from Malaysian companies and universities provided the contributors to the present volume with an important opportunity to review their data and test their arguments.

The program then turned to two days of academic seminars in which an unprecedented collection of expertise was available for presentation and discussion. Forty-two academic papers were presented by academic staff from the Malaysian and Melbourne campuses of Monash University's Faculty of Business and Economics, and by academic staff from seven other Malaysian universities: Universiti Kebangsaan Malaysia; Universiti Sarawak Malaysia; Universiti Multimedia; Universiti Putra Malaysia; Universiti Sains Malaysia; Universiti Utara Malaysia and the International Islamic University Malaysia. This volume publishes a selection of the best academic papers from the Kuala Lumpur symposium, which have been chosen to reflect the wide range of topical and significant themes that were presented and discussed. I am especially happy to introduce this volume because it brings to a wider audience a path-breaking achievement in collaboration between Malaysian and Australian scholars. The analysis of the dynamics surrounding modern Malaysian Business is very important for our region, and I am delighted that the Faculty of Business and Economics at Monash has had the privilege of bringing together so many noted scholars in pool their analysis and research.

Professor Gill Palmer
Dean, Faculty of Business and Economics, Monash University

1

Economic and social adjustment in Malaysia in the 'new' business era

Chris Nyland, Wendy Smith, Russell Smyth and Marika Vicziany

Introduction

This volume contains new research on a wide range of aspects of Malaysian business in the era that began with the Asian financial crisis of 1997–99. With due recognition of the period that preceded the crisis, the contributions are informed by a wish to identify what Malaysia needs to do to sustain economic growth, remain internationally competitive and further social stability in the post-crisis period. The papers recognise that while the Malaysian business environment requires further reform, especially in the areas of corporate restructuring, financial regulation and social protection, in the period of the crisis, the economic and social fundamentals of the society proved sound by contrast with a number of other states in the region. Malaysia was not compelled to seek the intervention of multilateral financial institutions and was able to sustain a high level of social stability through the crisis period. The government's bold initiatives of fixing the exchange rate of the ringgit and suspending the convertibility of the currency were initially greeted with cries of disbelief and denunciation. However, this soon gave way to congratulations with authorities such as Krugman (1999) and Eichengreen (1998) applauding Malaysia's confident response. With the passing of the crisis the IMF has acknowledged that its criticisms of Malaysia were excessive and that its own interventions not merely backfired but caused 'a bank panic that helped set off financial market declines in much of Asia' (Sanger 1998).

Malaysia's unconventional response to the crisis suggests that the community has developed a new level of confidence in its ability to adopt and sustain innovative policies even when these strategies challenge the international financial community. This confidence continues to be resented by international financiers and on occasion elicits strong criticism, as for example occurred when in February 2000 the government ordered the nation's 54 financial institutions to merge into just ten. Nevertheless, the sharpness of the recovery from the crisis has been perceived as evidence that Malaysian business has indeed entered a new era characterised by a high level of confidence in the nation's capacity to weather the external periodic shocks that are a feature of the current wave of globalisation. Whether this self-assurance is justified in the longer term will be tested when Malaysia is compelled to confront a major decline in its international export markets brought on by an OECD-wide recession.

At the conference that generated the papers in this collection, it was argued by Stephen Hess, Vice President and Senior Analyst of Moody's Investor Service in New York, that Malaysia has grounds for optimism regarding the long term. Hess noted that while Malaysia was caught up in the general panic that characterised the Asian financial crisis, the 'withdrawal of funds was not based on Malaysian fundamentals', which were sound (Hess 2000, p. 1). He also observed that Malaysia's fate was undeserved and was caused largely by the herd mentality of international financiers. Since the early 1980s, Moody's has regarded Malaysia as a country that belongs to the 'investment grade' of its international ratings. Whilst the ratings level was downgraded during the Asian financial crisis, Malaysia remained inside the 'investment grade' classification. Moreover, the government's intervention and handling of the crisis was, according to Moody's, exemplary in its firmness and competence and this itself reflected the underlying strengths of the Malaysian economy and its economic managers.

The effective approach, which Malaysia adopted in adjusting its macroeconomic policies, was matched by the manner in which it managed the distribution of the social costs of the crisis. While it is true not all suffered to an equal degree, the government, business and civil society together did manage to ensure that the costs were not borne primarily by the poor and dispossessed, as occurred in some neighbouring states with great consequent social costs. The importance of this factor in stabilising the business environment and establishing a sound foundation for future growth cannot be overemphasised when discussing whether Malaysia has entered a new era. Though it is clear that the social tensions of a multi-ethnic society remain a matter of deep concern, it is the case that Malaysia was able to weather the crisis without overt inter-ethnic conflict as, for example, occurred in Indonesia. The incidence of inter-ethnic hostility that occurred in March 2001 was quickly contained and appears to be a surface manifestation of unresolved issues arising from decades of industrial development, rapid urbanisation and the restructuring of the economy and the labour market, rather than being a response to the financial crisis.

That Malaysia successfully managed both the macroeconomic and social dimensions of the crisis bodes well for the nation's ability to move forward in the post-crisis era. In recent years much of the globalisation literature has focussed on the factors that determine the ability of nations to weather global shocks. The critical factor determining success appears to be whether the nation can combine rapid and decisive macroeconomic adjustments in the areas of fiscal, monetary and exchange rate policy, with the successful management of any social conflict that is triggered by the economic turbulence.

An outcome of particular importance that has been generated by the global shock debate is awareness of the fact that success at weathering such crises is very much dependent on the extent to which social tensions can be effectively managed. Dani Rodrik has asked why is it that of the 50 nations that had growth of 3 per cent or more through the period 1960–75, only nine were able to sustain this performance after 1975. His conclusion is that the primary factor determining whether or not nations were able to join the latter august group was the success they achieved in managing the social turbulence generated by the oil price rise of the mid- and late 1970s. Nations that were unable to handle this turbulence effectively found themselves greatly 'troubled' when compelled to adopt the monetary and fiscal policies required to ensure external balances, and it is notable that none of these 'troubled' states subsequently remained within the high growth league. Indeed, empirical evidence indicates that it was the conflict management factor that was of overwhelming significance in determining subsequent success. By comparison, government consumption, openness to trade, and the debt–export ratio were not statistically significant in determining which nations were able to weather the crisis and sustain their previous rapid advance into the post-1975 period.

Rodrik's historical evidence and Malaysia's proven success with managing both the social and macroeconomic variables that shape the business environment, and business relations within this environment, during the Asian financial crisis indicate the direction the nation needs to take in the post-crisis era. In short, it is imperative that Malaysia continues to reform macroeconomic, microeconomic and social instruments that can assist development while remaining acutely aware that the world market is both an opportunity for profit and growth and a source of upheaval and disruption. What this means is that economic, industrial and social instruments in the new era must be capable of stimulating business growth and be able to provide the economy and the wider society with the resilience needed to bear future periods of shock. At the time of writing, share markets around the world are in decline and we wait to see whether this decline will result in global recession. However, whether or not this happens on this occasion is beside the point. Sooner or later there will be a serious recession in the OECD world. Consequently, the new era must be a time of building and of preparation for when these export markets go into decline, of opening up to the world and of undertaking the institutional reforms needed to complement openness. In the case of the latter we endorse Rodrik's advice that institutional reform must involve (a) improving the credibility of the state apparatus and in particular the quality of the judiciary and public bureaucracy; (b) improving mechanisms of voice particularly in relation to non-elites; and (c) improving social safety nets and social insurance so that individuals are not left unprotected from the worst effects of global shock. It is with recognition both of the need for Malaysia to continue building sound business enterprises, and a business environment capable of ensuring sustained high growth and social protection, that the following papers have been prepared.

Contributions

The papers are arranged thematically. The first section contains papers that consider Malaysia's international competitiveness and discuss issues related to the nature of foreign enterprises conducting business in Malaysia. This is followed by a number of papers that explore the strategies of foreign firms operating in the manufacturing sector, the autonomy of operations of multinationals and the impact of concentration on profitability. The focus then moves to the specific managerial practices embraced by Malaysian firms and to questions of training.

Following this there are a number of papers that discuss some of the socio-political and financial issues that will shape economic development and the business environment in the new era. The papers in this section explore the value orientations of public servants, the effects of globalisation on Malaysian labour, the significance of Islamic work ethics for employment relations, the social costs of the crisis, and the functioning of the currency and financial institutions. The final paper discusses the complex interplay of Asian cultural values, political processes and economic development in the light of recent developments in Malaysian political representation.

Chapter two, by Wilson, uses shift–share analysis to compare the export growth performance of Malaysia with that of six other dynamic East Asian economies in the lead-up to the Asian financial crisis. As the author points out, this period was one of rapid domestic economic and trade liberalisation in many East Asian economies including Malaysia. Wilson's results show that throughout the second half of the 1980s, and the first half of the 1990s, Malaysia's relative export performance was quite good, particularly in traditional industries such as apparel and clothing. However, Wilson warns that if Malaysia is to continue to compete effectively, there is scope for further policy improvement in exports of organic chemicals in general and exports of electrical machinery to Japan and the European Union.

Chapter three, by Vicziany, Navaratnam, Wong and Thornton, presents the results of a survey of Australian companies regarding their attitudes to Malaysian business and the Malaysian economy in general. The results of the survey must be seen in light of the fact that it was conducted over the period November 1999 to March 2000 and that most of the responses were received before the signs of economic recovery were clearly visible. A main finding is that, although Australian companies see Malaysia as one of the more difficult markets in Asia, they also see it as one of the most profitable. The chapter provides a number of insights that both complement and challenge the findings of more detailed micro-studies in other parts of the book. It is argued, for example, that cultural constraints are not major impediments for Australian firms in Malaysia.

By contrast chapter four, by Dogan, Smyth and Wills, argues that at least for small and medium-sized ethnic Chinese firms, written contracts play a secondary role to informal understandings and that this is an important source of misunderstanding for Australian firms. The chapter is based on case studies of eight, predominantly small and medium-sized, Australian and Malaysian firms. It examines the transaction costs (or business costs) that Australian firms incur exporting to and investing in Malaysia. One of the study's main findings is that cultural differences are a significant cause of additional costs.

Edgington and Hayter in chapter five analyse 18 Japanese electronics firms in Malaysia to assess whether the crisis had any impact on the production and marketing strategies of these firms. Based on in-depth interviews conducted in May 1999, they conclude that Japanese firms were not adversely affected by the crisis. Indeed, they ascribe a greater impact to the decision to fully implement AFTA (the ASEAN Free Trade Area) in 2003. On balance, their research shows that Japanese managers were optimistic and viewed Malaysia as relatively well-positioned to facilitate a further increase in production by Japanese multinationals. The Malaysian government needs to respond to this optimism by upgrading the technical capacity of Malaysian companies that produce components for the Japanese and other multinationals.

Chapter six, by Rasiah, on the electrical industrial machinery industry, highlights the policy and size implications for this key player as a prime industrial export earner for Malaysia since the late 1980s. The author links the success of this industry to market friendly strategies in Malaysia's development policy of the New Economic Policy (NEP) era, which attracted a large volume of MNC investment. However, he points out a bias in government policy towards large and medium firms to the disadvantage of small and micro firms, most of which are owned by Malaysian Chinese and hence fell outside the *bumiputera* affirmative action agenda of the NEP. Despite this, his survey data indicates good performance by the small and micro categories. Growth trends in the industry relative to firm size are also examined.

Edwards, Adlina and Moss in chapter seven focus on the role of MNC subsidiary autonomy in promoting and sustaining the growth effects of foreign investment, a key element in Malaysia's NEP, which relied heavily on DFI for capital and technology transfers to transform itself from a commodity-based to a manufacturing-based economy. The chapter details results from a survey of MNCs in Malaysia and concludes that corporations that share corporate know-how, particularly in management and marketing expertise, and that give administrative authority to their subsidiaries, offer Malaysia more opportunities to benefit. It further concludes that the structure and strategy of the parents' international activities does influence subsidiary autonomy, albeit in limited areas such as marketing and product strategy in some cases.

Chapter eight, by Bhattacharya and Wong, examines the dynamics of profit in Malaysian manufacturing. Similar previous studies have found that profits persist above the long-run equilibrium level due to the monopoly power exercised by large firms, while others find little or no evidence to suggest the profit-concentration relationship is a long-run phenomenon. In their study, Bhattacharya and Wong found no evidence to support the view that the biggest firms are generating supra-normal long-run profits. Instead, their findings suggest that capital-intensive technology, labour productivity and foreign subsidiaries are the most important factors determining profits in Malaysia.

In chapter nine Richardson and Khong report the results of an empirical examination of the management techniques favoured by Malaysian business in the Klang Valley. More specifically they ask whether Business Process Re-engineering (BPR) is perceived as an effective tool of change management. The most popular management tools sequentially were found to be Management by Objectives, Total Quality Management, and Strategic Planning Tools, with BPR coming fourth. In answer to the question 'What techniques should be used which are not?' ISO 9000 was most highly rated, followed by BPR.

Weiler and Ham in chapter ten highlight the importance of ecotourism as a growth area in the Malaysian economy, due to Malaysia's heritage as a species-rich, tropical environment. This nature-based tourism relies on well-trained interpretive guides who can convey the ideals of environmental conservation and ecologically sustainable development to tourists. The chapter reports on an ongoing research project that monitors the development, delivery and outcomes of training programs for interpretive guides in developed, and developing tropical countries such as Malaysia.

Chapter 11, by Haidar, Pullin, Lim and Hughes, discusses the potential impact of public service moral values on Malaysia's economic growth and international competitiveness and argues that this enquiry is especially significant because government development plans have been the main engines of Malaysian economic growth since independence. Thus the value system of public servants is a crucial factor in achieving national economic and social goals. Conclusions are drawn from a study of municipal council officers in Penang, a key area of industrialisation and economic growth in the NEP era. The research indicates that the tradition of neutrality among Malaysian civil servants is giving way to a 'service' ethic in which officers see themselves as primarily serving the public interest, and, to a lesser extent, a 'responsive' ethic under which they show primary loyalty to the wishes of their superiors. This has occurred since the selection of councillors changed from a system of election to one of appointment.

Chapter 12, by Ramasamy, argues that economic growth and reform in Malaysia over the last decade have failed to accord adequate voice to the working class and that globalisation has subordinated the interests of women, migrants and plantation and manufacturing labour to the needs of capital and the state. Given this situation, labour has had to find alternative means of challenging the pro-business bias the author holds is manifest within state institutions. Echoing Rodrik, Ramasamy's fundamental point is that economic growth without redistribution does not serve the overall development process and that gaps between the classes need to be reduced.

Chapter 13, by Smith, Nyland and Adlina, examines the realities of Islamic identity for Malaysian workers and managers who participate in the Japanese management system of a Japanese–Malaysian joint venture. Based on anthropological fieldwork data, it compares Islamic and Japanese work ethics, details their commonality and shows how Malaysian state policy has managed to achieve DFI-led economic development while guaranteeing that the Islamic identity and lifestyles of its Muslim labour force would not be compromised within foreign-managed ventures. As such, it provides a case study of how the economic objective of growth has been reconciled with social concerns.

In chapter 14, Ishak draws some lessons from the crisis for the management of social policy in Malaysia. He notes that there were concerns that the crisis would lead to higher unemployment, increased poverty and might trigger racial conflicts and political instability, thereby making the country less attractive to foreign investors. While conceding that these fears proved misplaced, he suggests the crisis experience now requires the country to determine how it was that racial harmony was maintained. He also queries whether the social costs inflicted on the nation by the crisis are likely to have long-term political costs and concludes that the arrest of Anwar Ibrahim and his treatment by the judiciary are likely to have long-term economic costs.

Zubaidi, Azali and Habibullah in chapter 15 provide an econometric analysis of movements in the Malaysian ringgit. They argue that long-term trends are illuminating because they are potentially helpful to investors comparing expected returns on medium or long-term nominal bonds in different currencies. The chapter reviews the history of the ringgit, the different management strategies of the Malaysian government and Bank Negara Malaysia. As Malaysia is a small but open economy, which has witnessed considerable industrial growth during recent decades, this chapter makes a useful contribution to the much neglected question of Malaysian currency.

Chapter 16, by Avsar and Goss, investigates the phenomenon of increasing returns to liquidity in the Kuala Lumpur Options and Financial Futures Exchange using data from 1995 to 1999. They examine three distinct periods—which they term the 'launch' period, the 'mature' period and the 'crisis' period—and find no clear support for the hypothesis of increasing returns in the launch and crisis periods. However, there was strong support for the increasing returns hypothesis in the mature period. Avsar and Goss suggest the costs of liquidity were initially high because of high set-up costs, while liquidity costs were high in the crisis period because of uncertainty associated with the currency crisis. In the mature period, contract turnover exhibited strong growth and the costs of liquidity declined as the market expanded. The results for the mature period are consistent, with a tendency towards concentration in world futures markets and this is indicative of the growing maturity as well as the increasing globalisation of Malaysian business.

Chapter 17, by A. B. Shamsul, explores how the 'Asian values' concept has shaped Malaysians' cultural politics and consequently their response to the crisis. He argues that Malaysian business is not only about commercial activities but also about the business of politics and culture. Further, he suggests that the most successful business ventures in Malaysia are predicated upon making sense of the Malaysian Asian values paradigm and internal non-business dynamics. Having critiqued the authoritarian manner by which the notion of Asian values has often been utilised, Shamsul explores its significance in relation to the 'new politics' now manifest in Malaysia, wherein personality and politics are fused and developed into multiple trajectories but are concomitantly united in their opposition to the existing dominating state.

With the notable exception of Indonesia, the nations of East Asia appeared by 2001 to have successfully weathered the financial crisis of 1997–99. On April 2001, however, Thailand's central bank took a measure that it had avoided for three years, announcing it was propping up the baht to 'ease volatility' after the currency slipped below Bt45 to the US dollar. On the following day, in Kuala Lumpur, finance ministers from the Association of South-East Asian nations, China, South Korea and Japan met and expressed concern at the fact that Japan's currency was at its weakest point since January 1998, as were the Korean won and the baht, while the currencies of Singapore, the Philippines and Vietnam were approaching historic lows. This development was of particular concern to the finance ministers because they were acutely aware that recovery from the 1997–99 crisis had been rapid largely because the devaluation of their currencies had enhanced their competitiveness in the then booming United States economy and because they borrowed heavily in international markets to sustain their banks. By April 2001, however, the world economy was slowing and this was a development that begged the question of how Asia was to service its international debts if it could not sustain its export markets. Should the world economy continue to slow, surmounting this problem will be a major challenge to Malaysia. In meeting the associated difficulties it will need to confront the long-term economic and political problems generated by the crisis with all the resilience and innovation displayed during 1997–99. The papers in this volume suggest that Malaysia has the capacity to meet this challenge.

Bibliography

Beeson, Mark (2000), 'Mahathir and the markets: globalisation and the pursuit of economic autonomy in Malaysia', *Pacific Affairs*, 73 (3), Fall, 335–351.

DFAT (Department of Foreign Affairs and Trade) (1998), *Trade: Outcomes and Objectives Statement*, March, Commonwealth Government of Australia, Canberra.

Hess, Stephen (Vice President and Senior Analyst) (2000), Keynote speech *International Symposium on Malaysian Business in the New Era*, February, Kuala Lumpur.

Eichengreen, Barry (1998), 'Capital Controls: Capital Idea or Capital Folly', November, in Nouriel Roubini's Asian Crisis homepage: http://www.stern.nyu. edu/globalmacro/ Accessed 24 March 2001.

Krugman, Paul (1999), 'Capital Control Freaks: How Malaysia got away with economic heresy', 27 September in Nouriel Roubini's Asian Crisis homepage: http://www.stern.nyu.edu/globalmacro/ Accessed 24 March 2001.

Rodrik, Dani (1998), 'Globalisation, social conflict and economic growth', *The World Economy*, 21 (2), 143–158.

Sanger, David E. (1998), 'IMF Reports Plan Backfired, Worsening Indonesia Woes', *New York Times*, 14 January, in Nouriel Roubini's Asian Crisis homepage: http://www.stern.nyu.edu/globalmacro/ Accessed 24 March 2001.

Wessel, David and Bob Davis (1998), 'Currency Controls are Getting a Hearing Amid Asian Crisis', Staff Reports, *The Wall Street Journal*, 4 September, in Nouriel Roubini's Asian Crisis homepage: http://www.stern.nyu.edu/ globalmacro/ Accessed 24 March 2000.

2

Malaysian export competitiveness compared with the dynamic Asian economies: past performance and prospects for the next millennium

Peter Wilson

Introduction

This chapter looks at the export growth performance of Malaysia relative to a group of dynamic Asian economies (DAEs), consisting of Singapore, Thailand, Malaysia, Korea, Taiwan and Hong Kong, and assesses her prospects for maintaining export competitiveness in the new millennium. We employ a simple empirical technique to compare Malaysia's export performance in selected categories of manufactured goods relative to her key competitors in the markets of the USA, Japan and the European Union (EU) between 1983 and 1995. Our findings suggest that whilst Malaysia's performance between 1983 and 1995 was impressive compared with that of the other DAEs across both the product groups and markets considered here, there is some scope for policy action to improve her performance in the categories of office and data processing machines and in organic chemicals if she is to remain competitive in the new millennium.

We begin with some background on the competitiveness debate relating to the DAEs, followed by our empirical analysis. The chapter ends with some concluding remarks.

The dynamic Asian economies

Although there are a number of ways of grouping the more successful economies of East and South-East Asia in a rapidly changing world economy, the aggregation of the two most dynamic members of the Association of South-East Asian Nations (ASEAN)—Malaysia and Thailand—together with the established four (little) tigers or four dragons, or gang of four, is justified on the grounds that they have become increasingly competitive as a group, especially with respect to the markets of the EU, Japan and the USA.

Some of the economic characteristics of Malaysia and the DAEs are summarised in Table 2.1. All have undergone a period of rapid economic growth and structural change between 1983 and 1995 with Singapore, Taiwan, Korea and Thailand experiencing real GDP growth in excess of 7 per cent per annum on average over the period, while Malaysia and Hong Kong have very respectable figures of 6.9 per cent and 6.2 per cent. The share of manufacturing output in GDP in 1995, as an indicator of the extent of industrialisation achieved by the end of the period, ranges from 26 per cent for Singapore to 33 per cent in the case of Malaysia. The low figure for Hong Kong reflects the relocation of much of her manufacturing base across the border into China from the mid-1980s onwards as she *de facto* reintegrated economically with the mainland in advance of *de jure* reunification in 1997. In terms of income per capita, Singapore, Korea, Hong Kong and Taiwan would now be regarded as high-income economies while Malaysia and Thailand are designated middle income.

From the trade perspective, the DAEs became increasingly exposed to international trade and capital flows from the early 1980s, as measured in Table 2.1 by the trade to GDP ratio, and cumulative flows of foreign direct investment (FDI). Hong Kong and Singapore are especially open according to these measures, but note that the very high trade to GDP figure for Singapore somewhat exaggerates the contribution of trade to GDP, as the total export series includes a substantial quantity of *entrepot* re-exports and intermediate imports. Some economists have calculated a smaller value-added or net export series using the input–output tables to subtract the total direct and indirect import content of total exports of goods and services (see Peebles and Wilson 1996, p. 162). FDI has also played a major role in export-led growth in Singapore, whilst Taiwan, Korea and Hong Kong became increasingly important as suppliers of FDI to the region, including China. In the past Malaysia and Thailand have been relatively less outward-looking, preferring to exploit their large domestic markets through import substitution, but they too have substantially liberalised their foreign trade regimes since the mid-1980s and extended a more open arms approach to FDI.

During the 1980s and 1990s the DAEs also became more interdependent in trade and capital flows as a group and increasingly competed in similar goods and markets. There was a significant increase in the intensity of international trade, as measured by merchandise export flows, between the East Asian and South-East Asian developing countries of Indonesia, Malaysia, Thailand, Philippines, China, Singapore, Korea, Taiwan and Hong Kong by 1988, according to Hill and Phillips (1993). Moreover, by 1990 a substantial amount of the bilateral trade between these countries and the USA, Japan and the EU consisted of intra-industry trade as opposed to inter-industry trade, reflecting the increased sophistication of their manufacturing export structures (Chow et al. 1994).

Not surprisingly, the USA, Japan, and EU are important markets over this period,[1] both for Malaysia and the DAEs individually and also for the DAEs as a bloc.

Table 2.1: Economic indicators for Malaysia and the dynamic Asian economies 1983–95

	1983	1990	1995	1983–95
Malaysia:				
(1) GNP per capita (US$)	1,882	2,308	3,439	
(2) Manufacturing/GDP (%)	19	27	33	
(3) Trade to GDP (%)	91	137	174	
(4) Cumulative FDI (US$m)				9,997
(5) Real GDP growth (%)				6.9
Thailand:				
(1) GNP per capita (US$m)	799	1,526	2,729	
(2) Manufacturing/GDP (%)	22	27	29	
(3) Trade to GDP (%)	42	65	76	
(4) Cumulative FDI (US$m)				3,466
(5) Real GDP growth (%)				8.5
Singapore:				
(1) GNP per capita (US$m)	7,132	14,412	28,703	
(2) Manufacturing/GDP (%)	24	29	26	
(3) Trade to GDP (%)	288	303	284	
(4) Cumulative FDI (US$m)				32,105
(5) Real GDP growth (%)				7.4
Korea:	1,944	5,887	10,044	
(1) GNP per capita (US$m)	30	29	27	
(2) Manufacturing/GDP (%)	79	54	42	
(3) Trade to GDP (%)				−1,548
(4) Cumulative FDI (US$m)				8.7
(5) Real GDP growth (%)				
Taiwan:				
(1) GNP per capita (US$m)	2,808	8,045	12,390	
(2) Manufacturing/GDP (%)	36	33	28	
(3) Trade to GDP (%)	87	76	83	
(4) Cumulative FDI (US$m)				−15,938
(5) Real GDP growth (%)				7.9
Hong Kong:				
(1) GDP per capita (US$m)	4,841	13,101	21,382	
(2) Manufacturing/GDP (%)	23	18	9	
(3) Trade to GDP (%)	167	229	278	
(4) Cumulative FDI (US$m)				−6.2
(5) Real GDP growth (%)				8.0

Notes: Trade in (3) is exports plus imports in local currency; (5) is an annual average growth rate in national currency; US$ conversions use end of period exchange rates.

Sources: Asian Development Bank (1997), *Key Indicators of Developing Asian and Pacific Countries*, Manila.

Table 2.2: Malaysian and DAE exports to the USA, Japan and the EU as a proportion of their total exports

	USA	Japan	EU	Total
Malaysia:				
1983	16.4	23.3	14.5	54.2
1990	16.9	15.3	14.9	47.1
1995	20.3	13.0	13.3	46.6
Thailand:				
1983	18.1	14.2	21.4	53.7
1990	22.7	17.2	21.6	61.5
1995	21.5	17.0	15.0	53.5
Singapore:				
1983	23.4	8.6	11.1	43.1
1990	21.3	8.8	14.4	44.5
1995	20.4	7.5	13.5	41.4
Korea:				
1983	40.0	15.6	12.4	68.0
1990	29.9	19.4	13.6	62.9
1995	21.7	13.8	10.2	45.7
Taiwan:				
1983	50.5	11.2	11.4	73.1
1990	32.9	11.7	16.4	61.0
1995	27.7	10.6	7.9	46.2
Hong Kong:				
1983	31.3	4.7	14.5	50.5
1990	24.1	5.7	16.9	46.7
1995	23.1	5.2	14.2	42.5
Total DAEs:				
1983	35.2	11.6	13.1	59.9
1990	26.0	11.9	15.9	53.8
1995	22.9	9.8	13.9	46.6

Notes: The figures for Taiwan and Hong Kong are based on import data into other countries or to the world; the EU includes Belgium, Denmark, France, Germany, Greece, Ireland, Italy, Luxembourg, Netherlands, Portugal, Spain and the United Kingdom.

Sources: International Monetary Fund, *Direction of Trade Statistics*, Washington.

As the data in Table 2.2 suggests, despite some diversification from these markets by 1995, mainly by Korea, Taiwan and Hong Kong from the USA, exports to these three destinations by the DAEs as a whole still accounted for almost half (47 per cent) of their exports. The proportions going to Japan and the EU were more stable, but Thailand shifted from Europe to the USA and Malaysia shifted from Japan to the USA. Malaysia and the other DAEs have also become more competitive in a similar range of manufactured goods to these markets at the SITC two-digit level. A substantial proportion of both Malaysian and total DAE exports to these markets by 1995 were accounted for by organic chemicals, office and data processing machines, telecommunications and sound equipment, electrical machinery, apparel and clothing and miscellaneous manufactures.

Empirical analysis

Dynamic shift–share analysis is employed here specifically to compare changes in Malaysia's exports to the USA, Japan and the EU with the corresponding exports of a reference group, in this case the DAEs as a whole. Any difference between the performance of Malaysia in a given commodity group and destination and that part of the total change in exports that might be ascribed to the rate of export growth of the reference group as a whole—the share effect—is referred to as the export differential or shift effect and is measured in absolute dollar terms. A positive value implies an improvement in competitiveness relative to the reference group and a negative value constitutes deterioration in competitiveness.

The export differential is in turn accounted for by three additive factors: the industry mix effect, the competitive effect, and the allocative effect. The industry mix effect shows how much of the export differential is due to a divergence between the competing economy's economic structure and the reference group. It will be positive if the share of exports in this industry is larger than the reference group and its growth rate in the reference group is positive. The competitive effect, on the other hand, shows how much of the export differential is due to a difference between the export growth rate of the competing economy and the group. In other words, the contribution due to the special dynamism of that sector in the DAE compared with the average growth of that sector at the reference group level. Finally, the allocative effect shows how much of the export differential is attributable to a combination of economic structure (the industry mix effect) and competitiveness (the competitive effect). Full details of the shift–share methodology used here and the data sources are given in Appendix 2.1.

Shift–share is a relatively simple technique, but it has proved to be a useful tool for isolating trends in regional performance and for supplying data for policymakers to interpret changes in the industrial structure of their economies. Recent examples of its use in policy analysis include the Monetary Authority of Singapore (1998) and Khalifah (1996). The former uses the technique to identify those markets that are of growing importance to Singapore between 1991 and 1996, while the latter carries out a similar procedure for Malaysia between 1991 and 1993.

Most studies using shift–share methods are comparative static in that they only consider changes in exports between the beginning and the terminal years of the time period considered. In the context of export changes this was true of both Herschede (1991) and DBS Bank (1992). This is problematic because it cannot take into account continuous changes in the industry mix component and changes in the size of total exports in the country concerned. Only by applying an annual group growth rate to a country's exports at the beginning of the year can one accurately measure the share effect. Dynamic shift–share solves these problems by calculating the shift–share effects annually and summing over the whole period or sub-periods of interest. In this way both the industry mix and total group exports are adjusted continuously and annual growth rates are used. Thus, the dynamic approach is not only more accurate, especially when there are unusual years, such as when exports recover fast from a recession (Singapore 1986), it also enables years of transition to be more clearly identified.

Shift–share is a useful technique for descriptive analysis but it has a number of limitations. To begin with it does not itself identify the causes of any change in competitiveness, such as when there is a change in a country's real effective exchange rate, and any adverse movements can always be changed through the implementation of appropriate policies, including trade liberalisation, incentives for inward FDI, or export promotion.

Secondly, shift–share only captures one dimension of 'competitiveness', namely export performance in a product category relative to a specific reference group. A country would thus have a competitive advantage if the rate of growth of its exports were greater than the group's. It is possible, however, in a broader interpretation of competitiveness that a particular country might still have a competitive advantage if its export growth rate were less than that of the reference group, but the latter were high by world standards.[2]

Competitiveness is an illusive concept and can mean different things to different people. The criteria for replication of universal best practices and policy benchmarking of business environments in the world economy are constantly being re-assessed as globalisation proceeds and competitive performance and the role of industrial development policy are increasingly measured by world standards.[3] This has not been helped by a tendency to confuse competitiveness with the principle of comparative advantage. Trade economists, such as Paul Krugman (1994), have always been sceptical of this 'vulgar' analogy between competitiveness at the business level and competitiveness at the national level. Trade is not a zero sum game akin to a competitive sport. Every country has a comparative advantage in something, even if it is absolutely less productive than its trading partners. The trick is to ensure that prices and/or the exchange rate remain consistent with costs and productivity, and if a country falls behind relatively it should find something else to export.

Shift–share analysis is also sensitive to the level of aggregation of the data. The two-digit level still aggregates across quite a large range of product areas, so a country may have a comparative disadvantage in some categories but not in others. In our case the choice of product groups was based on the identification of those categories of manufactured goods at the

SITC two-digit level, which account for a substantial proportion of Malaysia's manufactured exports to the markets concerned. The choice of start and end years was dependent on the availability of comparative import data at the SITC two-digit level into the three markets by the DAEs. Unfortunately comparative trade data at a more disaggregated level is not readily available.

Empirical results

The export differential

Figure 2.1 provides a convenient visual presentation of the evolution over time of the export differential (ED) for Malaysia in each of the two-digit product categories to the markets of the USA, the EU and Japan respectively. To facilitate interpretation the EDs are left in absolute terms (millions of US$), but should be seen in the context of the scale used in each case. The task here is to ascertain whether there are any patterns in the profiles of the ED across markets and product groups, rather than focussing on individual years, which may give a myopic picture of Malaysia's export performance and be subject to data errors.[4] The full shift–share results, including the decomposition of the ED into its additive components—the industry mix effect (IME), the competitive effect (CE) and the allocative effect (AE)—are listed in Appendix 2.2.

Figure 2.1: The export differential for Malaysia relative to the DAEs 1984–95

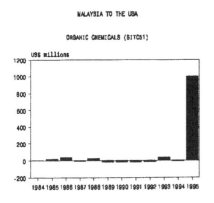

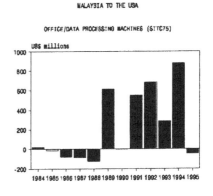

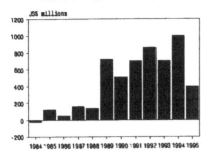

MALAYSIA TO THE USA

TELECOMMUNICATIONS/SOUND EQUIPMENT (SITC76)

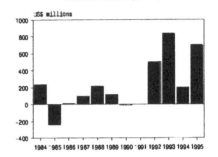

MALAYSIA TO THE USA

ELECTRICAL MACHINERY (SITC 77)

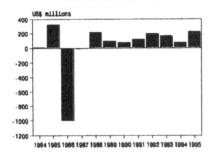

MALAYSIA TO THE USA

APPAREL AND CLOTHING (SITC84)

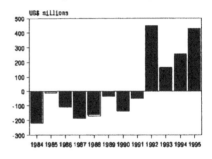

MALAYSIA TO THE EUROPEAN UNION

OFFICE/DATA PROCESSING MACHINES (SITC75)

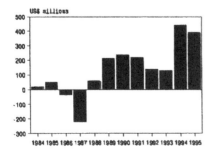

MALAYSIA TO THE EUROPEAN UNION

TELECOMMUNICATIONS/SOUND EQUIPMENT (SITC76)

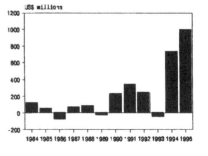

MALAYSIA TO THE EUROPEAN UNION

ELECTRICAL MACHINERY (SITC 77)

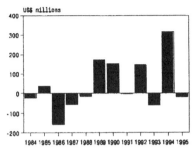

MALAYSIA TO THE EUROPEAN UNION

APPAREL AND CLOTHING (SITC84)

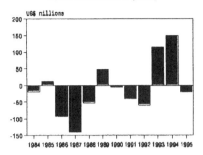

MALAYSIA TO THE EUROPEAN UNION

MISCELLANEOUS MANUFACTURES (SITC89)

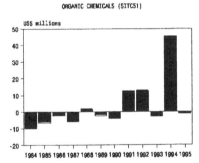

MALAYSIA TO JAPAN

ORGANIC CHEMICALS (SITC51)

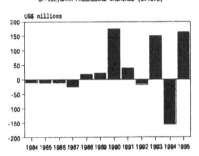

MALAYSIA TO JAPAN

OFFICE/DATA PROCESSING MACHINES (SITC75)

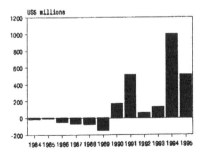

MALAYSIA TO JAPAN

TELECOMMUNICATIONS/SOUND EQUIPMENT (SITC76)

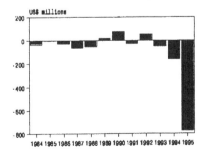

MALAYSIA TO JAPAN

ELECTRICAL MACHINERY (SITC 77)

As far as the aggregate export differentials are concerned, the results from Malaysia's perspective are striking, especially in SITC categories 75, 76 and 77. In office and data processing machines (SITC 75) there seems to be a clear switch to positive export differentials in the late 1980s in all three markets (1992 onwards for the EU). The star performer, however, is telecommunications and sound equipment (SITC 76) where the differentials are positive and sizeable over most of the period for the USA and EU, and from 1990 onwards in the case of Japan. Less clear-cut, but still impressive, is Malaysia's performance in electrical machinery (SITC 77), with positive differentials in the USA from the mid-1980s and mostly positive numbers over the same period with respect to the EU. Surprisingly, this success is not matched in the Japanese market.

For the other categories, there appears to be no obvious strength in organic chemicals (SITC 51) or miscellaneous manufactures (SITC 89) even when account is taken of the exceptional jump in the export differential for the former category to the USA in 1995, reflecting a sudden surge in exports in that year. Although the numbers are less startling, Malaysia's performance in the more traditional, labour-intensive category of apparel and clothing (SITC 84) is also positive in the fast-growing US market, if mixed in the EU. One should, however, bear in mind that this might have something to do with the fact that the reference point for Malaysia here is the DAEs, for whom this category has become a sunset industry. If the reference group had been ASEAN instead, one might expect Malaysia not to have performed as well as her lower wage neighbours of Indonesia and the Philippines.

Decomposition of the export differential

One of the key advantages of shift–share analysis is its ability to identify the pattern of a country's export growth relative to a reference group, in this case the DAEs, and to decompose this performance in terms of its export structure (industry mix effect), competitiveness (competitive effect) and the interaction of structure and competitiveness (allocative effect). This three-way decomposition can then be used as a guide to policy implementation. This decomposition is tabulated in Appendix 2.2.

Malaysia's success in SITC 76 and SITC 77 has been robust in terms of both the industry mix and competitive effects, and the allocative effects have been positive, although there does seem to be some scope for targeting changes in the industry mix for SITC 76 to Japan and SITC 89 with respect to the EU market. Malaysia has, however, been noticeably less successful so far in the area of organic chemicals (SITC 51), which would suggest policy action to improve both the industry mix and competitive effects. To some degree this might involve a continuation of policies that have been successful in Malaysia in the past, including a relatively open-arms approach to multinational corporations, trade liberalisation and openness, and an emphasis on training and education suitable to the creation of a relatively cheap but factory-skilled labour force. This would have the added benefit of diversifying Malaysia's market base and providing a further cushion to offset the negative effects of a regional slowdown. One of the lessons of the Asian crisis is that the Asian industrial miracle was built on a relatively narrow base. The contribution of these policies to Malaysia's growth and structural change has been well documented. In terms of education and training see, for example, Gan (1995), and with respect to trade liberalisation and foreign direct investment, Pussarangsri and Chamnivickorn (1995).

By contrast, for office and data processing machines (SITC 75), the export differentials have been positive, but the industry mix and allocative effects tend to be negative, so the positive export differential is primarily attributable to faster growth for Malaysia compared to the group (competitive effect). This suggests that Malaysia has not yet benefited as much as, for example, Singapore, from shifting resources into this fast-growing higher value-added electronics category. Indeed, one of the reasons Singapore has suffered less from the Asian financial crisis is her concentration in electronics exports, which were less adversely affected by the crisis (Monetary Authority of Singapore 1998).

For the office and data processing sector, however, it is more difficult to engineer a change in the industry mix than in the less sophisticated categories of manufactured goods since production requires a more sophisticated knowledge-based and creative labour force, a higher proportion of indigenous research and development, and a strong information technology environment for both production and marketing of the products. Unlike agricultural and resource-based production and relatively low value-added manufacturing, success in SITC 75 is much less a consequence of good industrial planning than providing a general environment in which MNCs can flourish and engender positive spill-over effects to the local economy.

In the end it will probably be the MNCs themselves that will determine the direction, composition and growth of such exports. Both Malaysia and Singapore have strategic plans to move up the value-added ladder. In Singapore this is to be achieved primarily through the attraction of foreign talent and the creation of a broad-based information technology culture, while the emphasis in Malaysia is directed more towards the provision of specific infrastructure (a multimedia super highway) and the attraction of high-technology research and development. The competition for such foreign resources is strong and the outcome is not certain, particularly in the wake of the capital and currency controls enacted by the Malaysian authorities in 1998. The continuation of long-term capital flows into the Malaysian economy is a major prerequisite for the deepening of her industrial structure, without which the associated local resources will be largely redundant.

Whilst Malaysia faces significant competition from regional players in its exports to developed-country markets, there is no doubt that she has also benefited significantly from the mutual effects of regional growth over the last two decades, especially with respect to her ASEAN partners Singapore, Indonesia, Thailand and the Philippines. In the manufacturing sector, much of the benefit of growing neighbours derives from the growth of intra-industry trade and the export of intermediate goods to be assembled into final products for sale to third countries, especially between Singapore and Malaysia. From an industry mix point of view this means that industrial policy should be based on the identification of specific products for specific markets in which Malaysia is likely to enjoy a competitive advantage, rather than on implementing general policies, such as those geared towards lowering production costs or facilitating exports, which may only stimulate growth in sectors, such as clothing and apparel (SITC 84), and are relatively slow growing in the DAE block as a whole. Similarly, the continuation of trade liberalisation, both unilaterally and under the umbrella of the ASEAN Free Trade Area (AFTA) is to be welcomed, but there may be gains from the targeting of investment by Malaysian companies overseas towards markets with potential positive export differentials. One possible model for this is Singapore's rationalisation policy to boost foreign-sourced income by encouraging its indigenous MNCs to engage in outward direct investment in the region. Recent evidence suggests a strong link between the direction of exports and the direction of overseas investments (see Monetary Authority of Singapore 1988, p. 30).

Conclusion

In this chapter we have looked at changes in the competitive position of Malaysia relative to six dynamic Asian economies exporting to the USA, EU and Japan between 1983 and 1995. This was an important period of dynamic change for this group as trade liberalisation and domestic economic reforms coincided with growing interdependence in the world economy through trade and capital flows. Our empirical results suggest that Malaysia's performance has been impressive across both the product groups and markets considered here. Not only was she able to maintain her position in the traditional apparel and clothing category in the US market, but also she posted strong positive export differentials in telecommunications and sound equipment and electrical machinery over the whole period, and in office and data machines from the late 1980s onwards.

Nonetheless, if Malaysia is to continue to compete effectively in the new millennium there does seem to be some scope for policy to improve the industry mix for SITC 76, 77 and 89 with respect to the EU market, and for exports of SITC 77 to Japan, and to address Malaysia's relatively poor showing so far in the area of organic chemicals (SITC 51). To some degree this might involve a continuation of policies that have been successful in the past. But in the case of office and data processing machines, where Malaysia's growth has been relatively fast compared to the DAEs, but her share in this sector has been less than that of her competitors, it is much more difficult to engineer a change in the industry mix since the production of these goods requires a more sophisticated knowledge-based and creative labour force, a higher proportion of indigenous research and development, and a strong information technology environment for both production and marketing of the products.

Appendix 2.1: Methodology and data sources

Shift–share analysis has been used extensively in regional analysis to analyse differences in regional and national growth rates in variables such as employment and productivity. For reviews of the basic methodology of shift–share, see Richardson (1978), Esteban-Marquillas (1972), Fothergill and Gudgin (1979), and more recently, Haynes and Machunda (1987) and Hayward and Erickson (1995).

Shift–share analysis is employed here specifically to compare changes in Malaysia's exports at the SITC two-digit level to the USA, Japan and the EU with the corresponding exports of a reference group, in this case the DAEs as a whole. The particular version of shift–share used in this chapter follows the national growth rate methodology of Richardson (1978) and Esteban-Marquillas (1972) but combines it with the more recent dynamic version of Barff and Knight (1988) and focuses on export growth over a period of time rather than employment change.

Let e = exports, i = export category at the 2-digit level, j = a competing DAE, then the change in exports of category i of competing economy j to a specific destination (USA or Japan or the EU). de_{ij} is given by the share effect s_{ij}, the industry mix effect m_{ij}, the competitive effect c_{ij} and the allocative effect a_{ij}:

$$de_{ij} = s_{ij} + m_{ij} + c_{ij} + a_{ij}$$

In other words, each sector of each DAE has a standard growth component given by s_{ij}, to which must be added the positive and negative contribution due to factors associated specifically with each DAE ($m_{ij} + c_{ij} + a_{ij}$).

s_{ij} represents the change in exports that would have occurred if the structure of exports in the competing DAE had followed the reference group (homothetic exports e'_{ij}) and its export categories had grown (r_{ij}) at the corresponding group rate r_{i0}:

$$s_{ij} = e'_{ij} r_{i0} \text{ where } e'_{ij} = e_{i0} \cdot e_{0j} / e_{00}$$
$$e_{i0} = \text{exports of i from the reference group 0}$$
$$e_{0j} = \text{total exports from the DAE}$$
$$e_{00} = \text{total exports from the reference group}$$

If $e_{ij} - e'_{ij}$ is positive the DAE is specialised relative to the group and vice versa if it is negative. Hence any difference between the actual change in exports in sector i of DAE j and the share effect s_{ij} represents the net shift or shift effect or export differential ed_{ij} ascribed to the specific characteristics of the individual DAE and is measured in absolute dollar values.[5]

$$ed_{ij} = de_{ij} - s_{ij} = de_{ij} - e'_{ij} \, r_{i0} = e_{ij} \, r_{ij} - e'_{ij} \, r_{i0}$$

A positive value for the export differential implies an improvement in competitiveness relative to the reference group and a negative value constitutes deterioration in competitiveness. The export differential is in turn accounted for by the three additive components m_{ij}, c_{ij}, a_{ij}.

The industry mix effect m_{ij} shows how much of the export differential is due to a divergence between the competing economy's economic structure compared to the reference group's. It will be positive if the share of exports in this industry is larger than the reference group's and the growth of exports of this industry in the reference group is positive:

$$m_{ij} = r_{i0} \, (e_{ij} - e'_{ij})$$

The competitive effect c_{ij} shows how much of the export differential is due to a difference between the export growth rate of the competing economy and that of the group: the contribution due to the special dynamism of that sector in the DAE compared with the average growth of that sector at the reference group level. If the DAE growth exceeds the rate for the group the effect is positive and it has a competitive advantage in that product category:

$$c_{ij} = e'_{ij} \, (r_{ij} - r_{i0})$$

Finally, the allocative effect a_{ij} shows how much of the export differential is attributable to a combination of economic structure and competitiveness: the industry mix effect and the competitive effect. It shows the DAE is specialised in those sectors in which it enjoys a competitive advantage. It will take on a positive value if either the competing economy specialises in exports in which it has a competitive advantage or produces little of the exports in which it has no such advantage:[6]

$$a_{ij} = (e_{ij} - e'_{ij}) \, (r_{ij} - r_{i0})$$

Export data at the SITC two-digit level for each DAE and for the group as a whole were extracted from import data into the USA, Japan and the EU in US$ from the OECD, *Foreign Trade by Commodities*, Paris. Since total exports by country and destination were not available from this source they were instead derived for each DAE in US$ by destination from export data from the International Monetary Fund, *International Financial Statistics*, Washington. The choice of start and end years was dictated by data availability.

Appendix 2.2: Shift–share results 1984–95

TO THE UNITED STATES (millions of US$)

ORGANIC CHEMICALS (SITC 51)

	1984	1985	1986	1987	1988	1989	1990	1991	1992	1993	1994	1995
IME	−1	1	8	0	4	3	−6	−7	−11	−1	−2	−3
CE	1	11	9	−2	7	−18	−18	−25	−2	95	−94	2089
AE	−1	8	23	−3	12	−3	6	17	2	−53	89	−600
ED	−1	20	39	−6	23	−18	−18	−16	−11	41	−7	1486

OFFICE AND DATA PROCESSING MACHINES (SITC 75)

	1984	1985	1986	1987	1988	1989	1990	1991	1992	1993	1994	1995
IME	−73	5	−76	−112	−142	−101	−66	−59	−135	−228	−165	−310
CE	222	−73	−247	530	214	3091	234	1266	1259	784	1336	343
AE	−131	55	242	−506	−202	−2378	−173	−655	−445	−270	−296	−82
ED	19	−13	−81	−87	−130	612	−6	552	679	286	875	−49

TELECOMMUNICATIONS/SOUND EQUIPMENT (SITC 76)

	1984	1985	1986	1987	1988	1989	1990	1991	1992	1993	1994	1995
IME	26	−1	−1	22	10	21	−59	55	241	20	481	47
CE	−147	168	51	109	94	368	229	220	213	239	231	122
AE	96	−46	−2	29	35	328	343	426	402	443	440	231
ED	−26	121	48	160	139	718	513	701	856	702	1152	401

ELECTRICAL MACHINERY (SITC 77)

	1984	1985	1986	1987	1988	1989	1990	1991	1992	1993	1994	1995
IME	481	−88	107	277	332	−38	−23	7	177	338	441	749
CE	−63	−39	−23	−46	−35	54	6	−1	163	272	−154	−38
AE	−181	−120	−74	−135	−79	99	9	−2	162	221	−84	−16
ED	237	−247	10	96	219	115	−7	4	502	831	203	695

APPAREL AND CLOTHING (SITC 84)

	1984	1985	1986	1987	1988	1989	1990	1991	1992	1993	1994	1995
IME	12	1	−1114	−31	−1	−16	12	2	−15	25	−7	17
CE	−22	261	−1808	39	269	149	85	157	291	205	127	297
AE	17	63	759	−14	−53	−38	−23	−42	−82	−69	−46	−94
ED	7	325	−2163	−6	215	95	73	118	194	161	74	221

TO JAPAN (millions of US$)

ORGANIC CHEMICALS (SITC 51)

	1984	1985	1986	1987	1988	1989	1990	1991	1992	1993	1994	1995
IME	-11	-9	-6	-6	-3	0	-3	-1	1	0	15	6
CE	9	15	12	0	6	-3	-2	15	12	-3	21	-5
AE	-8	-13	-8	0	-1	1	0	-1	1	0	10	-2
ED	-10	-7	-2	-6	2	-2	-4	13	13	-3	46	-1

OFFICE AND DATA PROCESSING MACHINES (SITC 75)

	1984	1985	1986	1987	1988	1989	1990	1991	1992	1993	1994	1995
IME	-10	-11	-11	-27	-30	-28	-20	-19	-16	-44	-101	-303
CE	21	-24	-36	281	735	280	405	99	-2	285	-94	818
AE	-20	24	35	-279	-688	-231	-211	-42	1	-92	41	-353
ED	-9	-12	-11	-25	17	21	174	38	-17	150	-154	161

TELECOMMUNICATIONS/SOUND EQUIPMENT (SITC 76)

	1984	1985	1986	1987	1988	1989	1990	1991	1992	1993	1994	1995
IME	-16	-10	-50	-114	-100	-54	12	8	3	17	318	367
CE	-35	26	-71	522	130	186	224	460	47	83	363	65
AE	34	-25	70	-481	-111	-141	-107	48	11	30	403	83
ED	-17	-9	-51	-74	-81	-8	129	515	61	130	1085	515

ELECTRICAL MACHINERY (SITC 77)

	1984	1985	1986	1987	1988	1989	1990	1991	1992	1993	1994	1995
IME	-25	17	-12	-57	-66	-33	-13	-42	-7	-51	-150	-422
CE	-16	-55	-58	-19	33	97	127	20	79	5	-261	-159
AE	6	36	43	13	-19	-43	-37	-7	-19	-2	-104	71
ED	-34	-2	-28	-63	-52	21	77	-28	53	-47	-307	-510

TO THE EUROPEAN UNION (millions of US$)

OFFICE AND DATA PROCESSING MACHINES (SITC 75)

	1984	1985	1986	1987	1988	1989	1990	1991	1992	1993	1994	1995
IME	-203	-17	-104	-181	-187	-55	-177	-149	-151	-63	-158	-327
CE	-239	61	-216	-194	507	354	457	717	1976	558	775	1116
AE	224	-55	210	190	-488	-335	-420	-620	-1377	-333	-362	-360
ED	-219	-12	-110	-185	-168	-35	-139	-51	447	162	254	429

TELECOMMUNICATIONS/SOUND EQUIPMENT (SITC 76)

	1984	1985	1986	1987	1988	1989	1990	1991	1992	1993	1994	1995
IME	0	1	-2	-74	-14	-1	49	33	-20	10	-22	164
CE	35	65	-35	-203	82	193	144	126	103	75	235	108
AE	-16	-13	0	54	-12	21	43	60	54	43	227	115
ED	20	53	-36	-223	56	213	236	220	138	127	441	386

ELECTRICAL MACHINERY (SITC 77)

	1984	1985	1986	1987	1988	1989	1990	1991	1992	1993	1994	1995
IME	38	11	49	116	82	29	81	93	70	38	429	821
CE	63	28	-71	-21	6	-34	86	129	92	-47	167	112
AE	30	19	-54	-18	5	-20	64	127	88	-36	137	91
ED	131	57	-77	78	92	-26	231	349	250	-45	733	1024

APPAREL AND CLOTHING (SITC 84)

	1984	1985	1986	1987	1988	1989	1990	1991	1992	1993	1994	1995
IME	-17	34	-157	-152	-45	20	-26	-61	12	5	20	-11
CE	-43	19	-4	277	84	297	270	86	183	-101	334	-7
AE	36	-16	3	-182	-52	-146	-91	-27	-48	38	-36	1
ED	-23	37	-158	-57	-12	172	153	-2	146	-58	318	-17

MISCELLANEOUS MANUFACTURES (SITC 89)

	1984	1985	1986	1987	1988	1989	1990	1991	1992	1993	1994	1995
IME	-18	11	-89	-144	-75	-14	-49	-51	-63	32	72	-53
CE	-7	16	-36	27	123	242	143	36	16	228	167	70
AE	7	-14	31	-23	-100	-181	-99	-25	-11	-145	-89	-36
ED	-18	12	-93	-140	-52	47	-4	-40	-59	114	150	-19

IME = Industry mix effect
CE = Competitive effect
AE = Allocative effect
ED = Export differential

Endnotes

[1] Membership of the EU is based upon the classification used in the International Monetary Fund, *Direction of Trade Statistics* 1993, p. vi, Washington, DC: International Monetary Fund; and the OECD, *Foreign Trade by Commodities* 1993, Vol. 5, Paris: OECD.

[2] I am grateful to an anonymous referee for this point.

[3] An assessment of seven different papers on international competitiveness contributed to the *Oxford Economic Bulletin* in 1996 can be found in Boltho (1996). The relationship between competitiveness and industrial policy in a changing world economy is also the subject of a recent UNIDO study by Sercovitch (1999).

[4] Where specific years produced exceptionally large values for the export differential, often because a discontinuity in the data produced an exceptionally large growth rate, the data was checked carefully but the differential values are capped at US$1,000 (millions) to retain the longer-term pattern in the graphs. The detailed and disaggregated nature of the data makes this inevitable, but in some cases there is a suspicion of recording error, particularly where a scale factor is involved.

[5] However, comparing absolute dollar amounts should be seen in relation to the size of the respective economies proxied by GNP or the volume of international trade.

[6] a_{ij} will be positive if the DAE is specialised, $(e_{ij} - e'_{ij} > 0)$, in those sectors of faster group growth $(r_{ij} - r_{i0} > 0)$, or if it is not specialised, $(e_{ij} - e'_{ij} < 0)$, in sectors in

which it is lacking in competitive advantages ($r_{ij} - r_{i0} < 0$). Contrary reasoning will produce a negative allocation effect.

References

Barff, Richard and Prentice Knight III (1988), 'Dynamic shift–share analysis', *Growth and Change*, 19 (2), 1–9.

Boltho, A. (1996), 'The assessment: international competitiveness', *Oxford Review of Economic Policy*, 12 (3), 1–16.

Chow, P., M. Kellman and Y. Shachmurove (1994), 'East Asian NIC manufactured intra–industry trade 1965–1990', *Journal of Asian Economics*, 5 (3), 335–348.

DBS Bank (1992), 'Singapore's export competitiveness vis à vis other Dynamic Asian Economies', *Singapore Briefing 29*, Economic Research Department, DBS Bank.

Esteban-Marquillas, J. M. (1972), 'Shift and share analysis revisited', *Regional and Urban Economics*, 2 (3), 249–261.

Fothergill, S. and G. Gudgin (1979), 'In defence of shift–share', *Urban Studies*, 16 (3), 309–319.

Gan Khuan Poh (1995), 'Human capital formation: a public policy approach', *The Singapore Economic Review*, 40 (2), 159–184.

Haynes, K. and Z. Machunda (1987), 'Considerations in extending shift–share analysis', *Growth and Change*, 18 (2), 69–78.

Hayward, D. and Rodney A. Erickson (1995), 'The North American trade of US states: A comparative analysis of industrial shipments 1938–91', *International Regional Science Review*, 18 (1), 1–31.

Herschede, F. (1991), 'Competition among ASEAN, China, and the East Asian NICs—a shift–share analysis', *ASEAN Economic Bulletin*, 7 (3), 290–306.

Hill, H. and P. Phillips (1993), 'Pattern of import penetration in East Asian industrialisation', *Asian Economic Review*, 7 (1), 1–23.

Khalifah, N. (1996), 'Identifying Malaysia's export market growth: a shift–share analysis', *Asia-Pacific Development Journal*, 3 (1), 2–8.

Krugman, P. (1994), *Peddling Prosperity*, New York: W.W. Norton.

Markusen, Ann, Hezi Noponen and Karl Driessen A shift–share interpretation', *International Regional Science Review*, 14 (1), 15–39.

Monetary Authority of Singapore (1998), 'Growth in Singapore's export market 1991–96, a shift–share interpretation', Singapore: *Economics Department Occasional Paper*, 4.

Peebles, G. and P. Wilson (1996), *The Singapore Economy*, Cheltenham, UK and Brookfield, US: Edward Elgar.

Pussarangsri, Bunluasak and Suchittra Chamnivickorn (1995), 'Trade liberalisation and FDI policies of ASEAN countries', *Singapore Economic Review*, 40 (2), 137–158.

Richardson, Harry (1978), 'The state of regional economics: A survey article', *International Regional Science Review*, 3 (1), 1–48.

Sercovich, F. (1999), *Competition and the World Economy—Comparing Industrial Development Policies in the Developing and Transition Economies*, Cheltenham, UK and Brookfield, US: Edward Elgar.

Wilson, Peter and Adrian Goh Kee Hsien (1998), 'The export competitiveness of dynamic Asian economies 1986–93: A shift–share analysis', *Journal of The Asia Pacific Economy*, 3 (2), 237–250.

3

Australian business attitudes to Malaysia

Marika Vicziany, Tan Sri Ramon Navaratnam,
Koi Nyen Wong and Tim Thornton

Malaysia bounces back

The Malaysian economy since late 1999 has been characterised by growing economic confidence and recovery and it has achieved this on its own, without the benefit of any IMF rescue package. The collapse that pessimists had been predicting never happened. Malaysia did not follow the Thai or Indonesian pattern and by late 1999 was on the cusp of another boom (Halls 1999; Jayasankaran 1999). Economic Darwinism emerged with a vengeance—Malaysia was now declared to be a sign of 'the survival of the fittest after the deluge'. After a great many unpredictable policy changes affecting the foreign investment climate[1] and a spell of being the 'most challenging market for custodians', Malaysia was declared to be 'stable' (Hyam 1999/2000). A report by Merrill Lynch in late 1999 went much further in describing Malaysia's recovery as 'one of the most impressive ever, with earnings per share growing by an annualised rate of 150 per cent' (Mitra 1999). More modestly, the EIU noted that the Malaysian recession had ended by the second quarter of 1999: growth rates had risen to 4.1 per cent, inflation was under control, interest rates were coming down and industrial production, sales and exports were strongly up, especially in the conductors (EIU 1999, pp. 3, 27–8). Recent figures indicate an even stronger recovery. According to an official report by the Government of Malaysia Department of Statistics, both imports and exports have been growing and the December 1999 trade figures show the largest monthly trade surplus on record (*New Straits Times* 5 February 2000). GDP was expected to grow by 6 per cent in 2000 and 6.7 per cent in 2001—and this is not a government prediction but the view of the Chase Manhattan Bank which is also saying that Malaysian growth is being driven by new investment rather than pump priming by the government (*Business Times* 11 February 2000).

The international rating agencies have also revised their opinion of the Malaysian economy. In late 1999, Morgan Stanley Capital International announced that on 31 May 2000 it would restore Malaysia to its former rating level (Hill 1999). This was not an isolated decision. At the end of 1999 Standard and Poor's (Lee 1999), Moody's and Merrill Lynch (Mitra

1999) also upgraded their rating of Malaysia. Standard and Poor's and Moody's, it needs to be remembered, had been severely criticised by the Malaysian government for downgrading Malaysia's rating in 1998. So the shift in attitude is especially important and reflects a positive reassessment of the Malaysian economy by some of its most influential critics. Hill reports that during the last quarter of 1999 'scores of fund managers were sniffing around Kuala Lumpur, contemplating a return to what used to be one of the largest and most liquid markets in Asia' (Hill 1999). She adds that Malaysia's impressive 'world-class infrastructure' is one factor bringing back foreign interest—and certainly infrastructure is one of the positive characteristics of the Malaysian economy that has impressed Australian firms. According to Hill, concerns about erratic shifts in government policy remain, but despite the storm that broke out over currency controls two years ago, foreign fund managers now look to the returned Mahathir government for stability and familiarity. But perhaps most telling of all, Hill reports that Malaysia has great appeal to foreign fund managers, information technology and electronics producers because, in the words of Pesaka Jardine Fleming's Weller, 'In terms of making money, Malaysia is a good place to be right now' (Hill 1999). And making money is what attracts all business, including Australian business.

Origins of this study

We decided to undertake a survey of Australian business attitudes to Malaysia in early 1999, long before the signs of economic recovery were visible. This decision was based on a number of considerations:

- it was clear to us that Malaysia was not the crisis-torn economy that Thailand and Indonesia represented, and so we were curious to find out what Australian companies thought of the Malaysian market;
- one of the authors of this paper had published similar studies about the Indian market, so we had some basis for cross-country comparisons;
- we were keen to learn what advantages and obstacles the Malaysian market might present to Australian firms thinking of moving production to off-shore facilities as part of their corporate strategies to become global competitors.

The survey results were collected from November 1999 to March 2000. Over this period of time there has been a growing consensus about the recovery of the Malaysian economy. The Australian firms we surveyed have an on-the-ground presence in Malaysia. According to the Australian–Malaysian Business Database, which we compiled,[2] 160 Australian companies have offices in Malaysia. All of these received a copy of the questionnaire by mail, and for the 70 firms that had email addresses, also by electronic means. Some contacts were followed up by fax and phone calls.

In addition to responses from relevant firms, we received replies from companies that were no longer Australian firms, or had left Malaysia, or had been amalgamated with other firms. These were eliminated from the database. For the purposes of this study, an Australian firm is defined as any Australian company or partnership that has an office in Malaysia, even if the majority ownership of the Malaysian enterprise is in non-Australian hands.

A total of 32 companies completed the questionnaire, making the response rate about 20 per cent. The majority of these firms, some two-thirds, are recent arrivals in Malaysia, having established themselves since 1991. Only 12 predate 1990, the earliest going back to 1972.

An economic profile of the Australian firms

Of the 32 firms, 12, that is 37.5 per cent, are involved in the Malaysian construction industry. We cannot say how this compares to the general profile of Australian firms present inside the Malaysian market because we do not have information about the industrial activities of those companies that did not respond to the questionnaire. The remaining Australian firms are involved in a wide range of economic activities, dominated by Information technology and Manufacturing (see Table 3.1).

Table 3.1: Australian firms inside Malaysia by areas of economic activity in 1999/2000

Type of activity	Number	Percentage
Construction	12	37.50
Information technology	6	18.75
Manufacturing	4	12.50
Miners/metals processing	2	6.25
Transport	2	6.25
Banking/finance	2	6.25
Tourism/recreation	1	3.12
Environmental engineering	1	3.12
PR consultant	1	3.12
Business/accounting consultant	1	3.12
Total	32	100.0

The majority of the Australian firms in Malaysia are small employers of labour in Malaysia compared with their labour force in Australia: almost three-quarters of the firms employed 100 or fewer people and another 25 per cent between 101 and 500 (see Table 3.2). The reasons for the smaller scale of operations in Malaysia are not known, but presumably reflect the relatively short time that the majority of Australian companies have been in Malaysia.

Table 3.2: Size of Australian firms in Malaysia according to the number of employees in Malaysia

No. of employees	No. of firms	Percentage of firms
Fewer than 10	9	28.12
11 to 100	14	43.75
101 to 500	8	25.00
501 to 1000	Nil	
1001 to 2000	1	3.12
More than 2000	Nil	
Total	32	100.00

Australian firms or citizens in about 60 per cent of cases own the majority of Australian companies in Malaysia. Other forms of ownership were scattered across a number of categories as Table 3.3 shows. In only two cases was the dominant ownership in the hands of a Malaysian firm and in three cases Australian–Malaysian ownership was shared.

Table 3.3: Ownership of Australian firms based in Malaysia

Types of business arrangements on the basis of who had majority (51 per cent+) ownership	No.	Percentage
An Australian firm or citizen	19	59.375
A Malaysian firm	2	6.250
A 50:50 Australian–Malaysian business	3	9.375
Corporate shareholders	3	9.375
An overseas multinational (non-Malaysian/non-Australian)	3	9.375
Publicly listed on Australian Stock Exchange	1	3.125
A non-multinational firm from some other country	1	3.125
Total	32	100.000

The labour force of these 32 Australian companies is overwhelmingly Malaysian. On average, the 32 Australian firms employ only 65 expatriate Australians—an average of about 2.03 per firm. The 23 firms that answered the question about the number[3] of Malaysian employees reported a total Malaysian workforce of 2,819. The largest employer of labour had only one expatriate Australian for every 233 Malaysian workers. Nor are the Australian firms large employers of labour from other Asian countries—of these there were fewer than the number of expatriates, namely 61 expatriate employees, or on average 1.9 per firm.

Business in Malaysia is profitable

Twenty-six of the 32 firms, or 82 per cent, reported that their business in Malaysia was profitable. Of these about 56 per cent (18 firms) said that they had become profitable within three years of doing business in Malaysia.

Another five firms, or 19 per cent, were profitable within five years. Two Australian companies took six years to show a profit and one firm was profitable within 20 years.

Only five companies reported that their Malaysian operations were not profitable (that is 16 per cent of the sample) and one firm was breaking even. Why these firms did not make a profit is a complex question and something that cannot be determined by a survey of the kind we undertook. However, we should note the following characteristics of the firms that were not profitable:

- all of them had entered the Malaysian market since 1990;
- three of them were involved in the construction industry;
- two of them were Australian–Malaysian partnerships.

The two variables of significance in these correlations are the last two. In the previous section we noted that 12 of the 32 Australian companies we surveyed were involved in the construction industry. So within that sector, three of the 12 were not making a profit—that is, 25 per cent were unprofitable. That is hardly remarkable given the difficulties the construction industry of Malaysia faced during the Asian currency crisis. What is remarkable is that the other nine firms involved in the construction industry were profitable. We know from in-depth studies conducted by one of the authors of this paper (Vicziany 2001) that many of the construction companies were able to ride out the difficulties of the Asian currency crisis in Malaysia by giving extended credit lines to their Malaysian customers. The bulk of these creative responses to the crisis worked very well. They not only kept both Malaysian and Australian firms afloat, but also allowed them to make profits.

The worrying variable here is the fate of Australian–Malaysian partnerships. In the previous section we noted that three of the Australian companies in Malaysia were partnerships, and we now learn that of these, two businesses, or 66 per cent, were not profitable. The survey results indicate the need for a very close examination of the nature of Australian–Malaysian joint ventures. However, at this stage it is too soon to say that the joint venture arrangement by itself accounts for the lack of profit.

Australian firms plan to expand their business in Malaysia

In view of the profitability of the Malaysian market for the over-whelming majority of Australian firms we studied (82 per cent), it came as no surprise that Australian firms in Malaysia were optimistic about the future. The majority, some 72 per cent or 23 firms, planned to expand their business dealings with Malaysia in the next 2–3 years. About a fifth (seven firms) have no such plans and another 6 per cent or two companies are unsure. Without in-depth interviews with the companies we cannot understand why some companies will expand their engagement with Malaysia whilst others have no such intention. In any case, the priority at this stage of research was more limited: we simply wanted to find out whether Malaysia was a profitable market or not and whether this had an influence on short- and medium-term corporate plans. Clearly the majority of Australian firms in Malaysia have a very positive view of their short- to medium-term prospects in Malaysia.

When asked about their plans in the next five to ten years, Australian firms remain overwhelmingly positive, with 63 per cent (20 firms) still reporting that they plan to expand and about 19 per cent (six companies) saying that they are unsure. Only a minority of four companies, representing 12.5 per cent of the sample, said that they have no plans to expand their Malaysian business.

Of the 23 firms that plan to expand their interests in Malaysia in the short term (namely the next two to three years), a majority of 19, or 83 per cent, are also planning to increase their investments in the short term. These plans were obviously in place before the Asian currency crisis, but by the start of the survey in October 1999 these firms had decided to proceed with their plans.

Expectations about the performance of the Malaysian economy are also high, with 78 per cent of Australian firms (that is 25 companies) reporting that they expect the demand for their goods and services in Malaysia to recover in the next two to three years.

Australian perceptions about economic reforms

We asked five different questions pertaining to the process of economic reform in Malaysia:

- Is enough being done to increase accountability and transparency in the distribution of government contracts?
- Is enough being done to reform the banking and financial sector?
- Is enough being done to increase domestic competition with *bumiputera* firms?
- Is enough being done to increase domestic competition with non-*bumiputera* firms?
- Are government policies sufficiently attractive to foreign firms?

The responses showed that Australian firms are divided on the question of how extensive the reform process has been. More Australian firms have a positive view of banking and financial reforms in contrast with negative views about accountability/transparency in government contracts, competition with *bumiputera* firms and government policies to bring foreign capital into Malaysia. On none of the five questions, however, did the majority of Australian firms believe that sufficient reform had taken place. Just over half of the Australian companies thought that not enough had been done to achieve transparency/accountability and more competition with *bumiputera* firms and 40 per cent said that not enough had been done to promote the inflow of foreign capital.

This does not mean that Australian firms were unaware of the economic reforms undertaken by the Malaysian government. From in-depth interviews with Australian firms in Malaysia (Vicziany 2001) we know that they do follow the economic policies of the Malaysian government fairly closely and a very active Australian trade office in Kuala Lumpur also keeps them well briefed. The publication of the Department of Foreign Affairs and Trade in Canberra has also given proper recognition to the reforms occurring in Malaysia (Trade and Economic Analysis Branch, 1999, p. 23). Another conduit for current information is Mr Alistair Maitland, formerly of the ANZ–Grindlays Bank and now one of the two foreign directors on the Board of Danaharta. Mr Maitland is a regular speaker at business briefings in Australia and has taken great pains to publicise the extent of the reforms and the painstaking nature of the process itself.[4] The Australia–Malaysia Business Council and its Malaysian counterpart are also important avenues of information between the government and the private sector (Australia–Malaysia Business Council Newsletters 1999–2000).

Despite this, Australian firms are of the opinion that the reform process still has a long way to go. A surprisingly large percentage of firms are also 'unsure' about what the reform process has achieved. When asked about whether the government of Malaysia had done enough to promote competition with non-*bumiputera* companies, 13 Australian firms, or 40 per cent, said that they were not sure (Table 3.4 below). The concept of 'uncertainty' needs to be understood not as something that stems from a lack of knowledge by Australian companies but rather as a result of their hesitancy about the ability of government policies to make a difference.

Table 3.4: Perceptions about economic reforms in Malaysia: Responses to the questions is the Malaysian government doing enough to increase/improve...

	Yes	No	Not sure	No replies	Percentages of Yes/No
17a Accountability/transparency	5	17	9	1	16.00 / 53.13
17b Banking reforms	14	12	3	3	44.00 / 37.50
17c Competition with *bumiputera* firms	4	18	10	Nil	12.50 / 56.25
17d Competition with non-*bumiputera* firms	4	12	13	3	12.50 / 37.50
17e Policies to bring in foreign capital	9	13	9	1	28.13 / 40.63

Of course, Australian firms are impatient for economic reform is not really surprising—companies throughout the world appear to be impatient with governments and their economic policies. This impatience is usually more noticeable in the case of foreign firms, which perhaps do not have enough inside knowledge of their host societies to make them more cautious. In Malaysia, India, China and other Asian nations, economic reform has to proceed in a manner that is not too rapid or too disruptive. The timing and sequencing of reform is a critical issue in ensuring the maintenance of social and political stability in these multiracial societies.

It is important to note that Australian firms do not reserve their concerns exclusively for the Malaysian government. They are also critical about the role and responsibilities of the IMF and G-7 countries, as responses to Question 18 in the survey indicated.

At the suggestion that reforming the international financial architecture was a prerequisite for more confidence in Malaysia, more Australian firms strongly supported the statement (50 per cent), while others thought this was not important at all (25 per cent). Another 25 per cent were relatively neutral.

Opinions about the IMF were also critical, with 22 firms, or 69 per cent, reporting that the IMF was not doing enough to prevent volatile capital flows in the future. When asked about the G-7 countries 66 per cent of Australian firms also reported that not enough was being done to prevent volatile capital movements in the future.

In contrast to these criticisms of the international institutions, more Australian firms believed that the Malaysian government was doing enough to prevent another crisis (13 firms or 41 per cent) than those who thought that not enough was being done (8 firms or 25 per cent). Another 11 companies, or 34 per cent, were relatively neutral on this question.

On the other hand, Australian companies were most critical about the corporate and banking sectors: about half of the firms (15) thought that the corporate sector was not doing enough, and 17 firms felt that the banks had not reformed themselves sufficiently. Those who thought that enough was being done by the corporate and banking sectors were a minority of 16 per cent and 9 per cent respectively.

A general conclusion that emerges from this is that on balance Australian companies have divided views about the nature and success of economic reform in Malaysia. They distinguish between reforms of different kinds. Whilst being sympathetic to many of the initiatives of the Malaysian government, Australian companies remain critical of the *bumiputera* policies and the lack of accountability and transparency. But Australian firms reserve their strongest criticism for the Malaysian corporate sector and multilateral institutions such as the IMF. Flowing from this, only a third of Australian respondents thought that the risk of a recurrence of a crisis in Malaysia had been greatly diminished as a result of the lessons learned during the recent crisis. A large number of Australian firms, 47 per cent of the sample, strongly disagreed with this proposition.

The negative perceptions of risk and reform, however, did not have a negative impact on plans for further business or investment in Malaysia, as we saw in the previous sections of this chapter. Indeed, the pragmatic strategies of Australian firms took them in the direction of increasing their engagement with Malaysia. One possible reason for this could be that whatever criticisms the Australian firms have about the limitations and slowness of reforms, Malaysia is regarded as a good market for Australia because of a range of positive considerations. The next sections discuss the relative ease of the Malaysian market and the nature of the constraints in that business environment.

Malaysia is not the most difficult market

We asked the Australian firms to rank the Asian markets from one to six in order of descending levels of difficulty. From the returns it is clear that the majority of Australian firms do not operate in sufficient markets to fill this grid. Hence we have eliminated the fifth and sixth categories and will report only on the four most difficult markets in Asia.

Malaysia is not regarded as the most difficult market in Asia. It is superpassed by Indonesia and Thailand in this regard. At the same time, it is not an easy market and was mentioned more often than India, China, Vietnam and many others. Malaysia was mentioned 11 times in the top three categories of most difficult markets in Asia compared with China (seven), India (one), Japan (two) and Vietnam (five). As a percentage of the possible number of answers this amounts to about 11 per cent. Indonesia was mentioned in 15 per cent of cases and Thailand in 17 per cent. Malaysia was also mentioned most often as the fourth most difficult Asian market by eight companies (25 per cent of the sample) and with twice the frequency of Indonesia. The remaining 24 firms spread their complaints more evenly across the region. In summary, in a grid of 128 possible entries Malaysia was named as a difficult market a total of 19 times, or in 15 per cent of cases.

The conclusion from this is complex: Malaysia is not regarded as an easy market. Indeed it is regarded as relatively difficult but not as difficult as Thailand and Indonesia. However, perceptions of difficulty are not the primary considerations that drive entrepreneurs. Indeed, the high level of difficulty could well motivate a Schumpetarian entrepreneur to take on a particular problem or market for a whole range of complex reasons. Whether or not an entrepreneur will do so will be determined by other factors, including the profitability of a market. Furthermore, despite relative levels of difficulty, all markets have factors that foster or hinder the involvement of foreign firms. It is to these considerations that we now turn.

What is attractive about the Malaysia market?

What did Australian firms find attractive about the Malaysian market? Most of the variables we selected did not solicit a particularly strong response. Direct government policies designed to encourage foreign companies, incentives and research and development policies were not regarded as important by the majority of firms. In the case of access to raw materials and third markets, only a third of Australian companies attached any importance to these. As we see in Table 3.5, the strongest appeal of the Malaysian market comes from its geographical location, with half of Australian firms saying that this was an important factor. Oddly, however, seven firms, or 22 per cent, did not respond to this part of the questionnaire. We assume that these and the other seven firms who circled number '3' in the range of survey values did not particularly care about geographical location—this comes to a total of 44 per cent of the sample. Finally, the quality of human resources in Malaysia was regarded as very important by some 40 per cent of the respondents, but this is a percentage well below what we expected. The image Malaysia has in international markets led us to anticipate a more enthusiastic response to this particular factor. Malaysia's reputation as one of the Asian markets in which labour is of a relatively high quality is based on the success of the information technology industry in Penang and the fact that Malaysia attracts a large number of unskilled migrant workers from nearby Indonesia and Bangladesh.

Table 3.5: Attractiveness of the Malaysian market

Attractive variables	Not at all	Neutral	Strongly Agree*
Government attitudes to research and development	22	5	5
Malaysian government incentives	15	8	8
Access to raw materials/resources	11	7	11
Ease of access to third markets	8	10	11
Quality of human resources	4	14	13
Geographical location	2	7	16

* Where the answers do not total 32, it is because not all companies answered all survey questions.

Companies that operate at the international level are more inclined to be preoccupied with the constraints they face in overseas markets, rather than what attracted them to that market in the first place. The question of constraints is dealt with in the next section.

The constraints of the Malaysian market

We tested for a range of factors that could act as obstacles to doing business in/with Malaysia:

• infrastructure constraints;
• informational constraints;
• human resource constraints;
• government constraints;
• cultural constraints.

In all cases we asked the question: 'To what extent have the following factors affected your business with/in Malaysia?' Respondents were asked to circle a number from one to five as appropriate to each factor: Numbers one and two were at the bottom end of the scale representing the response that 'x was not at all' a constraint, and numbers four and five the top end of the scale indicating 'x strongly affected business'.

Infrastructure constraints

One of the most revealing points about this survey is the extent to which Australian firms are happy with the basic infrastructure of Malaysia—the ports, airports, roads, telecommunications, marketing and distribution facilities and research and development facilities (see Table 3.6). The overwhelming majority of firms reported that these were 'not at all' constraints in their activities. This is remarkable mainly in contrast with other parts of Asia, in particular India, where infrastructure bottlenecks constitute perhaps the single largest group of constraints facing Australian companies in that market (Vicziany and Chatterjee 1999).

Table 3.6: Infrastructure constraints
Australian firms which reported that these factors did not at all obstruct their business in Malaysia

	Number	%
Problems with ports	30	94
Problems with airports	28	88
Problems with marketing infrastructure	24	75
Problems with roads	23	72
Problems with telecommunications	23	72
Lack of research and development infrastructure	21	66

Human resource constraints

Again in contrast to India, where Australian firms report major difficulties with local labour, in Malaysia human resource constraints are much less severe (see Table 3.7). In the Indian case, the difficulty arises from a lack of basic training amongst the semi-skilled workforce, an antiquated system of trade union legislation, and unfair dismissals, which give rise to labour unrest. Whether or not it is economically beneficial to the Malaysian labour force for Australian companies to be so satisfied with Malaysian labour is a question beyond the scope of the present paper. All we can say is that 99 per cent of the respondents did not see industrial relations as major constraint.

Nor was there much local resistance to continuous training—only 16 per cent reported this to be a problem. In contrast to this, 44 per cent of Australian firms reported difficulty with obtaining and keeping trained labour. This reflects the considerable degree of job-hopping and head-

Table 3.7: Human resource constraints
Number and percentage of Australian firms that strongly agreed the following were serious obstacles to business in Malaysia

	Number	%
Obtaining and keeping trained labour	14	44.00
Availability of engineers	8	25.00
Availability of scientists/researchers	6	19.00
Resistance to continuous training	5	16.00
Facilities for expatriate families	2	6.25
Industrial relations problems	1	3.13

hunting in Malaysia as firms seek to attract skilled labour. Even so, the majority of firms (56 per cent) did not see this as a problem. About a quarter of respondents also reported serious constraints in the supply of engineers but an overwhelming 75 per cent did not agree that this was a constraint.

These responses are not incompatible with broad trends of the Malaysian economy. Although Malaysia has been a labour-scarce economy for some years, she also imports labour from Indonesia and Bangladesh. These arrivals have augmented the local labour force and so Australian firms have not experienced serious labour supply difficulties. In fact, various site visits to Australian factories in Malaysia in 1999 by one of the co-authors of this chapter indicated that some of the migrant labour will need to be shed as mechanisation and automation accelerate.[5]

The lack of concern on the part of Australian companies about the availability of scientists and researchers is also not surprising, if we assume that research and development is conducted not in Malaysia but abroad. Less than one-fifth of the respondents viewed this as a constraint. This might be unexpected by some observers, given the buoyancy of Malaysia's information technology sector and the assumed demand for scientists and researchers which this could generate (*The Economist* 5 February 2000). The buoyancy of Malaysian information technology, however, does not in itself tell one much about the locus of innovation and research and development. Most research and development probably originates abroad. So in this instance, the lack of complaint on the part of Australian companies might indeed be the very reason the Malaysian government should be worried. The government has announced that the development of a 'knowledge-based economy' is one of its priorities, but this will be difficult to achieve if research and development is largely imported.

Informational constraints (Table 3.8)

Fewer than a quarter of the respondents thought that information about the Malaysian market was a constraint, whether it was information about specific markets or government policies or the reliability of information. But the returns on this matter need to be considered in conjunction with the next subheading in this part of the survey, namely cultural constraints. It is often suggested that market information can be poor or misleading if foreign companies fail to understand the real intentions of government and the host society. So under the heading of 'cultural constraints' we included questions about this. Only 27 per cent of Australian firms thought that understanding the real intentions of local partners was a problem, but that rose to 41 per cent when it came to understanding the real intentions of government policies (refer to the section below on cultural constraints).

Table 3.8: Informational constraints
Number and percentage of Australian companies who strongly agreed that the following were constraints on business in Malaysia

	Number	%
Reliability of business information	8	25
Access to market-specific information	5	16
Access to information about government policies	6	19

Cultural constraints

Beginning with the work of Hofstede in 1980, there is now a considerable international literature about the problems of cross-cultural communication when companies carry out operations in foreign markets (Hofstede 1980/1984, chapter 6). This part of the survey demonstrated that Australian firms had varying experiences, depending on exactly which dimension of the Malaysian business culture was involved. When it came to language barriers, understanding the real intentions of local partners and the question of a local research and development culture, the majority of Australian firms did not identify these as problems. Again, the fact that Australian firms are not especially concerned about the lack of a research and development culture does not necessarily mean that Malaysia is well supplied in that regard. As we suggested earlier it could mean that Australian firms are not research and development oriented, or that if they are, this kind of work is done elsewhere.

The response to the question about political risk and uncertainty in Malaysian is worthy of attention. The survey coincided with the ongoing trial of Anwar Ibrahim and the Malaysian elections. The international press frequently exaggerates these events because their drama makes them newsworthy. It is then often wrongly assumed that because these events have been prominent in the international media, including the Australian media, they also impinge on the political stability of Malaysia. As it happens, over half of the Australian companies surveyed by us did not regard political risk and uncertainty as a constraint on business, and another 25 per cent were neutral on this issue as Table 3.9 below shows. Only a minority of 22 per cent strongly agreed with the proposition that this adversely affected their business. This is certainly a large 'minority' but is counterbalanced by the fact that an overwhelming 78 per cent of Australian firms did not see political risk and uncertainty as a constraint in their business operations in Malaysia.

But views on the cultural obstacles were divided, as a comparison of Parts 1 and 2 of Table 3.9 shows. When it came to the question of unethical business practices, Table 3.9 Part 2 shows that half of the Australian firms identified this as a problem, with only a third saying that it was not an issue. The question of business ethics was the largest single constraint of all the cultural factors we tested for. We return to this question of business ethics below.

Table 3.9: Cultural constraints: Part 1
Australian firms which reported that the following factors were 'not at all serious' obstacles to business in Malaysia compared with those who 'strongly agreed' that they were major constraints

	Not at all		Strongly agree	
	No.	%	No.	%
Language barriers	22	69	1	22
Political risks and uncertainties	17	53	7	9
Lack of R&D culture	16	50	3	22
Understanding real intentions of local partners	16	50	7	22

Table 3.9: Cultural constraints: Part 2
Australian firms which reported that the following factors were 'not at all serious' obstacles to business in Malaysia compared with those who 'strongly agreed' that they were major constraints

	Not at all		Strongly agree	
	No.	%	No.	%
Unethical business practices	10	31	16	50
Understanding real intentions of government Policies	16	50	9	28
Contracts	12	38	9	28

On the matter of understanding the real intentions of government policies, the majority of Australian companies were not concerned. Only 28 per cent of Australian companies felt that this was a constraint. Nevertheless, the Malaysian government might still wish to address the question of how to improve the awareness of this not insignificant minority of foreign firms.

Finally, cultural differences in the understanding and importance of contracts is widely regarded by Western companies as a bottleneck to business in Asia, so we also tested for this. However, Table 3.9 Part 2 of this survey shows that more Australian firms were comfortable with Malaysian contracts (12 firms or 38 per cent) than those who saw this as a barrier to business (9 firms or 28 per cent).[6] Moreover, more firms had a neutral position on this (34 per cent) than had complaints. This is a highly interesting survey outcome as it contradicts what we know from in-depth interviews with Australian firms in the Malaysian market and also other Asian markets (Vicziany 2001; Dogan, Smyth and Wills, chapter 4 in this book). The stereotypical view is that there is a fundamental clash of cultures between the Western and Eastern business styles. The Western, European approach is supposed to place a great emphasis on the written contract, with a tendency to seek legal redress as an early option when things start to go wrong. In Malaysia, and Asia more generally, the written contract is not supposed to have that kind of authority. According to the cultural stereotype, verbal undertakings, trust and personal loyalties all play a more important role in Asia than in the 'West'.

The survey results reject these culturally-based explanations. We would like to put forward an alternative hypothesis to explain the outcome of this study. The business culture of Malaysia and Australia may not be as wide apart as is commonly believed, for the following reasons:

- like India, Malaysia has a long history of involvement in international commerce and foreign companies;
- the legal and accounting traditions in the business world of Malaysia are dominated by professional norms influenced by Western business practice;
- the latter influence is quite powerful given the number of Malaysian professionals trained abroad, especially in Australia.

Government constraints

The most serious constraints in the Malaysian market appear to relate to government regulations. More Australian firms were worried about these than were concerned about compared to the cultural factors for which we tested (see Table 3.10). At the top of that list are the regulations about *bumiputera* ownership, with 56 per cent of Australian firms agreeing strongly that this was an obstacle. This was followed by 53 per cent of Australian companies regarding government regulation in general as a serious constraint on business. The majority of firms, by contrast, did not view restrictive local equity rules as a major constraint. Nevertheless, a significant minority of 47 per cent did report this as a serious problem.

But government policies were not regarded as equally difficult. On the question of unpredictable policy changes acting as a constraint on business, only a minority of Australian firms—some 38 per cent—thought that this was an important barrier. The overwhelming majority were either neutral or dismissive on this point.

Again, only a quarter of Australian firms were worried about laws concerning the employment of *bumiputeras* and import tariffs, and less than a fifth recorded intellectual property rights as an obstacle.

Finally, limitations on the repatriation of profits bothered hardly anyone, with only two out of 32 companies (6 per cent) reporting concerns in this area. It is important to note, once again, that when it comes to any aspect of

Table 3.10: Government constraints
*Number and percentage of Australian companies which 'strongly agreed'
that the following factors were obstacles to business in Malaysia*

	Number	%
Regulations re *bumiputera* ownership	18	56
Bureaucratic regulations	17	53
Restrictive local equity	15	47
Unpredictable policy changes	12	38
High tariffs on imports	8	25
Regulations re *bumiputera* employment	8	25
Uncertain protection of intellectual property	6	19
Difficulty in repatriating profits	2	6

the Malaysian economy that impinges immediately on the profitability of
Australian firms and their capacity to collect that profit, there was a high
level of satisfaction with Malaysia. It is probably the case that the optimistic
view Australian firms have of the prospects of the Malaysian market is
driven by a handful of considerations such as this.

The impact of the Asian currency crisis

In early 1999, the Australian government announced that the Asian
currency crisis afforded special opportunities for the Australian corporate
sector. We were, therefore, interested in finding out what impact the Asian
currency crisis had on Australian business firms based in Malaysia.
Specifically, we asked respondents to 'assess the impact of the Asian
currency crisis on your business in Malaysia during the last two years'.

The majority of the firms, 18, that is 56 per cent, said that the crisis had
been 'not at all' positive. But interestingly enough, as many as seven
companies, or 22 per cent, strongly agreed that the effect had been positive.
Of these seven firms, three were involved in information technology
industries, two in minerals and metal processing, and one in the manufacture
of components. That some Australian information technology firms
benefited from the crisis is not surprising. The information technology
industry in Malaysia has been booming and, crisis or no crisis, the demand
for information technology goods and services in Malaysia and throughout
the world has not abated. To what extent that demand was driven by fears
about the Y2K bug is unknown. Determining the reasons behind the
responses from the other four companies would require more detailed
investigation.

The other interesting aspect of this part of the survey was the
contradictory opinions about fixed exchange rates and currency
convertibility. It would be reasonable to assume that the firms who
perceived fixed exchange rates to be beneficial might also regard suspension
of currency convertibility as a positive thing. Fifteen firms, or 47 per cent,

said that the fixed exchange rate policy of the Malaysian government had helped their business. Only a third said that fixed exchange rates had not been helpful. We would have predicted that a sizeable number of firms would, therefore, agree that the suspension of currency convertibility was also helpful. But oddly enough, only five, or 16 per cent of the sample, did. A much larger number of companies—16 firms or 50 per cent—reported that they had not been assisted by the suspension of currency convertibility.

Perhaps the discrepancy can be accounted for in the following way: the suspension of currency convertibility affected the perceptions that international business had about the long-term commitment of the Malaysian government to the open market economy regime of the previous decades. This shook confidence in the Malaysian market, and probably had an adverse impact on all foreign firms in Malaysia in a diverse number of ways. On the other hand, Australian firms might have regarded short-term and practical measures such as imposing fixed exchange rates, more positively. Because fixed exchange rates replaced the wild fluctuations in the months leading up to this decision by the Malaysian government, Australian firms might well have seen this measure as establishing some kind of short-term certainty and predictability, hence their positive view of the decision (see Table 3.11).

Table 3.11: Impact of Asian currency crisis
Australian companies which reported that the following aspects of the Asian currency crisis had been 'not at all' helpful to their business in Asia, compared with those who strongly agreed that they had been positive

	Not at all		Strongly agree	
	No.	%	No.	%
Has the effect been positive?	18	56	7	22
Did suspension of currency convertibility help your firm?	16	50	5	16
Has the fixed exchange rate helped your firm?	10	31	15	47
Has the main impact been on Malaysian partners?	6	19	13	41

Of the minority of firms that had a positive view of the suspension of currency convertibility, three provided more detailed explanations of why this was so:

- two said that it had created a more stable environment for their business ;
- a third firm said it helped their international competitiveness.

Another two companies, which had a neutral view of the suspension of currency convertibility, also noted:

- the movement of funds had been made easier, although their firm had not directly benefited from this;
- a second firm reported that it had helped to devalue their inventory.

Conclusion

Australian firms have found the Malaysian market to be a profitable one and one that does not restrict their ability to repatriate profits. They had plans to expand their involvement and investment in Malaysia before the Asian currency crisis and they have not changed these plans as a result of that crisis. These plans are driven, more than anything else, by the profitability of the market. Australian optimism about the Malaysian market was also based on:

* the country's good infrastructure;
* its human resources base;
* its geographical proximity to Australia;
* the absence of language barriers;
* a business culture compatible with the Australian law of contract;
* political stability;
* a government willing to undertake ongoing economic reform.

All these positive views existed alongside the opinion that whilst Malaysia was not Asia's most difficult market, it was certainly a market that was not especially easy. Only Thailand and Indonesia were regarded as more difficult than Malaysia.

At the same time, Australians believed that the process of economic reform in Malaysia had not gone far enough, but they were more critical of the corporate sector than of government efforts. Business ethics, in particular, ranked high on the list of constraints. They were equally critical of the IMF and G-7 countries, neither of which had done enough to help stabilise the world economy within which Malaysia operates. When it came to business constraints within the Malaysian market, Australian firms were most concerned about government regulations—the bureaucratic environment in general and laws about *bumiputera* ownership.

Australian optimism about Malaysia was also tempered by the belief that a recurrence of the economic crisis of 1998–99 has not been totally eliminated as a result of the lessons learnt and the reforms instituted during the last few years. The Asian currency crisis itself did not have a positive impact on the majority of Australian firms, with only five firms reporting that they had actually benefited from it. The Malaysian government's response to the crisis also divided Australian opinion: the majority of firms reported that the suspension of currency convertibility had not been useful, but on the other hand a large proportion of companies had found the imposition of fixed exchange rates helpful.

We cannot pretend to have resolved all the issues thrown up by this survey. This chapter is the first in a series of business surveys we plan to undertake. Perhaps some of the issues will be explained more adequately in subsequent reports. We are also conscious of the limitations of all questionnaires. In their nature, they cannot provide in-depth explanations.

For greater depth, we need detailed case studies. About four case studies have been undertaken (Vicziany 2001), but these may not be typical of the experience foreign firms have of the Malaysian market.

On the other hand, the questionnaire was able to provide an overview of the things that bother Australian firms. Some of the concerns are likely to be shared by other foreign companies in Malaysia. As a result, the survey helps to identify areas that need to be addressed by the Malaysian corporate and government sectors. The following list identifies areas in which Australian firms signalled the need for change:

- more engineers and more highly skilled labourers in general need to be trained—this is supported by anecdotal evidence from Australian companies about the skilled labour shortages which they typically face in Malaysia;
- government regulations concerning foreign equity and joint ventures between foreign and Malaysian firms need to be reviewed, especially the regulations about *bumiputera* ownership;
- the matter of business transparency and accountability needs to be placed at the top of the government's reform agenda in order to overcome the perception that business practices in Malaysia are unethical.[7]

Of these, perhaps the latter is the one that has attracted the greatest amount of international comment. One reason is that of the 52 countries ranked by Transparency International in 1999, Malaysia appears on the wrong side of the average—it is ranked as number 32 and not far removed from unfavourable perceptions of South Korea, Thailand, Philippines and Indonesia at 34, 39, 40 and 46 respectively. In challenging Singapore's business dominance in South-East Asia, Singapore's ranking as nine provides an unwelcome contrast for the Malaysian government (Aziz 1999). This is not the place to engage in a discussion of the relative accuracy or fairness of the measures used by Transparency International. We acknowledge that there is a valid debate on this issue. However, whatever the limitations of the work by Transparency International and similar organisations, the question of business practices in Malaysia needs to be addressed because Australian firms perceive this to be a problem. What the appropriate policy response to this might be, however, is beyond the purposes of this chapter.

On the subject of relations between foreign and Malaysian companies, a fundamental disagreement clearly exists between the priorities and perceptions of the Malaysian government and foreign firms—especially on the matter of the *bumiputera* ownership laws. In September 1999, the Malaysian Prime Minister restated the commitment to the *bumiputera* policies until such time as the *bumiputera* control 30 per cent of the 'national wealth' (EIU 1999, p. 22). Given that current estimates indicate that only 20 per cent of the corporate wealth is in the hands of indigenous groups, foreign firms would be better off simply accepting these policy measures as one of the parameters within which they must work if they find the Malaysian market attractive. And as the present survey shows, there are compelling reasons why Australian companies do find Malaysia an attractive market. As in other parts of Asia, national priorities that involve matters of socio-economic equity are not negotiable. Social development policies cannot be put on the same plane as tariff, tax or interest rate policies and the sooner this is accepted by foreign firms the better.

At the same time, we need to recognise that the Malaysian government, consistent with its pragmatic policies and practices, is involved in an ongoing process of reviewing economic liberalisation and the country's success in attracting foreign capital. In early 2000, the Malaysian government asked the National Economic Consultative Council to review the *bumiputera* policies with a view to improving the economic climate for the next ten years. As we argued earlier in this chapter, Australian companies are reasonably well informed about current government policies and priorities. However, they do not appear to have a strong sense of the extent and direction of ongoing policy revisions. Perhaps Australian companies could be given a greater sense of the dynamism of planned policy changes in Malaysia through special high level, Government of Malaysia briefings.

On balance, the survey suggests that Australian firms have a very positive attitude towards doing business in Malaysia. The reasons for this—profitability, growth, easy repatriation of profits, political stability, good infrastructure, and the use of the English language—need to be made more widely known in the Australian and the international business communities. However, for this information to carry weight it is desirable that the Malaysian government demonstrate that independent external assessors have collected the information. Perhaps is this one role that foreign scholars working on Malaysia can play.

Endnotes

[1]	In September 1998 the Malaysian government introduced a one-year hold on the repatriation of foreign assets, in addition to suspending convertibility of the ringgit. In February 1999, a sliding exit tax replaced the former—on profits remitted out of Malaysia in under 12 months, the charge was 30 per cent and on profits repatriated after 12 months, this fell to 10 per cent. By the end of September 1999, a uniform ruling was introduced—all remitted profits would incur a 10 per cent tax.
[2]	The database team consisted of Associate Professor Marika Vicziany (Monash Melbourne, Team leader), Mr Tim Thornton (Monash Melbourne), Mr Nar Chin Sun (formerly of Monash Malaysia) and Mr Koi Nyn Wong (Monash Malaysia).
[3]	The other firms reported percentages and gave ranges rather than exact figures.
[4]	Interviews with Mr A. Maitland, May 1999, Melbourne.
[5]	Fieldwork in Kuala Lumpur and Melaka by M. Vicziany in February 1999.
[6]	This paper diverges from the earlier, preliminary report by the authors in February 2000 on this particular topic. The larger survey diminished the importance of contracts as a cultural barrier to commerce.

7   On the basis of a poll of 19 registered political parties, the Malaysian chapter of Transparency International concluded, 'Most Malaysian parties, including the main component parties of the ruling coalition, have made no commitment to promote greater transparency and accountability' (Transparency International 1999).

References

Australia–Malaysia Business Council Newsletters 1999–2000.

Aziz, Tunku Abdul (1999), 'Malaysia: Living with perceptions—the importance of transparency', *A Transparency International Working Paper*, Berlin, October.

Business Times (2000), 'Chasing the right investment', 11 February.

The Economist (2000), 'Asia online: The riger and the tech', 5 February.

EIU (Economist Intelligence Unit) (1999), *Country Report, Malaysia and Brunei, 4th quarter 1999*, London.

Halls, Mike (1999), 'Malaysia opens up again', *Corporate Finance*, November, 180 (57).

Hill, Christine (1999), 'Punishing capital controls with kindness', *Institutional Investor*, New York, 33/12, December, 105–112.

Hofstede, Geert (1980/1984), *Culture's Consequences: International Differences in Work-Related Values*, Beverly Hills: Sage Publications.

Hyam, Tim et al. (1999/2000), 'After the deluge only the fittest have survived', *Global Investor*, 128, December–January.

Jayasanakaran, S. (1999), 'Politics confuse rosy outlook', *Far Eastern Economic Review*, 162 (43), 28 October.

Lee, Peter (1999), 'Being rational about recovery', *Euromoney*, London, 368, December, 93–98.

Mitra, Sabyasachi (1999), 'Moody's raises rating outlook: but lack of reform, politics remain barriers', *Reuters News Service*, 8 October.

Navaratnam, Ramon (1999), *Healing the Wounded Tiger: How the Turmoil is Reshaping Malaysia*, Malaysia: Pelanduk Publications.

New Straits Times (2000), 'RM72.3b surplus in 1999', 5 February.

Trade and Economic Analysis Branch (1999), *Trade Winds: East Asia—Recovery Underway*, December.

Transparency International, Malaysian Chapter (otherwise known as The Kuala Lumpur Society for Transparency and Integrity) (1999), Press Release, Kuala Lumpur, 26 November.

Vicziany, Marika (2001), 'Long-term trends in the Australia–Malaysia business relationship', forthcoming.

Vicziany, Marika and Chatterjee Samirb (1999), 'Australian business attitudes to India in the late 1990s', in S. Neelmagham et al. (eds), *Enterprise Management: New Horizons in Indo-Australian Collaboration*, New Delhi: Tata McGraw Hill.

4

Transaction costs of cross-cultural exchange: Evidence from Australia–Malaysia case studies

Ergun Dogan, Russell Smyth and Ian Wills[1]

Introduction

From a purely contractual perspective, parties to a transaction need to undertake a number of costly activities. These include (Eggertsson 1991, s.1.4; Wills 1997, s.5.6):

- identification of exchange partners;
- measurement of the quantity/quality dimensions of the good or service exchanged;
- definition of the parties' rights and obligations in respect of whatever is exchanged, making provision for anticipated contingencies;
- revelation of the parties' willingness to pay or to accept; and
- after the parties agree to the exchange contract, enforcement of the parties' rights and obligations, which must include performance monitoring and imposition of penalties for contract violations.

When a firm is contracting with exchange partners from a different culture, the costs involved in performing these activities are higher. The abilities of firms involved in international exchanges to understand and subsequently reduce the costs stemming from cultural differences with their foreign trading partners is therefore important in determining each firm's competitiveness in a global economy.

In the aftermath of the Asian crisis the competitiveness of Malaysia's export sector has taken on increased importance. As is well known, before the crisis most South-East Asian countries had been growing at very high rates; with the crisis this came to a sudden halt. In the case of Malaysia the crisis disrupted the country's drive to achieve developed country status by 2020, the so-called Vision 2020. A higher volume of international trade can be expected to increase employment and output; it will also help Malaysian firms to remain competitive in the future. Increased exposure to foreign trade creates dynamic benefits because of the positive effect of international competition on firm efficiency and productivity, which are key factors for survival in international markets.

Small and medium-sized enterprises (SMEs) can play a crucial role in this process. There are no reliable aggregate statistics on the number of

SMEs in Malaysia, but a survey in 1994 suggested that the number was about 12,000. SMEs constituted 84 per cent of all manufacturing enterprises, employed 33 per cent of the manufacturing workforce, and produced 28 per cent of total manufacturing value-added (Foong 1999). According to Foong (1999, p. 81): 'The relatively low contribution of Malaysian SMEs to the total value added of the manufacturing sector is seen as a bottleneck in achieving the rapid industrialisation of the nation'. This bottleneck could be addressed through an increase in SME exports and imports. Given that the share of SMEs in Malaysia's total exports is only 15 per cent, well below the 26.1 per cent average for a sample of OECD countries (Hall 1995), a lot could be achieved by increasing the involvement of SMEs in international trade. Hall (1995, p. 5) emphasises the importance of SME involvement in trade for APEC countries such as Malaysia.

From an APEC perspective, the main driving issue is the move toward increasing economic interdependence, open regionalism and the liberalisation of flows of goods, services, resources and capital. The enormous potential for SMEs to contribute to the economic development of the region will be under-utilised if SMEs are not able to take advantage of the opportunities created, or able to adapt to the competitive pressures that open regionalism brings.

This chapter reports the results of a study of the transaction costs of cross-cultural exchange, drawing on interviews with senior management in a small sample of Australian and Malaysian firms. The study uses a contractual approach, consistent with the above framework, to investigate the ways in which cultural differences add to the costs of exchange between Australian and Malaysian firms. The issue of cross-cultural exchange has received extensive theoretical treatment;[2] however, there are no empirical studies of the cultural impediments to contracting between Australian and Malaysian firms.

Our results should be of assistance to policy makers and commercial trade organisations in designing policies to lower or eliminate cultural barriers, which in some cases are preventing SMEs in Malaysia from entering international markets and/or increasing their share of foreign trade. In this respect an understanding of how cultural differences contribute to transaction costs will assist in the formulation of corporate and government policies to increase the international competitiveness of Australian and Malaysian firms. The chapter describes the analytical framework used and the study's methodology and the firms surveyed, reports empirical findings from our interviews with the sample firms, and summarises the main conclusions of the study and limitations of the research.

Analytical framework

Consider the activities that a firm needs to undertake once it has decided to export or invest overseas. These include (see Teece 1986):

• identifying possible foreign business partners;

- communicating information about the item of sale and its performance features;
- ascertaining the formal and informal rules applying to foreign business dealings;
- negotiating a contract/choosing a foreign business partner; and
- monitoring and enforcing the contract, once agreed.

This study focuses on the costs of cross-cultural exchange after a possible business partner has been identified, that is, activities 2–4 above. The process of choosing a business partner, involving investigation of the credibility and capabilities of various candidates, is not complete until contract negotiations are successfully concluded.

As indicated in the introduction, the costs involved in the above activities are greater when the exchange is cross-cultural. From the perspective of an Australian firm contemplating business dealings in Malaysia, either its employees must acquire the necessary communication skills, or Malaysians must be hired to represent its interests, raising principal–agent problems, which are also part of the transaction costs of exchange. For this reason, previous studies that report interviews with Australian firms involved in Malaysia suggest that, at least in the initial stages, the costs of contracting with a Malaysian partner represent high barriers to entry (Stokie 1995; Smyth and Wills 2000).

The distinction made between the contracting activities 2–4 above separates recognisably different information-gathering and -exchange activities; there is no necessary implication that the management of a firm engaged in overseas contracting will see activities 2–4 as separate, or undertake them in the order given above. Nevertheless, the distinction is useful as a step towards identifying the most serious technical and/or behavioural barriers to lower-cost exchange between Australian and Malaysian businesses.

Communicating information about the item of sale and its performance

One source of transaction costs is imperfect information about the item exchanged. These costs exist irrespective of the contracting environment, but are often magnified in cross-cultural exchange. Previous research suggests that in Asia, Australian firms find it hard to communicate information about technologies. There is a common perception in Asia that Australian technologies are not as good as technologies from Europe, Japan or the United States. For instance, Vicziany (1993) suggests that this has been one of the major difficulties Australian firms have encountered in India. She states (1993, p. 42): 'The chief advantage which German companies have had over their competitors was the international reputation of German engineering and technology'.

On the Malaysian side, firms often have problems in getting their partners to understand the difficulties faced in production. Smyth and Wills (2000) argue that Australian firms often have a better understanding of the problems faced by their counterparts in Malaysia than do competitors in

Europe and the United States, and this gives Australian firms a competitive edge. The population and market size in Malaysia are similar to Australia's, and it is likely that because of geographical proximity Australian firms have a better understanding of the climatic conditions in Malaysia than European or American competitors. However, cultural and religious differences make it just as difficult for a Malaysian firm to get an Australian partner to understand certain work practices, such as those related to the Muslim faith, as a partner from Europe or the United States.

Ascertaining the rules and norms applying to business in Malaysia

Once a firm has made investments (for example, an Australian firm investing in training of Malaysian staff or installation of equipment in Malaysian premises) dedicated to a one-to-one relationship with a business partner the firm is vulnerable to 'hold-up'. In the example given, because the relationship-specific investments may have little or no value in their next-best uses, the Malaysian partner, citing changed circumstances, can try to force the Australian firm to accept a less favourable deal than previously agreed. Thus a firm incurring relationship-specific investments will demand safeguards to prevent its overseas counterpart from attempting to appropriate all or most of the profits associated with these assets (Klein et al. 1978). These safeguards can take the form of legally-enforceable contracts, or extra-legal private ordering arrangements (Noorderhaven 1996).

Smyth and Wills (2000) found that one reason many Australian firms prefer to invest in Malaysia, rather than other Asian countries, is that the legal system is based on the common law. However, for Australian firms the actual form of legal agreement might be quite different, depending on with whom they are contracting. Handshake deals and personal relationships are more important in South-East Asia than in Western countries (Hamilton 1991; Thompson 1996). Such informal contracting mechanisms are likely to create additional (including psychological) costs for Australian firms that are more comfortable with a written contract than an extra-legal private agreement (Thompson 1996). At the same time, it has been argued that some Asian firms resent being obliged to sign a written contract, for two reasons. First, it implies the other party does not trust them (Kao 1991). Second, it suggests that the other party is not committed to developing a high level of personal trust needed to create an effective working relationship (Thompson 1996).

Negotiating a contract/choosing a business partner

Several researchers have distinguished between individualist and collectivist societies (see Hofstede 1980; Doney et al. 1998). Others have emphasised that Asian societies stress 'collectivist values' while Western societies stress 'individualist values' (see Shi 1999; Smith 1999). The distinction between individualism and collectivism influences the ease with which a party can ascertain whether the other is a credible contractor;

collectivist norms provide greater assurance that the other party's motives are benevolent. For instance, Williamson (1985, p. 122) states 'the hazards of trading are less severe in Japan than in the United States because of cultural and institutional checks on opportunism'.

Cultural differences are also an impediment to the development of trust in inter-firm relationships. It is argued that trust lowers transaction costs in uncertain environments (see Dore 1983; Noordewier et al. 1990). Trust depends on shared expectations about behaviour (Zucker 1986). Thus a firm from Australia, where individualist values are dominant, will find it difficult to establish credentials as a reliable contractor in a country such as Malaysia, where collectivist values are important. This is because trust is a prediction process; it stems from expectations about how another party will behave based on past behaviour (Deutsch 1960; Good 1988). This takes time to establish when the firms come from different contracting cultures, because of the lack of shared expectations about behaviour.

Monitoring and enforcement of the contract

Monitoring and enforcement costs are also likely to be larger when the exchange is cross-cultural. Access to local knowledge has been shown to be an important determinant of whether joint ventures between international and local companies are successful in the Asia–Pacific region (Lasserre 1999). But it is often difficult for 'outsiders' to get access to reliable local information. Thompson (1996) makes the point that if a firm in Australia wants information about the financial health of a client or prospective partner it can obtain this information from formal sources such as professional credit rating agencies. Credit rating agencies are rarely used in South-East Asia because the ratings are based on publicly available company reports that are themselves regarded as unreliable. Monitoring costs can be high when the foreign firm does not know where to look. One way for a foreign firm to access local information is to appoint an agent, but, as indicated above, the resulting principal–agent problems also add to the transaction costs of cross–cultural exchange.

The value of litigation for enforcing contracts might also differ between collectivist and individualist societies. Trubisky et al. (1991) argue that the method of conflict resolution in collectivist and individualistic cultures is different. Their study found that individualistic cultures, such as Australia and the United States, emphasise direct and explicit methods of conflict resolution, like litigation; collectivist cultures, such as those in Asia, prefer to avoid direct conflicts. There is also evidence to suggest that preference for conflict avoidance differs within collectivist cultures. For instance, in a comparative study of Japanese and Malaysian managers, both from what are regarded as collectivist cultures, Wafa et al. (1999) found that Malaysian managers preferred less direct forms of conflict resolution (such as mediation through a mutual business associate) than their Japanese counterparts. This can be frustrating, and costly, for firms from individualist cultures. Australian firms are likely to prefer immediate court-imposed solutions when, for example, payments are not made, rather having to invest time in less formal mediation.

Methodology

The cross-cultural costs of exchange between Australian and Malaysian firms were investigated through interviews with senior managers of five Australian firms doing business in Malaysia and three Malaysian firms with business links to Australian firms. The five Australian firms were selected based on preliminary discussions with two informants: staff at Export Access, an Austrade-funded export consultancy affiliated with the Australian Chamber of Manufactures, and a private trade consultant who has a long association with the Australia–Malaysia Business Council. These interviews were conducted in Melbourne between November 1998 and March 1999. The interviews with the Australian firms were with either the Managing Director or Marketing Manager for Asia. The Australian companies that we interviewed were either small or medium-sized firms that lacked substantial in-house expertise on international business and had few established links to accounting, legal and consulting firms. This meant that senior management had an active on-going role in managing the foreign venture. Thus, in contrast to larger firms where senior executives often withdraw after the initial negotiation phase, the managers that we interviewed had intimate knowledge of problems in both the negotiation period and ongoing difficulties in the management of their Malaysian activities. The Malaysian firms were selected from those listed in the 1999 edition of the Federation of Malaysian Manufacturers Directory as having links to Australia. Interviews with these firms were conducted in Kuala Lumpur in December 1999 and January 2000.

The Australian respondents were asked open-ended questions about: how they established a contract with a Malaysian partner; how they communicated product quality; how they determined the formal and informal rules governing business dealings in Malaysia; how they monitored the Malaysian partner; and how they took steps to enforce agreements. In the interviews, the emphasis was on pinpointing how, and in what ways, each of these aspects of the contract differed in their business dealings in Malaysia compared with their business dealings in Australia. The interviews with the Malaysian firms were conducted with the benefit of information obtained from the Australian interviews. We asked the Malaysian managers similar questions, and invited them to comment from their perspective.

Characteristics of the firms

In order to protect the confidentiality of the firms, in this chapter each is identified by a number. Firms I–V are Australian; firms VI–VIII are Malaysian.

Firm I is a medium-sized firm that provides refrigeration services. It has a joint venture with an ethnic Chinese firm based in Singapore; the Chinese firm has a branch in Malaysia. They have one Australian employee based in Malaysia full-time and the office of its Malaysian partner performs all the administration.

Firm II is a manufacturing firm that produces specialised equipment for factories and also sells and installs its production technology in the factories of other manufacturers in Australia. Just prior to the Asian crisis, it entered into a contract to install its production technology in an ethnic Chinese business in Malaysia. The contract also covered training for the employees of the Malaysian firm to service the production equipment once installed, and assistance with marketing the product in Malaysia.

Firm III produces plastic products. It has been exporting plastics technology and raw materials for moulding to Malaysia since 1993. In 1994–95 firm III was doing AU$1 million worth of business per annum in Malaysia. However, since 1996 it has been involved in a strategic withdrawal because it considered that the returns were not good enough. However this might change; firm III is currently looking for a Malaysian JV partner.

Firm IV supplies small components used in assembly-line products such as cars and computing equipment. It first entered the Malaysian market in 1994–95 and now has contracts with Mitsubishi and NEC. It has a joint venture subsidiary in Malaysia that employs three people and, on paper, at least 51 per cent is owned by its *bumiputera* agent.

Firm V manufactures and services a high-technology product. It differs from the other Australian firms in the sample to the extent that it is part of a group of companies, with headquarters in Germany, which produce a similar product with an annual turnover of more than AU$180 million worldwide. Firm V appointed agents and resellers in Malaysia, Indonesia, Thailand and Taiwan when it started exporting in 1993. In 1995 it set up a fully-owned subsidiary in Kuala Lumpur.

Firm VI is a large publicly listed Malaysian firm with close ties to the government. The National Investment Fund for *bumiputera* holds a controlling interest and of its nine-member board, eight directors are *bumiputera* and one is ethnic Chinese. It has a long and close association with, and substantial investment interests in, Australia.

Firm VII manufactures rubber products and is based in Kuala Lumpur. It has a joint venture with an Australian firm in Kuala Lumpur, producing rubber moulds for export in the Asia-Pacific region that was formed after the Asian crisis. Firm VII also exports rubber products to a number of European countries and Australia.

Firm VIII, based in Kuala Lumpur, manufactures and exports pipes and fittings to a number of countries in Africa, Europe and the Asia-Pacific region. Firm VIII has been exporting to Australia for six years, with three main customers, a Malaysian-owned Australian firm and two Australian-owned firms.

Empirical findings

Communicating information about the item of sale and its performance

The Malaysian senior managers had mixed views on the relative performance of Australian technologies. The Chief Financial Officer of firm VI thought that in many areas Australian technology was world class. The Chief Executive Officer (CEO) of firm VII thought that, in general, Japanese technologies were better than Australian technologies, but added that it depended on the industry concerned. The CEO of firm VIII considered that Australian technologies were good, although in certain areas German technologies were superior. In our earlier interviews with the Australian firms, the Managing Director of firm III expressed the view that Malaysian firms prefer to purchase technologies from Australian firms rather than Japanese firms because Japanese firms sell 'old technologies'. The Malaysians tended to agree with this observation, stating that one of the main advantages of dealing with Australian firms, relative to Japanese firms, is their willingness to transfer technologies. Each emphasised the flexibility and willingness of Australian firms to provide training and after-sales support for their technologies. In contrast, the CEO of firm VII complained that Japanese firms give minimal after-sales support; in other words, if there is a problem with their technologies, they give very short and specific answers when asked for information, and if pushed for further details most of the time will not elaborate.

Firms II, III and IV all attempted to offer superior customer service as a way of maintaining goodwill and reducing the chance of contractual misunderstandings. For firms II and IV this took the form of marketing advice and free seminars. Firm III, which marketed itself on its willingness to service its product, built the cost of providing the additional service into the contract. Its customers could often buy the product cheaper, but knew they wouldn't get the same after-sales support. In contrast, firm V took advantage of the good reputation that German technology has in Asia and used its German connections to market its product in Malaysia. The Managing Director considered 'it is a definite advantage to have German technology' when selling his product in Malaysia.

The Malaysian managers had differing views about getting Australian partners to understand the difficulties faced in production in Malaysia. The CEO of firm VII stated that their Australian joint venture partner was sympathetic when they faced production problems and attributed this to the fact that their partner was in a similar line of production. The Chief Financial Officer of firm VI expressed the view, based on his experience, that Australian firms were too quick to judge Malaysian firms by the standard of developed countries rather than developing countries, which meant their demands and expectations of the performance of their Malaysian partners were too high. Our interviews with Australian firms also suggested that some failed to appreciate the difficulties facing their Malaysian counterparts, particularly following the Asian financial crisis. For instance, when, following the Asian financial crisis, firm II's client failed to make some payments and requested more time to meet its obligations under the contract, the General Manager put this down to the client attempting to get a 'financial edge'.

Failure to appreciate all of the performance dimensions of international contracts of concern to exchange partners is not restricted to Australian firms. The Australians found it difficult to communicate their concerns about price–quality trade-offs to their Malaysian counterparts. Firm I is a good example of this problem. It employs an expatriate manager in its Malaysian joint venture to ensure high quality service to its customers; it thus has higher overheads, which means that it finds it difficult to compete with local companies on price. The Managing Director of firm I expressed frustration that local Malaysian customers were often only concerned with price and not service quality. As a result, firm I concentrated its Malaysian business on multinational firms that it deals with in Australia; the Managing Director believing that the multinationals understand the reasons for its higher prices and are willing to pay more for superior service. Thus firm I mostly avoided having to communicate with Malaysian firms about the price–quality performance dimensions of its product service.

Ascertaining the rules and norms applying to business in Malaysia

Our initial interviews with Australian firms suggested that the Malaysian party often views the contract as encompassing the points written in the agreement, plus others that were verbally stated during discussion, assumed to be agreed upon but not written in the contract. This means that the written contract is just a general guide as to what was agreed; negotiations continue after the contract is signed. We interviewed a Melbourne solicitor, with extensive experience in Malaysia, for this project. He said that, in his experience, confusion about the contents of the contract was the source of most misunderstandings for Australian firms.

A common complaint from the Australian firms that we interviewed is that the contract is never final. The experience of firm II is an example of the problems that can be caused because of misunderstanding about the scope of the contract. The price agreed in the written contract was the lowest at which firm II was prepared to sell, but the Malaysian customer took this as a starting point to negotiate a lower price to install the production technology. As a result, negotiations about price continued for 18 months after the contract was signed, with what the Malaysian partner viewed as everyday business practice in Malaysia being regarded as unethical by the Australian partner.

When we asked the three Malaysian managers about the different concept of the contract in Chinese culture the CEO of firm VII suggested that the Chinese concept of the contract is not as important on the Malaysian side as it once was, particularly among the younger generation. By this, he meant that managers are now much more willing to specify all the terms of the agreement in a written contract. The senior managers we spoke to in both firms VI and VII said they were happy to specify everything in the written contract. The Chief Financial Officer of firm VI made the further point that small entrepreneur-owned Chinese firms sometimes use the different notion of the contract as a veil to obtain a financial advantage. This suggests that some hold-ups over the terms of the contract might be manufactured rather that the result of innocent cultural misunderstanding in such firms.

The CEO of firm VIII went further and suggested that on average Malaysian firms were less principled than Australian firms in doing business. He stated: 'The Australian firms we deal with are more direct and more open. We talk about the matter, we agree and that's it. If we have any trouble we can talk to them'. In contrast, the CEO of firm VIII reported having problems with local customers, when purchasing their products, reneging on contracts. This is significant, remembering that firm VIII is a Malaysian firm.

The comments of the Malaysian managers suggest a tentative hypothesis. As the Australian firms in our sample were all dealing with Malaysian firms much smaller than firms VI–VIII, there may be an inverse relationship between the use of the Chinese notion of the contract and the size of the firm. In larger firms, the Western notion of contract is more accepted. The education of senior management in different-sized Malaysian firms could also be important. The senior managers in firms VI and VII were Western educated and the senior manager in firm VIII had worked for an Australian firm in Malaysia for several years. On the other hand, the Australian firms interviewed were mainly dealing with Malaysian firms where senior management was not Western-educated.

Negotiating a contract/choosing a business partner

Our Australian and Malaysian interviews highlighted the differences between direct (Australian) and indirect (Malaysian) approaches to negotiation, reflecting individualist and collectivist cultures. Wafa et al. (1999, p. 432) state: 'members of individualist cultures tend to stress the value of straight talk and tend to verbalise overtly their individual wants and needs, while members of collectivist cultures tend to stress the value of contemplative talk and discretion in voicing one's opinions and feelings'. The interviews we conducted with the Malaysian firms confirmed this observation.

Australians' direct approach in negotiation can alienate the Malaysian partner from the beginning. The CEO of firm VII made the point: 'we often feel intimidated when the other person has a direct approach, especially during discussion of contracts. Australians, in particular, like to argue to win. In Chinese culture it is important to get to know the person first and then do business if you feel comfortable'. This point was also stressed by a private trade consultant with several years of experience in Malaysia, whom we interviewed in Melbourne. He emphasised the importance of personal relationships and non-legal private orderings as the basis of formal contracts; in collectivist cultures budgets are often heavily weighted towards information exchange activities. This can increase the costs of initial negotiations for the Australian firm; for instance, the Managing Director of firm V reported spending 90 per cent more on entertainment expenses in Malaysia than in Australia.

Another consequence of the importance of personal relationships in contracting in Malaysia is that finding, and negotiating with, a Malaysian partner is time-consuming. For example, firm III is interested in forming a joint venture in Malaysia, but has not found the right partner, despite speaking to about 15 companies between 1993 and 1996. Before firm VII entered into a joint venture with its Australian partner, there was a one-year period between the initial expression of interest from both parties and the commencement of serious negotiation. While this familiarisation period adds to the initial cost in terms of entertainment and negotiation expenses, it has benefits in the long run because success stories where the firm 'jumps into the market' in Malaysia, seem to be rare (Thomas 1993; Wheeler 1993). Firm II illustrates the perils of jumping in without first getting to know the other party. Firm II met a customer in its first trade delegation with Export Access and agreed on a contract straight off. It has since had many problems with late payments or non-payment. The General Manager of firm II expressed regret that he did not take longer to get to know the potential pitfalls.

Our interviews with the Malaysian managers revealed perceptions that Australian firms were reluctant to commit senior personnel to the Malaysian market, in particular in the initial negotiation period. The CEO of firm VII said that in his experience Australian firms sent senior personnel in the beginning as a 'show of good faith', and then left negotiation to middle management. He didn't think this was a problem because he had a good working relationship with the Australian middle managers with whom he had dealt. However, the Chief Financial Officer of firm VI complained that few senior decision-makers in Australian firms come to get first-hand experience of the Malaysian market.

The commitment of senior management can be an important ingredient in building international relationships in the period prior to the establishment to the contract, particularly given traditional Asian respect for leadership (Smith 1999). While senior management involvement entails a high cost in the short term, previous research on Australian companies in Asia suggests that the commitment of senior personnel can 'open doors' and facilitate the formation of personal relationships that reduce delays in reaching agreements. For example, Vicziany (1993, p. 51) reports that the visits to Delhi of the Managing Director of Atlas Air, an Australian air conditioner firm, were extremely important in expediting government approval for the firm's Indian joint venture.

Monitoring and enforcement of the contract

One issue foreign firms face is whether to have an agent or other representative in the Malaysian market to undertake contracting with Malaysian firms. When firms do have agents, monitoring the agent is an important issue. Firm V used agents in its initial involvement in Malaysia in 1993–94. In its initial period of investment it built performance criteria into its agent's contract. However, the high costs of monitoring the agent made it more attractive for firm V to set up a fully-owned subsidiary. The Managing Director summed this up as follows:

> Our biggest problem was we could see potential for our product
> that wasn't being realised by the dealers. We invested [in a fully-
> owned subsidiary] to protect our reputation and because we
> weren't happy with what the agent was doing. With our product, it
> is important to have a follow-up service, but the agent was not
> providing this.

Firm IV has had more success with using an agent. Firm IV met their
agent (who is a *bumiputera*) while in Malaysia investigating business
opportunities. He wrote a letter to the sales manager stating that he would
like to represent firm IV in Malaysia, and gave certain reasons why he felt
he could be of benefit. Firm IV could see advantages in having a
bumiputera as an agent and hired him. It has used the agent to overcome its
lack of local knowledge. The sales manager of firm IV explained that their
bumiputera agent has a valuable network of family and friendship
connections to senior people in the Malaysian government.

Firm IV uses a 'carrot and stick' approach to monitoring its agent. It has
a nominal joint venture that is 51 per cent owned by its agent in order to
comply with the Malaysian government's *bumiputera* equity regulations for
preferential treatment. The Australian firm, however, put up all the capital
for the Malaysian venture, and in practice the Australian firm retains 100 per
cent control. The Australian firm has a share transfer form signed by its
agent, which it keeps in its Australian office. If the agent ever attempted to
exercise control consistent with his 51 per cent share, the Australian firm
would execute the share transfer form, which would give it majority equity
in the joint venture. At the same time, firm IV gives its agent financial
incentives to reward good performance. To this point firm IV has given him
5,000 shares in the Malaysian subsidiary as bonuses, with the promise of
further equity in the Malaysian venture for continued good performance.

In the case of enforcement, firms II and IV both reported that it is
difficult to get companies in Malaysia to pay their accounts. The sales
manager of firm IV stated:

> The biggest difficulty we find there [i.e. Malaysia] is getting the
> companies to pay their bills. It's worse than here [i.e. Australia].
> It's not in their culture to come on too strong and say if you don't
> pay your bills we will cut off your supply. They tend to say we
> will do that tomorrow or later.

This reflects the preference in collectivist cultures for alternative forms of
mediation. The solicitor we interviewed in Melbourne said that in his
experience litigation is regarded as a last resort by Malaysian firms and that
cultural factors are one of the main reasons for the growing popularity of
alternative dispute resolution in Malaysia. He suggested that one common
alternative form of dispute resolution is for the parties to use a go-
between—a third party that both can rely on and respect, which is often a
clan or family elder.

Firms II and IV have responded differently to the non-payment issue.
The General Manager of firm II preferred to avoid legal action if possible.
His view was that the best approach is to get a large up-front deposit that

would hurt the other party financially if it reneged on the contract. In the contract firm II had in Malaysia, it took a 10 per cent deposit. The General Manager stated he did not believe this was enough. In a new contract in the Philippines, firm II is asking for a 50 per cent deposit. On the other hand, in one case, firm IV has taken legal action after failing to get a customer to pay its account; it is suing for 14,000 ringgit (AU$6,000). When we suggested that this was not a large amount to go to court over (given the potential legal costs), the sales manager of firm IV said the intention was to send a signal that the firm was prepared to take court action.

Conclusion

Like the preceding study by Smyth and Wills (2000), this study finds that exchange between Malaysian and Australian firms involves significant transaction costs. This study identifies cultural differences that magnify these costs.

Our results suggest that the cultural differences most likely to create major transaction costs in exchanges between Malaysian and Australian firms are, first, the predominance of collectivist values in Malaysia and individualist values in Australia, and second, the different notions of contract in (Chinese) Malaysian and Australian business. On the first point, Malaysian firms, being part of a collectivist society, give more emphasis to getting to know prospective exchange partners and to establishing mutual trust before doing any business. This means that Australian firms (or firms that come from an individualist society) have to spend extra time and money to establish a contract with Malaysian firms. The collectivist nature of the Malaysian society, which emphasises mediation rather than direct confrontation, also makes it difficult for Australian firms to use legal means to settle disputes and enforce contracts.

With respect to the different notions of contract in Malaysian and Australian business, we have mixed evidence. Our interviews with Australian firms indicate that conflicting interpretations of the scope of contracts can create major problems and costs for Australian firms. On the other hand, the interviews with Malaysian firms suggest that larger Malaysian firms are willing to abide by Western-style written contracts, and that acceptance of the Western notion of a contract is related to firm size and to the education level of Malaysian managers. If this is so, disputes over contract interpretation between Malaysian managers and their counterparts from individualist societies like Australia can be expected to decrease over time as the proportion of Malaysian business people with educational exposure to Western notions of the contract increases. Also, the international competitiveness of both Malaysian and Australian firms could be increased by educating managers in both countries about the understandings of contract and contract enforcement common to potential foreign business partners.

In the aftermath of the Asian crisis of the late 1990s, cultural barriers to international exchange by Malaysian firms, especially SMEs, take on added significance. Subject to more detailed empirical studies of international contracting by Malaysian firms, it appears that cultural differences create substantial costs for Malaysian firms dealing with foreign partners; such costs may be important barriers to the international competitiveness of Malaysian firms. If this is so, Malaysia's policy makers and commercial trade organisations will need to create specific educational, commercial and legal instruments to assist firms in lowering cultural barriers to expanded trade.

The small number of Australian and Malaysian firms sampled, and the absence from our samples of small Malaysian firms and large Australian firms, mean that our findings cannot be generalised to cover the full range of firm-to-firm dealings between Malaysia and Australia. A logical next step would be to test our initial conclusions about how cultural differences add to the transaction costs of international exchange by surveying larger and more diverse samples of firms in Malaysia, Australia and other regional countries. Our results should help in the design of survey questionnaires for such a project.

Endnotes

[1] This chapter is part of a broader project on the 'Business Environment of Malaysia' being undertaken by the Asian Economies Research Unit, within the Economics Department, Monash University. It builds on results initially reported in Smyth and Wills (2000) and draws on the interviews reported in that paper. We thank Teng Goh, Len Phillips and Paul White for making themselves available for interviews. We also especially thank the representatives of the firms sampled in this study for giving us their valuable time. These people for obvious reasons must remain anonymous.

[2] See Doney et al. (1998) for a recent review.

References

Deutsch, M. (1960), 'The effect of motivational orientation upon trust and suspicion', *Human Relations*, 13, 123–139.

Doney, P., J. Cannon and M. Mullen (1998), 'Understanding the influence of national culture on the development of trust', *Academy of Management Review*, 23 (3), 601–620.

Dore, R. (1983), 'Goodwill and the spirit of market capitalism', *British Journal of Sociology*, 34, 459–482.

Eggertsson, Trainn (1991), *Economic Behaviour and Institutions*, Cambridge: Cambridge University Press.

Foong, S.-Y. (1999), 'Effect of end-user personal and systems attributes on computer-based information system success in Malaysian SMEs', *Journal of Small Business Management*, 37 (3), 81–87.

Good, David (1988), 'Individuals, interpersonal relations and trust', in Diego Gambetta. (ed.), *Trust Making and Breaking Cooperative Relations*, New York: Basil Blackwell, pp. 31–48.

Hall, Chris (1995), 'APEC and SME policy—suggestions for an action agenda', Australian APEC Studies Centre Issues Paper No 1.

Hamilton, Gary (ed.) (1991), *Business Networks and Economic Development in East and South-East Asia*, Hong Kong: Centre of Asian Studies, University of Hong Kong.

Hofstede, Geert, (1980), *Culture's Consequences: International Differences in Work-Related Values*, Beverly Hills: Sage Publications.

Kao, Cheng-shu (1991), 'Personal trust in large businesses in Taiwan: A traditional foundation for contemporary economic activities', in Gary Hamilton (ed.), *Business Networks and Economic Development in East and South-East Asia*, Hong Kong: Centre of Asian Studies, University of Hong Kong.

Klein, B., R. Crawford and A. Alchian (1978), 'Vertical integration, appropriable rents and the competitive contracting process', *Journal of Law and Economics*, 21 (2), 297–326.

Lasserre, P. (1999), 'Joint venture satisfaction in Asia-Pacific', *Asia Pacific Journal of Management*, 16 (1), 1–28.

Noorderhaven, Niels (1996), 'Opportunism and trust in transaction cost economics', in John Groenewegen (ed.), *Transaction Cost Economics and Beyond*, London: Kluwer.

Noordewier, T.G., G. John and J. R. Nevin (1990), 'Performance outcomes of purchasing agreements in industrial buyer–vendor relationships', *Journal of Marketing*, 54 (4), 80–93.

Shi, He-ling (1999), 'Micro aspects of the Asian crisis', in *Proceedings of the 1999 Industry Economics Conference*, Melbourne: Productivity Commission, pp. 55–62.

Smith, Wendy (1999), 'Management in Malaysia', in Malcolm Warner (ed.), *Management in Asia-Pacific*, Melbourne: Business Press Thomson Learning, pp. 244–259.

Smyth, Russell and Ian Wills (2000), 'The transaction costs of doing business in Malaysia' in Ron Edwards, Chris Nyland and Max Coulthard (eds), *Readings in International Business: An Asian Perspective*, Sydney: Prentice Hall, pp. 33–47.

Stokie, Martin (1995), 'Australia Malaysia relations—A commercial perspective', unpublished manuscript accessible at website www.cmsb.com.my/sponsor/maf/comper/htm .

Teece, D (1986), 'Transaction cost economics and the multinational enterprise—an assessment', *Journal of Economic Behaviour and Organisation*, 7 (2), 21–45.

Thomas, T. (1993), 'It's no holiday in Malaysia', *Business Review Weekly*, 13 March, pp. 4–6.

Thompson, A. (1996), 'Compliance with agreements in cross cultural transactions: Some analytical issues', *Journal of International Business Studies*, 27 (2), 375–390.

Trubisky, P., S. Ting-Toomey and S.-L. Lin (1991), 'The influence of individualism, collectivism and self-Monitoring on conflict styles' *International Journal of Intercultural Relations*, 15, 65–84.

Vicziany, Marika (1993), 'Australian companies in India: The ingredients for successful entry into the Indian market', in Marika Vicziany (ed.), *Australia–India Economic Links: Past Present and Future*, Nedlands: Indian Ocean Centre for Peace Studies, University of Western Australia, pp. 24–83.

Wafa, Syed Azizi, Roselina Ahmad Saufi and Tan-Hong Lee, (1999), 'A comparative study of Japanese and Malaysian conflict resolution styles', in Ron Edwards and Chris Nyland (eds), *Preparing for 2000: Opportunities and Challenges for International Business in the Asia Pacific Region*,

Proceedings of the Annual Academy of International Business South-East Asia Region Conference, Melbourne 8–10 July 1999, Vol. 1, pp. 431–438.

Wheeler, C. (1993), 'Canadian firms find patience is the key to success in Malaysia', *Financial Post*, 28 August, p. 4.

Williamson, Oliver (1985), *The Economic Institutions of Capitalism*, New York: Free Press.

Wills, Ian (1997), *Economics and the Environment: A Signalling and Incentives Approach*, St Leonards: Allen and Unwin.

Zucker, Lynne (1986), 'Production of trust, institutional sources of economic structure, 1840–1920', in Barry Staw and L. L. Cummings (eds), *Research in Organisational Behaviour*, vol. 8, Greenwich, Connecticut: JAI Press.

5

Japanese electronics firms in Malaysia: After the financial crisis

David W. Edgington and Roger Hayter[1]

Introduction

In this chapter we examine the strategies of 18 Japanese electronics firms in Malaysia following the financial crisis of 1997–8. Our aims are to assess the impact of the crisis upon their production and marketing strategies, and attitudes to Malaysia as a host country location. Our theoretical perspective on Japanese direct foreign investment in the Asia-Pacific region and the broader impacts of the financial crisis are explored elsewhere (Edgington and Hayter 2000; forthcoming). In this chapter, we report on interviews we conducted with factory managers of Japanese subsidiaries in May 1999. These included the assembly plants of large Japanese consumer firms, parts suppliers and integrated circuit assemblers (see Table 5.1) and we believe this sample of firms to be broadly representative of subsidiaries in this sector. During 1998, electronics firms comprised 43 per cent of all Japanese-affiliated firms operating in the manufacturing sector. On a broader scale, Japanese firms in Malaysia accounted for an estimated 28 per cent of total cases of approved DFI between 1992 and 1997 and 20 per cent by value (JACTIM 1998).

The results reported in this chapter suggest that, overall, Japanese firms were not adversely affected by financial crisis of 1997–98. Rather, the move to fully implement AFTA (the ASEAN Free Trade Area) in 2003 was perceived to have more of an effect upon investment decisions and production plans than the Asian financial crisis itself. Such a finding has implications for both theory and policy in Malaysia. Thus, while traditional 'globalisation' theory might imply that multinational firms might 'take flight' and abandon South-East Asian countries such as Malaysia in light of the crisis, the reality is more complex. On the one hand there is certainly a new sentiment among Japanese investors that a severe over-capacity of electronics production existed in the ASEAN region, especially in relation to likely market growth. This was due to the rapid build-up of electronics investments in the first half of the 1990s. On the other hand there is also a feeling that a sudden flight of capital will not occur in the immediate future, either from Malaysia or from other ASEAN countries. Nonetheless, all Japanese firms are now carefully examining their long-term options throughout the ASEAN region. Japanese managers we interviewed in Malaysia were optimistic overall about Malaysia's prospects and viewed it as relatively well-positioned to take further rounds of production from the

Table 5.1: Japanese electronics companies interviewed, May 1999

A. Consumer electronics
    Aiwa Electronics
    Alps Electronic
    Casio
    Hitachi Air Conditioning Products
    Hitachi Consumer Products
    Hitachi Electronic Products
    Matsushita Precision Industrial Company
    PJVM (Philips and JVC Video Malaysia)
    Pioneer Technology
    Sharp Manufacturing Corporation
    Sharp–Roxy Electronics Corporation

B. Industrial electronics
    Fuji Electric
    Fujitsu Microelectronics
    Hitachi Semiconductor
    KUB-Fujitsu Telecommunications
    Meisei Electric

C. Parts suppliers
    Tatura Acoustic Industry
    Nichibei Parts

headquarters of Japanese MNEs. This was especially the case should the Japanese yen continue to strengthen in the next few years and make the existing exports of electronic products from Japan unprofitable. However, Japanese managers expressed the view that in order to maximise benefits from such positive prospects the Malaysian government would need to pay more attention to strengthening its own 'base of industry'. In other words, policy should be directed towards upgrading the technical capacity of Malaysian component firms in addition to the current focus on aggressively pursuing a new generation of high-technology industries in Malaysia's high profile 'multi-media corridor'.

The remainder of this chapter reviews the history of investment by Japanese electronics firms in Malaysia, and then examines the particular impact of the financial crisis of 1997-98 on the 18 firms in the authors' study. A subsequent section deals with the future attractiveness of Malaysia as an investment destination and production location. This is necessarily more speculative and uses qualitative responses from the Japanese factory managers interviewed. These responses raise the possibility of Malaysia's becoming a source of more sophisticated parts and sub-assembly components for other Japanese assembly factories located in South-East Asia, Europe and North America. The implication of these findings for Malaysian government policy is addressed in the conclusion.

History of Japanese electronics FDI in Malaysia

Japanese interest in producing electronics in Malaysia has gone through a number of stages over the last 25 years or so. The first generation of Japanese DFI (direct foreign investment) in Malaysia took place during the 1960s. It was based mainly on utilising either local raw materials for export production (such as timber and rubber production) or for import substitution production in the face of high tariffs on imported consumer items (televisions, refrigerators and other domestic items) (Lim and Ping 1983; Lim and Fong 1991). Giant multinational enterprises (MNEs) such as Sony and Matsushita set up joint venture subsidiaries at that time with medium-scale capacity in order to produce consumer electronics for local markets. In the 1970s, these and other firms also established parts and component companies. This decade also saw the rapid growth of large-scale, export-oriented integrated circuit (IC) assembly by companies such as Hitachi and NEC (Piei 1990). Studies conducted in this period typically reported very few linkages with local subcontractors, low levels of localisation of research, design and development, and limited promotion given to Malaysian staff or engineers (Fong 1990; Aoki 1992). In all, the 'first generation' of investments involved 'classic' assembly-oriented and low valued-added production typified by Japanese offshore production in Asia and other parts of the world (see Edgington 1991; 1993).

However, following the rise of the yen (*endaka*—yen appreciation) in 1985 there was a 'new wave' of large-scale assembly production aimed at overseas export markets, especially involving television and video cassette recorder production in Penang, the Klang Valley (Selangor) and at Johor Bahru (Ikuta 1997; Edgington and Hayter 2000). At the same time, changes in Malaysian investment facilitation provisions (the Promotion of Investments Act and deregulation of foreign equity ownership guidelines) encouraged further inward direct investment, and created a 'bandwagon' effect among Japanese electronics companies (Anazawa 1994). Consequently, by 1987, Malaysia had become one of the world's largest exporters of semiconductors and the third largest producer of video cassette recorders (VCRs) after Japan and the United States. Malaysia also became the world's largest exporter of room air conditioners. JETRO (Japan External Trade Organisation) surveys showed that there were over 1,400 Japanese firms in Malaysia in mid-1999, of which around 800 were in the manufacturing sector. The biggest manufacturing category comprised the production of electronics and electrical parts. The local factories of Matushita Electronic Industries Corporation alone were said to account for about 3–4 per cent of Malaysia's total exports (interview with Secretary General of the Japan Chamber of Trade and Industry, Malaysia, Kuala Lumpur, May 1999). In the 1990s, firms such as Hitachi also began to 'deepen' their involvement in local manufacturing by producing more sophisticated products such as key VCR components, recording heads and tape drive mechanisms (interview with senior executive of JETRO, Kuala Lumpur, May 1999). This most recent set of Japanese investments in consumer electronics has made Malaysia the third-largest exporter of VCRs and CTVs (colour television) in the world after Japan and South Korea (O'Connor 1993; Ikuta 1997; Ling and Yong 1997).

Moves towards localisation

During the late 1980s and early 1990s, Japanese small and medium-scale firms (SMEs) also carried out larger investments in Malaysia, aimed primarily at making components (such as hard disc drives and motors) to supply local subsidiaries such as the export trade. Moreover, a general move to higher levels of investment and sophistication throughout the industry led to localisation in terms of design engineering capacity and operation of manufacturing. The indigenous Malaysian component industry also began to respond to the growing number of assembly investments after 1987. While some local firms aimed to supply specialised parts for export-oriented semiconductor operations, the bulk of their local operations consisted of a range of generic parts, such as resistors, diodes, capacitors, transformers, power supplies, coils and filters, and loudspeakers. Many local firms began supplying these components to satisfy the large demand from Japanese VCR manufacturers (O'Connor 1993). Aoki (1992) recounts how in the late 1980s, for almost the first time, Japanese electronics firms attracted to Malaysia began to form local networks of parts and component-making local firms involved in parts procurement. Other studies also found that local subcontracting arrangements evolved rapidly in the immediate post-*endaka* period. Dobson (1993), however, argued that Japanese firms continued to function in more exclusive ways than American firms in Malaysia, relying mainly upon 'in-house' or *keiretsu*-style production networks of the earlier generation of subsidiaries and their almost exclusively Japanese suppliers. Her finding was that this occurred mainly because of Japanese firms' protracted reliance upon Japanese ex-patriot managers, who typically lacked any local networks, and in part also because of a general diffidence towards non-Japanese products. Ernst (1994) has pointed out that, while Japanese firms traditionally exhibited very low interaction with local firms, critical changes were made after 'second *endaka*' (yen appreciation) of 1993. At that time, Japanese subsidiaries in Malaysia, and more widely throughout other ASEAN locations, were under considerable pressure to reduce their imported inputs from Japan and to increase their reliance on sourcing regional components. While this involved a further round of new investments by small to medium-sized Japanese component suppliers in the mid-1990s, it also involved upgrading of local firms willing and able to service the expanded investments of Japanese electronics MNEs.

A more recent survey of local procurement behaviour by Japanese firms (Ling and Yong 1997) suggests that Japanese firms have indeed sought higher levels of components locally, or at least from surrounding Asia-Pacific countries rather than Japan. They distinguish this position with that of US electronics firms in Malaysia, which were concentrated mainly in the production of semiconductors or the manufacturing of computer parts such as hard disk drives and communications components. The input requirements of these US firms were specialised and tended to come from other US affiliates located in third countries. By contrast, Japanese firms in Malaysia produced consumer electronics, such as colour TVs or VCRs, or generic electronic goods such as magnetic heads, computer-display monitors, and television sets, and imported only about 45 per cent of their local content from Japan. These findings imply that inputs from affiliates in third countries were less important for Japanese electronics firms than for US firms, and that components for Japanese manufacturers came substantially from sources external to the firm rather than from within the same firm's overseas networks. In contrast to popular belief regarding tightly-knit Japanese supply chains, usually organised within *keiretsu* groups, the experience of their electronic affiliates in Malaysia suggests a gradual 'opening up' to inter-firm sourcing from non-affiliated companies, either in Malaysia or nearby Asia-Pacific countries than US firms in the same broad industry. Thus Ling and Yong (1997) report that 40 per cent of total inputs by value of Japanese subsidiaries were inter-firm, compared with 74 per cent in the case of US subsidiaries in Malaysia. The major reason why the US and Japanese affiliates sourced differently was dissimilarities in their sectoral specialisation within Malaysia. Thus, because US affiliates were mainly concentrated in semiconductor production, their operations occurred higher up the value-added chain and so they tended to use inputs only from their own proprietary sources. However, Japanese firms operated in the consumer electronics sectors and had more opportunity to source generic parts and components as well as intermediate products further down the value-added chain from outside their traditional production networks, either in Malaysia or from countries in North-East or South-East Asia.

Ling and Yong (1997) also noted that where 'backward linkages' were successfully made by Malaysian supply firms to the local Japanese assemblers, it was partly due to a fairly aggressive 'vendor-development program' begun by the Malaysian government after the mid-1980s recession to promote local Malay SMEs. Japanese 'buyer firms' in government-approved schemes were eligible for tax breaks in return for local procurement. The vendors were often small firms registered with Malaysia's MITI's (Ministry of International Trade and Industry) subcontracting network under the *paying*, or umbrella concept, designed to build linkages between large MNEs and local SMEs. Examples of local Malaysian inputs bought by Japanese electronics firms include moulded compounds for plastic casings, silicon wafer packaging materials, solder for joints, spare parts and components, supportive tools, industrial chemicals, lubricants, ancillary materials and final packaging and shipping materials. While these are all low to medium value-added components, the Japanese firms we surveyed were generally open to further domestic sourcing as more materials and components of high standards became available locally.

Interestingly, in light of debates about the efficacy of host country 'industrial policy' in shaping MNE and SME outcomes, Jomo et al. (1997) have argued that Malaysian local content rules have been relatively successful. This has especially been the case for the government's system of supplying export credit refinancing facilities to foreign investors in return for higher local content in assembly operations. However, they also note that Malaysian policies in favour of *bumiputera* (indigenous Malay) enterprises at the expense of Chinese-Malaysian firms may have worked against fostering a viable local parts industry. Support for local ethnic Malay business reflected the overall development strategy implemented since 1970 to carry out the NEP's (New Economic Program) redistribution objectives, particularly those aimed at increasing the share of Malay ownership in the economy. In effect, any attempt to foster local industry in Malaysia has been subordinated to vested (ethnic) 'political' interests that prioritised the promotion of a Malay rentier business community rather than the emergence of an efficient industrial policy *per se*. Because of this the objectives of Malaysian industrial interventions have been quite different from those of industrial policies applied elsewhere in the Asia-Pacific region. The NEP was primarily focussed on redressing socio-economic imbalances, not on gaining international competitiveness for new industrial activities. Jomo et al. (1997) also argue that difficulties in increasing local sourcing have existed in Malaysia mainly because local suppliers were unable to attain and maintain, sufficiently high technical standards in the light of rapid product development. Other studies that assessed the position of local sourcing of parts and components from the vantage point of the mid-1990s (just prior to the Asian financial crisis) confirmed this state of affairs. Ling and Yong (1997), for instance, argued that while progress had been made in raising local content in low-to-medium technology products, developing a full network of high quality local vendors would probably take a long time.

The future attractiveness of Malaysia

By the mid-1990s, scholars such as Guyton (1995) were beginning to question whether Malaysia's high rates of Japanese electronic industrial investment could be sustained. It was clear that Malaysia had gained mass-production factories for export, mainly thanks to lower wage costs and Malaysia's access to the generalised system of preferences (GSP) privileges. These two factors played a significant part in shaping Japanese MNEs' regional production strategies in the years following 1985. The tariff exemptions offered to poor nations by industrialised countries under GATT's GSP enticed Japanese MNEs to relocate their production to low-wage nations, with the intention of exporting the majority of finished goods to the EU (European Union) and North America, especially as a counter-action to European and American protectionist trade policies. Guyton's study indicated that the 1989 lifting of GSP privileges from South Korea, Singapore and Taiwan—due to their achieving industrialised status—was an important factor that led to a shifting of some Japanese investments from those countries to Malaysia. The companies we interviewed also revealed that Malaysia's GSP quota played a role in its being selected over other ASEAN countries, as it tended to be more generous. Still, by the mid-1990s it was also apparent that China was a potential competitor to both Malaysia and other ASEAN countries for assembly-based Japanese DFI in electronics and other industries (Yam 1997). Guyton (1995) commented that 'in light of this evidence, it will be interesting to see what impact the imminent review and ultimately removal of Malaysia's GSP privileges will have upon Japanese companies' investment strategies'; and 'with the combination of rising labour costs and a labour shortage in Malaysia, it is not surprising that multinationals are beginning to look to poorer, lower cost countries such as China, Vietnam and India, which will retain their GSP status for some time to come' (pp. 69–70).

Japanese electronics firms whose tax-incentive 'pioneer status' in Malaysia had expired or was about to expire at the end of the 1990s, expressed their concern to the authors that any reinvestments may not be entitled to further tax incentives in Malaysia. The period of tax relief under the 'pioneer status' incentive is five years, which may in some cases be extended for a further five years (Rasiah 1995). Some indicated that tax-incentive programmes in other countries, particularly Taiwan, were more extensive. Many Japanese firms also complained rather bitterly about local ethnic Malay work habits that were very different from those of North-East Asian cultures. For instance, the larger Japanese firms have had to increase the facilities offered to employees to compete for increasingly scarce factory labour (for instance gyms, rest rooms during Ramadan when Muslims fast during the day). Another contentious issue was the tendency for 'job hopping' among young ethnic Malay operatives and even engineers, rather than the displays of long-term loyalty to their company that would be typical in Japan (see Oizumi 1995). While 'job hopping' reflects the very real shortage of trained skilled labour and management in Malaysia, it undermines Japanese interest in long-term training programmes. Still, while these tensions might have 'bubbled close to the surface' in the middle of the decade, they were completely swept away by the deep impact of the Asian financial crisis, which broke first in neighbouring Thailand during July 1997, and the need for a strategic re-evaluation of local Malaysian operations (Mallet 1999; Navaratnam 1999). This chapter now turns to the findings of the authors' survey findings from interviews with the 18 Japanese electronics firms.

Impact of the Asian financial and currency crisis

The interviews all took place with Japanese managers of electronics firms in Malaysia (usually the Chief Executive Officer) who were first contacted by mail, often after introductions were initiated through their headquarters offices in Japan. Interviews lasted approximately one hour, and Malay or Chinese managers were introduced to the authors in the case of the larger assembly factories. The sentiments recorded in this section on the impact of the currency crisis, and in the next section on the future prospects for Malaysia as a host country for Japanese investment, were in all cases taken from the comments of Japanese managers.

The first area on which managers were asked to give comments was the recent currency crisis in Malaysia and the rest of South-East Asia. In general, their responses revealed that the lowering of the Malaysian ringgit to a stable level by the Malay government in 1998 had the effect of inducing overall investor confidence. This was confirmed by a wider survey of Japanese firms by the Japanese Chamber of Trade and Industry in Malaysia (JACTIM) (1999). Nonetheless, the dramatic drop in the value of the ringgit from 1997 to 1998 and the slump in the local economy impacted on the 18 Japanese electronics firms in a variety of ways. First, the worst affected were the small to medium-sized parts and components firms who had come to supply affiliated Japanese assembly firms (see group C, Table 5.1). These were, and still are, dependent entirely upon sales in local currency and have had to renegotiate sales contracts with the major assemblers (such as Sony and Matsushita), as well as taking measures to increase productivity. Where relations with large-scale assembly firms were long-standing the 'core' assembly firms often took steps to assist their suppliers, especially by renegotiating input prices. As one SME supplier in our survey remarked.

> The major impact here has been on the cost side. As the ringgit fell against the Singapore dollar, then the cost of our key components started to rise in 1997, and our profitability fell. But even the price of Malay components involves a substantial import of raw materials, and so even local products such as metal and plastic started to rise in price. So, the value of our income has been reduced, and costs have risen. We have passed some of those costs onto our purchaser, Sony. The emphasis recently has been how to contain our local costs. We have the decentralised capacity to do this from our Japanese headquarters (Interview with Japanese SME supplier in audio-visual consumer sector).

A second group of companies, those established in the first generation of investments prior to 1985 and traditionally selling to local markets along import substitution lines, often found their local sales value declining dramatically, and had to resort to higher levels of exports in order to survive. Many companies found that their local sales in consumer items plummeted during late-1997 and early-1998 as the financial crisis worsened in Malaysia and as consumer spending on their products all but dried up. In these circumstances the headquarters of the company in Japan often 'came to the rescue' by placing new orders from within the wider corporate global network (Edgington and Hayter forthcoming). Certain firms have taken even more drastic steps, especially those that had lost profitability in Japan. Sony, for instance, has now closed two of its five consumer electronics factories in Malaysia, and another in Indonesia. This was part of Sony's overall 10 per cent cut to its global workforce, and a reduction of manufacturing facilities from 70 to 55.

A final group of companies, and those which were in the majority in the authors' surveys, were export-oriented firms (either among the silicon chip factories which started in the 1970s or 1980s, or the 'new wave' consumer goods production post-*endaka*) have taken advantage of the lower-valued ringgit, and the growing American market, and have even expanded their sales of consumer and industrial products out of Malaysia. The windfall from the currency devaluation has been tempered, however, by the negative influences of: (1) the more general 'price crash shock' of falling consumer electronics prices due to a global oversupply and declining markets in Asia, Russia and Brazil in 1998; (2) the 'loan repayment shock' of increased borrowing costs incurred by local factories in yen or US dollars; and (3) the 'input price shock' of expensive imported parts and components following the fall in the value of the ringgit. Many export companies lamented the fact that they could often only keep about 50–60 per cent of the currency devaluation windfall because of the relentless pressure from headquarters to reduce prices worldwide following the Asian financial crisis. As a manager of a VCR factory commented:

> All our export contracts are written in US$ so theoretically the 30 per cent decline of the ringgit should have given our factory more of a financial surplus. But, overall demand for VCRs is down. Also, prices have been crashing as this market is very competitive, and so we have to follow the pricing strategies of our competitors—Sony, Korean and Taiwanese products and so on. We were asked by head office to reduce our product price in 1997, another 20 per cent in 1998, and another 20 per cent this year— which will be impossible! (interview with Japanese manger of VCR factory).

A longer-lasting legacy of the financial crisis has been lower market expectations, a realisation that excess production capacity now existed in the entire ASEAN region, and increased competition for further rounds of investment from headquarters between the factories of Japanese overseas networks, and even between overseas factories and 'home factories' in Japan. The likely commencement of AFTA (ASEAN Free Trade Agreement) in 2003 also led to a closer examination of the strengths and weaknesses of individual factories within the network of electronics firms. Some downsizing and production adjustment will almost certainly take place after 2003. The outcome for any particular country in ASEAN will depend upon local conditions with regard to productivity, currency values, localisation, and the costs of imports (Tan 1996).

We will now examine how Japanese companies in the Malaysian electronics sector viewed their particular prospects in the foreseeable future, in light of this new trade environment.

Prospects for Malaysia

Despite some apprehension over AFTA, the overall sentiments revealed by the field research and interviews was that Japanese-controlled Malaysian factories in the global networks of major electronics firms were well positioned to take further rounds of investments in new added-value production and local upgrading. A number of positive sentiments were expressed along the lines that local factory levels of productivity were now as high as in Japan, and secondly (perhaps even more importantly), there was a well-developed local components production capacity. Local Malaysian firms could supply plastics, rubber and paper products, and electronics parts up to a certain level of sophistication, and these products were widely available. This degree of localisation in Malaysia compared favourably with that in other parts of ASEAN, such as Indonesia and the Philippines, and even China, despite labour costs being lower in these other countries. While labour costs might be lower in these countries, too many expensive and semi-sophisticated materials, parts and components could not be found locally. As a Japanese VCR factory manager observed:

> Localisation in our factory is about 70 per cent for VCRs. The magnetic-head chip still comes from Japan, as well as the two cylinders for the drive. But even some local products will have Japanese parts inside them so it is difficult to work out the final level of localisation. The CD rom drive is more sophisticated and so uses less local components—probably about 70 per cent of its components come from Japan. But nearly all the local plastic and metals come from Malaysian firms or from Thailand and Indonesia. Indeed, one of the great selling points in Malaysia for DFI is that there is the likelihood of allowing a high local content, as the quality of local suppliers here is much better than what you could find in Indonesia, Thailand or mainland China. We will certainly stay here because of the many local parts suppliers nearby. We have three subcontracting companies here in Malaysia. We can cooperate with them in terms of financing and technology. We can provide training for their staff, provision of components, and so on. We would never consider operating in either Indonesia or the Philippines, as bringing in parts would be so expensive. So far, the Philippines are only good for cheap-wage assembly operations (interview with VCR factory manager).

However, many Japanese managers were willing to express certain negative sentiments about their Malaysian operations, and some argued that there was no guarantee that Japanese electronics firms would continue to invest in Malaysia and upgrade their existing factories to more added-value production. Thus, beyond the concerns raised by Guyton (1995) over the loss of GSP status, some managers considered that much depended upon improved skill formation of the local labour force. Others considered important an expanded capacity of local supply firms to innovate and produce new designs alongside their Japanese assembly firms—in other words, to operate more akin to subcontractors in Japan. Moreover, continued reservations were made by some managers about the stability of basic infrastructure in Malaysia, such as electricity supply. For instance, by contrast to neighbouring Singapore, the concern over occasional 'brown-outs' and electricity load shedding in Malaysia appears to have delayed significant 'next stage' upgrading, such as the production of 'wafers' as part of integrated chip (IC) manufacturing at existing Japanese plants in Penang and elsewhere.

Surveys of Japanese investor intentions (Tejima 1992) often suggest that the present large-scale assembly production of electronics in Malaysian subsidiaries for global markets may decline over the next decade in favour of locations in China (where assembly production is aimed at Asian markets) and in Mexico (for NAFTA markets). However, there remains a substantial opportunity for Malaysia to shift away from assembly production *per se*, to a new role: that of an international procurement centre for Japanese electronics firms, supplying parts and components to a wide overseas network of assembly factories. Survey results collected by Ling and Yong (1997) showed that East Asian NIEs (newly-industrialising economies), such as Korea, Taiwan and Hong Kong, in that order, were already developing as electronics suppliers for Japanese assembly companies in Malaysia. By way of illustration, Korean vendors supplied Japanese firms in Malaysia that produced mainly consumer-electronics products and telecommunications equipment. Taiwanese suppliers specialised in telecommunications equipment and components for television and computer manufacturing. Hong Kong vendors supplied components for Japanese semiconductor manufacturers. The replacement of traditional Japanese supply firms in Malaysian production networks with North-East Asian, ASEAN or Chinese components was expected to accelerate as more supporting industries developed in the Asia-Pacific region. This trend was already well established for some of the firms in the authors' survey. Responses from the Japanese firms interviewed suggested that if more local and regional vendors emerged with high enough standards and adequate capacity to supply Japanese firms, and if they were able to provide cost advantages without sacrificing quality, this would give advantage to the procurement of components by Malaysian subsidiaries. Moreover, instead of developing further assembly production, Malaysian investments in the future could focus on the adding of local value to components and the export of sub-assemblies to Japanese assembly subsidiaries elsewhere in the global production network. Against this optimistic scenario, there was also the very real possibility of short-term loss of jobs if Chinese firms (rather than Malaysian component producers) competed in final assembly and supply components to Malaysia. Nonetheless, most respondents were optimistic as long as local firms could upgrade their technology to enable such value-adding.

Conclusions

This study set out to ask to what degree changes in the underlying assumptions about the sustainability of Japanese electronics investments in Malaysia were shaken by the Asian financial crisis of 1997–98. The results showed that despite the difficulties of traditional import-substitution-based companies, the lowering of the ringgit to a stable level by the Malaysian government in 1998 buoyed overall investor confidence. Beyond this, Japanese electronics firms perceived that Malaysia had important potential within the post-AFTA network, mainly because of high rates of factory productivity and access to local components, either within Malaysia or in neighbouring Asia-Pacific countries.

For this potential to be realised, however, three initiatives can be suggested. First, in general the Malaysian government can still do more to strengthen local supplier networks. For instance, stronger partnerships could be fostered to promote links between Japanese investors and domestic suppliers of parts and components. Second, a key issue for the future of the electronics industry is to ensure that Malaysia produces the human resources needed to keep the industry competitive. Despite training allowances introduced by the government since 1988, the lack of a large mass of skilled labour in Malaysia to provide the base of advanced industrialisation is glaring. Finally, more attention has to be given to encourage Japanese firms to undertake research and development in Malaysia. So far, the amount of Japanese-based electronics research and development undertaken in Malaysia has been quite limited. This reflects not only the ineffectual incentives from the government, but also the concentration of Japanese investment in low-cost assembly for export, apart from IC wafer production and the manufacture of hard disk drives. Nonetheless, many Japanese companies have begun to establish 'design and develop' operations for adaptive research and development and have fine-tuned generic products to local-market tastes and regulations. Still, there is probably more scope for government–private sector joint ventures, and the government needs to determine how to provide stronger encouragement to research and development within the private sector. Such a strategy means, of course, a shift in research and development priorities, and a more pragmatic conceptualisation of industrial policy. Thus, the government needs to pay at least equal attention to upgrading the technology levels of existing support industries (and to developing new local Malaysian firms in advanced technology sectors) as attracting a new generation of foreign MNEs into its recently completed 'multi-media corridor' south of Kuala Lumpur (Cyberjaya). Rather than generous tax concessions and other investment incentives for building up software technology, a more balanced, prosaic approach would appear appropriate to move Malaysia further up the production value-added scale.

Endnotes

[1]   The authors would like to express their gratitude to the many managers both in Malaysia and in Japan who granted the interviews on which this research is based, and to many government employees in Penang and Kuala Lumpur. Our special thanks go to Dr Morshidi Sirat, Dean of Humanities, Universiti Sains Malaysia, for hosting David Edgington in Penang during May 1999, and for providing logistical support above and beyond the call of duty. Dr Marika Vicziany kindly hosted David Edgington at Monash University during August 2000, when the bulk of this chapter was written.

References

Anazawa, M. (1994), 'Japanese manufacturing investment in Malaysia', in K. S. Jomo (ed.), *Japan and Malaysian Development: In the Shadow of the Rising Sun*, London: Routledge.
Aoki, T. (1992), 'Japanese FDI and the forming of networks in the Asia-Pacific region: experience in Malaysia and its implications', in S. Tokugawa (ed.),

Japan's Foreign Investment and Asian Economic Interdependence: Production, Trade and Financial System, Tokyo: University of Tokyo Press.

Dobson, W. (1993), *Japan in East Asia: Trading and Investment Strategies*, Singapore: Institute of South-East Asian Studies.

Edgington, D. W. (1991), 'Japanese direct investment and Australian economic development', in J. Morris (ed.), *Japan and the Global Economy: Issues and Trends in the 1990s*, London: Routledge.

—— (1993), 'The globalisation of Japanese manufacturing companies', *Growth and Change*, 24, 87–106.

Edgington, D. W. and R. Hayter (2000), 'Foreign direct investment and the flying geese model: Japanese electronics firms in Asia-Pacific', *Environment and Planning A*, 32, 281–304.

—— (forthcoming), 'Japanese direct foreign investment and the Asian financial crisis', *Geoforum*.

Ernst, D. (1994), 'Carriers of rationalisation: the East Asian production networks of Japanese electronics firms', Working Paper 73, The Berkeley Roundtable on the International Economy, Berkeley: University of California.

Fong, C. O. (1990), 'Multinational corporations in ASEAN: technology transfer and linkages with host countries', in L. Y. Soon (ed.), *Foreign Direct Investment in ASEAN*, Kuala Lumpur: Malaysian Economic Association.

Guyton, L. E. (1995), 'Japanese FDI and the transfer of Japanese consumer electronics production to Malaysia', *Journal of Far Eastern Business*, 1 (4), 63–97.

Ikuta, M. (1997), 'Japanese direct investment and its impact upon the Malaysian urban system', in proceedings of the Third Ritsumeikan-UBC Seminar, *Canada and Japan in the Pacific Rim Area: Focusing on the Multicultural Society and Global Cities*, Kusatsu, Shiga.

Japanese Chamber of Trade and Industry, Malaysia (JACTIM) (1998), *Malaysian Economy in Figures*.

—— (1999), *Results of a Survey on the Influence of Strengthening the Foreign Exchange Regulation*.

Jomo, K. S. et al. (1997), *South-East Asia's Misunderstood Miracle: Industrial Policy and Economic Development in Thailand, Malaysia and Indonesia*, Boulder: Westview Press.

Lim, L. Y. C. and P. E. Fong (1991), *Foreign Direct Investment and Industrialisation in Malaysia, Singapore, Taiwan and Thailand*, Paris: OECD.

Lim, C. P. and L. P. Ping (1983), 'Japanese direct investment in Malaysia, with special reference to Japanese joint ventures', in S. Sekiguchi (ed.), *ASEAN–Japan Relations: Investment*, Singapore: Institute of South-East Asian Studies.

Ling, S. L. M. and Y. S. Yong (1997), 'Malaysia: electronics, automobiles, and the trade–investment nexus', in W. Dobson and C. S. Yue (eds), *Multinationals and East Asia Integration*, Singapore: Institute of South-East Asian Studies.

Mallet, V. (1999), *The Trouble with Tigers: The Rise and Fall of South-East Asia*, London: Harper Collins.

Navaratnam, R. (1999), *Healing the Wounded Tiger*, Subang Jaya: Pelanduk Publications.

O'Connor, D. (1993), 'Electronics and industrialisation: approaching the 21st century', in K. S. Jomo (ed.), *Industrialising Malaysia: Policy, Performance, Prospects*, London: Routledge.

Oizumi, K. (1990), 'Malaysia', *Journal of Japanese Trade and Industry*, 14 (2), 18–20.

Piei, M. H. (1990), 'Malaysia–Japan economic relationship: trends, issues and prospects', in Sumantoro (ed.), *ASEAN–Japan Relations*, proceedings of an intra-universities seminar on ASEAN–Japan relations, Bandung: Padjadjaran University.

Rasiah, R. (1995), *Foreign Capital and Industrialisation in Malaysia*, Houndmills: St. Martin's Press.

Tan, J. L. H. (ed.) (1996), *AFTA in the Changing International Economy*, Singapore: Institute of South-East Asian Studies.

Tejima, S. (1992), 'Japanese foreign direct investment in the 1980s, and its prospects for the 1990s', *Exim Review*, 11 (2), 25–51.

Yam, T. K. (1997), 'China and ASEAN: competitive industrialisation through foreign direct investment', in B. McNaughton (ed.), *The China Circle: Economics and Electronics in the PRC, Taiwan, and Hong Kong*, Washington: Brookings Institute Press.

6

The importance of size in the growth and performance of the electrical industrial machinery and apparatus industry in Malaysia

Rajah Rasiah[1]

Introduction

The electronics industry has been the prime export earner in Malaysia since 1987, accounting for over 70 per cent of manufactured exports and over 50 per cent of overall exports in 2000.[2] It contributed over a quarter of Malaysia's manufacturing value-added, fixed assets and employment in 2000. Two important issues are critical here in explaining the successful expansion of the electric and electronics industry in Malaysia. It is argued that these achievements have been driven by market-friendly strategies that attracted large multinational corporations (MNCs) from abroad (see Sheperd 1980; World Bank 1993). The first implies general policy neutrality towards the industry while the second argues that policy stimulated the expansion of large MNCs into the industry. However, unlike the South Korean and Taiwanese experiences, where large and small firms respectively spearheaded manufacturing expansion, the significance of size in Malaysia's manufacturing growth is still unclear. To obtain a careful analysis, this chapter attempts to examine the significance of size on the growth and performance of the electrical industrial machinery and apparatus industry, which is one of the sub-sectors within Malaysia's leading manufacturing industry, that is electric and electronics.

This chapter is divided into two main sections. The first examines policy biases facing the electric and electronics industry. The second discusses the growth trends in the industry based on firm size. Four categories of size are used in the chapter: micro, small, medium and large.

The regulatory environment

The development of small to medium industries (SMIs) in Malaysia's manufacturing sector was initially constrained by weak government-support instruments. During the colonial era, the British introduced financial support for craft and other small industries under the Rural Industrial Development

Authority (RIDA), largely to reduce discontent among the Malays (see Rasiah 1995, chapter 3). Such lukewarm initiatives were continued with greater financial support after independence under the Rural Development Ministry. It was not until the late 1970s that official policy attempted to earmark SMIs for support, but their development remained uncoordinated and cumbersome until SMI activities were given direct prominence by the Ministry of Industrial Development, following the launching of the Industrial Master Plan in 1986.[3] At this time, the umbrella concept of marketing—originally introduced in 1983—was augmented with the Subcontract Exchange Program (SEP) in 1986 and later with the Vendor Development Program (VDP) in 1992. In addition to the extension of export-oriented double tax deductions to SMIs from 1986, the government introduced the Industrial Technical Assistance Fund (ITAF), complementing credit guarantee supports in the late 1980s. A separate Small and Medium Industries Development Corporation (SMIDEC) was incorporated in the 1990s under the Ministry of International Trade and Industry (MITI) to govern their activities. However, official state policy tended to discourage local SMIs with a size above mandatory registration levels, as the experienced ones were dominated by Chinese ownership and these generally preferred to remain small to avoid the ethnic equity conditions imposed by the Industrial Coordination Act of 1975.[4] It is only in Penang, where local state autonomy has promoted better government business coordination, that the development of strong SMI supplier firms has been observed (see Rasiah 1999).

Being generally small and medium in size, and dominated by Chinese ownership, local machine tool firms faced the same fate as most SMIs. Much of the initial federal support for the evolution of machine tool firms came indirectly, but in some sense fortuitously as we shall see below. There were no clear efforts to attract electronics firms with the aim of spawning local subcontractor firms when the government first launched its export-oriented industrialisation policy following the Investment Incentives Act (IIA) in 1968. The early electronic components MNCs only began relocating in Malaysia after the Free Trade Zone Act of 1971 and the subsequent opening of the zones in 1972. Although Matsushita Electric commenced production in 1965 in Selangor, it was not until the early 1970s that the first major wave of electric and electronics firms located their production in Malaysia. Nevertheless, government efforts to woo export-oriented manufacturing firms have been critical in at least four important ways.

While big potential for the development of SMIs emerged following the growth in demand generated from the relocation of foreign electric/electronics subsidiaries, the regulatory environment generally hindered their development until the late 1980s. Large firms enjoyed considerable advantage over small firms in their access to pioneer status, the Investment Tax Allowance (ITA), free trade zones (FTZ) and licensed manufacturing warehouse (LMW) incentives (see Rasiah 1995).[5]

The electronics component firms who came to Malaysia in the initial wave were large, with employee numbers exceeding 500. As a symbolic gesture, the Penang government opened Penang Electronics in 1970, which operated briefly before closing down. The Japanese-owned Clarion was the first foreign electronics component firm to start operations in Malaysia arriving in 1971. National Semiconductor of the United States was the first semiconductor firm to build its factory in Malaysia, commencing production in 1972. A combination of lucrative incentives directed at firms that generated larger employment and investment levels, and the labour-intensive production technologies associated with electronics assembly in the 1970s and early 1980s, skewed the industry towards large firms (see Rasiah 1993; 1996).

Given the lack of production experience in electrical industrial machinery and apparatus manufacture prior to the 1970s, local initiatives in the industry only began to emerge in Malaysia after the redeployment of production by foreign MNCs. With the exception of showpiece industries and other scattered small-scale efforts, local involvement in electronics component manufacture did not grow significantly until the late 1980s. Being small and largely owned by local Chinese capital, electrical industrial machinery and apparatus firms generally enjoyed little government support until this time. In fact, the industry only received a boost when it was classified among the industries to be promoted in the Industrial Master Plan of 1986. Being complementary to the operations of strategic industries such as electronics, the industry enjoyed similar incentives to theirs, although the extent of foreign direct investment in electrical and industrial machinery and apparatus was extremely small at the time. The Promotion of Investment Act of 1986 offered the industry equal duty exemptions, if located in free trade zones (FTZs) or licensed manufacturing warehouses (LMWs), and export incentives, such as the double tax deduction on exports and export credit refinancing. These policies and the Plaza Accord of 1985 (under which the value of the currencies of South Korea, Taiwan, Japan and Singapore rose), the withdrawal of the Generalised System of Preferences (GSP) from the Asian Newly Industrialised Economies (NIEs) and agglomeration effects from clustering attracted large and medium foreign firms to Malaysia, especially from Japan and Taiwan, from the second half of the 1980s. However, biases against micro and small firms remained, despite policy instruments to promote them from the 1980s.

Federal policy instruments generally offered little stimulus for the growth of micro and small electrical industrial and apparatus firms in Malaysia. Against this general trend nationally, changes in production organisation began to affect the size configuration of the electrical industrial machinery and apparatus firms in Malaysia, especially from the mid-1980s. With considerable assembly and test upgrading, as well as aspects of redesigning taking place in Malaysia, local state initiatives began to stimulate the development of institutional networks to enable greater deepening of the value-added chain in Malaysia. Especially the local state of Penang began to promote clustering with emphasis on local SMIs. Using considerable autonomy, Penang aggressively pursued such opportunities. Here, government–business initiatives led to the formation of the Penang Skills Development Centre (PSDC) in 1989. Several other aspects of infrastructure were strengthened so that large foreign MNCs could externalise substantial aspects of production, which had been internalised in the past because of the uncertainties associated with an underdeveloped local structure. Such production segments were dissimilar but complementary to the operations of the main electronics component firms in Malaysia. Hence, production reconstitution in firms led to the outsourcing of electrical industrial machinery and apparatus operations by MNCs, generating substantial demand for proximate supplying. SMIs began to figure considerably in the supplier chains of MNCs.

The lack of similar strong networks in the Kelang Valley, Negeri Sembilan, Melaka and Johore discouraged the strong development of electrical industrial machinery and apparatus firms in these areas. With the exception of Penang, local micro and small electrical industrial machinery and apparatus firms in the rest of Malaysia generally faced difficulties in accessing government support. Especially Chinese-owned micro and small electric industrial machinery and apparatus suppliers faced considerable problems in their efforts to supply multinationals in locations outside Penang. The lack of state support left them facing severe market failure[6] problems, although ethnic congruence with the generally ethnic Chinese purchasing officers in the multinationals has helped reduce transaction costs involving local sourcing. Not only are electronics component multinationals badly positioned to identify micro and small-scale firms' potential capabilities, as this would require detailed scrutiny and monitoring, but also they receive little encouragement to participate in such developments, which can be risky and uncertain. Hence, outside Penang, few links have been forged between foreign MNCs and local micro and small electrical industrial machinery and apparatus firms. Micro and small firms not only face financial problems—including accessing subsidised loans and technical assistance from the credit guarantee schemes and the industrial technical assistance fund (ITAF)—but they are also insufficiently prominent to attract the attention of potential multinational clients. Indeed, interviews show that the list of micro and small firms promoted by the federal government includes relatively few electrical industrial machinery and apparatus firms operating in the Kelang Valley. Where there has been active state promotion, such as by the *bumiputera* venture trust Permodalan Usahawan Nasional Berhad (PUNB), stringent ethnic-based conditions apply.

Overall, the lack of political support has been a key factor in restricting the establishment and strengthening of sourcing relationships between MNCs and local micro, small and medium electrical industrial machinery and apparatus firms. The intermediary coordination role played by the Penang Development Corporation (PDC)[7] in Penang has been missing elsewhere in Malaysia. Lacking state efforts to institutionalise risks, MNCs in the Kelang Valley, Negeri Sembilan, Melaka and Johore reported that they lacked the motivation to develop links with and promote local electrical industrial machinery and apparatus capabilities.[8] Unlike in Penang, where a proactive state leadership has played a critical role in stimulating links between local firms and MNCs, state leadership in other parts of Malaysia has generally avoided such a role (see Rasiah 1999). Since the federal state, *de facto*, has generally been the active governance agent in the rest of West Malaysia, national considerations embedded in the New Economic Policy (NEP)[9] and its successor (see Hua 1983; Jomo 1986), the National Development Plan (NDP),[10] have dictated the promotion of local sourcing. *Inter alia*, ethno-class differences restricted the effectiveness of the nationally coordinated VDP and SEP.

The federal state has only been slightly more successful with the promotion of the VDP than with the SEP, which involved the electrical/electronics industry. However, anchor companies[11] began to support small and medium firms with equity of not less than $100,000 ringgit with *bumiputera* participation in equity and employment of 70 per cent and 55 per cent respectively. Participation in this programme within the electronics industry has so far largely involved consumer and industrial electronics firms. Few links have been established with microelectronics firms. Sapura and Sharp were the initial anchor firms. This programme has helped to create the first generation of *bumiputera*-controlled suppliers within a short time in the electrical and electronics industry. The government planned to create 80 new vendors during the Sixth (1991–95) and Seventh (1996–2000) Malaysia Plans (Vijaya Letchumy 1993, p. 14). Subsidised loans and technical assistance offered through ITAF and venture companies such as PUNB have been critical for their development.

The extension of financial incentives and the Endaka effect from the Plaza Accord of 1985 stimulated a massive relocation of North-East Asian firms to Malaysia, which included MNCs—primarily medium and large firms in the electrical industrial machinery and apparatus industry. The expansion of especially Japanese and American MNC production operations in the electrical and electronics industry generated sufficient demand to attract machinery and apparatus suppliers from Japan and Taiwan. Given the incentives and longer learning experience enjoyed by foreign medium and large suppliers, most local micro and small firms were disadvantaged.

Socio-political divergence in Malaysian industrial locations outside Penang between the micro, small and medium business communities stifled the development of the complementary institutions required to support the growth of micro and small electrical and industrial machinery firms. An important reason for this divergence was that the political interests of the United Malays National Organisation (UMNO)-dominated leadership and the generally Chinese-dominated ownership of micro and small firms both at the state and federal levels were contradictory. With weak inter-ethnic collaborative relations at the micro and small firm levels, the middle-class Chinese business community involved in the electrical industrial machinery and apparatus industry enjoyed little government support. Federal financial incentives associated with support for SMIs also hardly reached Chinese owned micro and small electrical industrial machinery and apparatus firms in Malaysia outside Penang. Thus foreign-owned medium and large firms have tended to enjoy greater financial incentives from the Malaysian government than micro and small firms.

Growth and performance

Because of the general bias of government policy towards large and, to a lesser extent, medium firms, one would expect the relative contribution of micro and small firms to the overall electrical machinery and apparatus industry to be smaller than in Taiwan, where the policy environment does not discriminate between micro, small and medium firms. This section presents statistics on the contribution of the electrical machinery and apparatus sub-sector to overall electronics and manufacturing output, the relative contributions of the different employment size categories, analysed in terms of the number of establishments, value-added, employment and fixed assets, and growth and performance of these categories. All statistics used are annual figures, calculated at 31 December each year.

The total number of electrical machinery and apparatus establishments grew from 20 in 1988 to 116 in 1995. Micro firms with an employment size of less than 50 made up 55.0 per cent of the establishments in 1988, the share falling to 26.9 per cent in 1992 before rising to 60.3 per cent in 1995. Medium firms with 100–499 employees contributed the next highest category, 25.0 per cent in 1988 and 21.6 per cent in 1995, and were the largest category in 1994 with 44.4 per cent of firms. Large firms with 500 employees and above were the least in number, contributing 5.0 per cent of total firms in 1988 and 7.8 per cent in 1995.

The total value added of the electrical industrial machinery and apparatus industry, based on 1985 prices, rose from 67.4 million ringgit in 1988 to 343.8 million ringgit in 1995. Medium firms contributed most to electrical machinery and apparatus value-added in the period 1988–89 and 1994. The large firm category was the leading contributor in 1990–92 and 1995. The small firms' contribution to total value-added was the least in 1995.

The electrical industrial machinery and apparatus industry contributed a total of 2,783 employees in 1988, reaching 18,318 employees in 1995. Large firms contributed most to electrical machinery and apparatus employment in 1988 and in the period 1990–95. Medium firms contributed least to employment in the period 1988–89. Micro and small firms also contributed little to overall employment figures.

The total fixed assets of the electrical industrial machinery and apparatus industries increased from 48 million ringgit in 1988 to 315 million ringgit in 1995. Medium firms were the largest contributors in the period 1988–90 and 1993–94. The medium firms category also contributed most to total fixed assets in 1990 and 1994. Large firms became the largest contributor in the period 1991–93 and in 1995. Fixed asset levels in the categories of medium and large firms expanded sharply in the period 1994–95 because of the big influx of new firms. Micro and small firms contributed least to overall fixed assets. Interviews with industry officials suggest that the fluctuations between size categories could be the result of some firms' graduation into higher categories and also result of the birth of new firms.

The measurement of total factory productivity (TFP) requires special caution as the specific characteristics and structures of particular industries need to be addressed.[12] Apart from the usual deficiencies associated with TFP measures (see Rasiah 2000b), a number of practical issues relating to this data deserve attention. First, technological differences —both product and process technologies—vary substantially between the different size categories.[13] It is impossible to distinguish these differences at the ISIC five-digit level. Second, fluctuations in market demand are intense when they involve large export-oriented firms facing a very liberal tariff environment. Smaller firms—engaged in infrequent demand situations and as suppliers to larger firms—tend to face externally generated destabilising effects. Third, despite their production inflexibility, large firms show stronger resilience when facing financial destabilisation unless they are exposed to high loan–equity ratios. Fourth, according to interviews with officials from three firms in each of the size categories, the first category of micro firms is characterised by relatively higher turnover rates because of firms ceasing operations or firms graduating to higher employment size categories following expansion.[14] Micro and small firms may have been severely affected by the presence of relatively newer firms as well as the absence of some successful ones moving on to higher size categories. Most of the firms in the micro and small size categories perform simple subcontract operations for medium and large firms, and specialise in lower value-added activities. These firms enjoy hardly any financial incentives. Therefore the analysis of the TFP and TFP growth (TFPG) measures in this chapter must be treated with caution.

The measurement of growth rates and productivity is also affected by the use of industry level deflators, which rely on aggregate price movements rather than prices facing firms in the specific size categories. Interviews showed that most micro and small firms are engaged either in the manufacture of simple industrial machinery and apparatus or are supplying apparatus to bigger firms operating in Malaysia. Medium firms with 100 to 499 employees also export, but are diversified over a number of activities, which reduces their market risk. Large firms tend to specialise in the high volume assembly of electrical industrial machinery and apparatus.

Table 6.1 presents the growth rates of value-added, inputs, labour, capital and TFPG. It can be seen that TFPG recorded negative rates in all categories for the period 1988–91. Large firms recorded the biggest decline with their value-added growth driven primarily by strong growth in labour, inputs and capital utilisation. Small firms recorded a decline in TFPG because of growth in inputs and the factors of labour and capital when value-added actually declined. Although the value-added of small firms achieved positive growth in the period 1988–91, it was still exceeded by growth in labour, material inputs and capital. Micro firms experienced rapid growth in labour and material inputs.

Table 6.1: Growth of the Malaysian industrial electrical and apparatus industry 1988–95 (logarithmic growth rates)

a: Size—Micro firms

	1988–91	1991–93	1993–95
Value-added	0.08	−0.01	0.09
TFP	−0.30	−0.09	−0.27
Inputs	0.11	−0.03	0.13
Labour	0.21	0.05	0.12
Capital	0.06	0.06	0.12

Note: Fewer than 50 employees

b: Size—Small firms

	1988–91	1991–93	1993–95
Value-added	−0.07	0.29	0.10
TFP	−0.47	0.23	0.15
Inputs	0.12	0.27	0.01
Labour	0.22	0.10	−0.05
Capital	0.06	0.16	−0.02

Note: 50–99employees

c: Size—Medium firms

	1988–91	1991–93	1993–95
Value-added	0.07	0.18	0.02
TFP	−0.26	−0.09	0.01
Inputs	0.10	0.11	0.03
Labour	0.14	0.07	0.02
Capital	0.09	0.09	0.00

Note: 100–499 employees

d: Size—Large firms

	1988–91	1991–93	1993–95
Value-added	0.33	0.15	0.07
TFP	−0.82	0.12	−0.14
Inputs	0.30	0.04	0.10
Labour	0.63	−0.02	0.07
Capital	0.21	0.01	0.05

Note: 500 or more employees
Source: Data from Statistics Department, Malaysia.

The TFPG of small and large firms achieved positive rates in the period 1991–93. High growth in value-added of small firms helped achieve strong TFPG, while big improvements in use of inputs, labour and capital largely explain the positive TFPG of large firms. Medium firms and micro firms recorded negative TFPG. Medium firms faced high growth in inputs, capital and labour, while micro firms experienced a decline in value-added in the period 1991–93.

Micro firms and large firms recorded negative TFPG in the period 1993–95 primarily because of faster growth in the use of input and factors of production (see Table 6.1). Small firms achieved strong TFPG following the especially strong improvements in the utilisation of inputs and the factors of labour and capital. In fact, labour and capital utilisation in this category declined in the period 1993–95 as high labour turnovers and rising capacity utilisation helped lower factor use.[15]

Micro firms show the highest birth and mortality rates as some new firms enter then exit production. Others graduate to higher categories as they expand. Small firms are engaged in both subcontracting and original equipment manufacturing activities for export markets. Products assembled include power-driven machinery, automated and electrical machinery and tools. The products range from simple graters and power tools to boiler machines and fully-automated semiconductor assembly machinery. Most of the firms in the large and medium categories are foreign-owned and enjoy export-oriented incentives while local firms dominate the micro and small categories. While most large and medium firms enjoyed tax holidays, only a handful of small firms received investment tax allowances.[16] Except for 1994–95, when some firms expanded and moved from micro to small and medium categories and the large firms rationalised to trim their headcounts, the number of firms in these categories has been stable with a gradual increase in new firms over the years.

The breakdown of the contribution of firms size categories into TFP levels, material inputs, labour and capital is shown in Table 6.2. Small firms showed the highest TFP levels in 1989, followed by micro firms. Material inputs accounted for the most growth in large, micro and medium firms. On average only about a quarter of value-added growth in all size categories came from disembodied technical change in 1989.

The contribution of the TFP level fell for all categories in 1991 compared with 1989. Small firms' TFP level fell from more than a quarter to a fifth in 1991. Material inputs and labour for small firms expanded their shares by 3.0 and 4.2 per cent respectively.

The TFP levels of all size categories rose slightly in the period 1991–93. However, only small firms experienced a rise in TFP levels in 1995—exceeding the TFP levels of micro firms. Improvements in the use of material inputs, capital and labour helped improve small firms' TFP levels in 1995.

However, with the exception of small firms, the overall TFP levels in all size categories were fairly stagnant throughout the period 1989–95,

Malaysian business in the new era

Table 6.2: Composition of growth, Malaysian industrial electrical and apparatus industry 1989–95 (per cent)

a: Size—Micro firms

	1989	1991	1993	1995
TFP	25.1	24.5	25.4	25.0
Inputs	28.4	28.4	28.0	28.0
Labour	22.2	22.6	22.4	22.6
Capital	24.3	24.5	24.3	24.4

Note: Fewer than 50 employees

b: Size—Small firms

	1989	1991	1993	1995
TFP	27.5	20.6	22.2	25.7
Inputs	24.9	27.9	23.5	22.1
Labour	24.1	28.3	26.4	25.0
Capital	23.4	23.2	27.8	27.2

Note: 50–99 employees

c: Size—Medium firms

	1989	1991	1993	1995
TFP	23.9	23.3	24.2	23.9
Inputs	27.7	27.7	27.4	27.4
Labour	22.5	22.8	22.6	22.8
Capital	25.9	26.1	25.8	25.9

Note: 100–499 employees

d: Size—Large firms

	1989	1991	1993	1995
TFP	24.4	23.8	24.7	24.4
Inputs	29.1	29.1	28.6	28.6
Labour	22.8	23.1	22.9	23.1
Capital	23.8	24.0	23.8	24.0

Note: 500 or more employees
Source: Data from Statistics Department, Malaysia.

suggesting that the relative share of disembodied technical progress has not changed much, irrespective of firm size. The same seems to hold for technical progress embodied in capital and labour. The contribution of inputs in value-added remained stable throughout the period 1989–95 in all size categories except small firms. The TFP levels of small firms fell sharply in the period 1989–91 before improving in 1991–93 and 1993–95. Overall, inputs, labour and capital accounted for between 75 and 80 per cent of the contribution to value-added growth, with TFP only accounting for 20–25 per cent of value-added growth in the period 1989–95.

While the contribution of TFP levels to value-added does not establish the significance of size as a factor in performance, the generally-observed specialisation of firms in each of the employment size categories in different products suggests that scale effects may still be important. Further research is necessary before such a statement can be validated. Future research should also examine the movement of particular cohorts of firms between size categories before the conjectures introduced earlier can be refuted or reinforced. Therefore, unlike the cases of South Korea (large firms) and Taiwan (small and medium firms), where the drivers of manufacturing expansion are clear, this exercise does not establish the clear dominance of any particular size.

It should also be noted that there has been a trend towards rationalisation in the industry. For example, the average employment per firm fell in 1995, largely due to a decline in the largest category of 1,000 or more employees.[17] The large firms category experienced a sudden rise in the period 1991–94 because of the relocation of high-volume foreign machinery assemblers with more than 1,000 employees. Overall, it seems that scale may not be a critical variable in the electrical industrial machinery and apparatus industry, though, its effects might become apparent if specific products are examined.

The rationalisation tendencies with falling employment size began first in the electronics component sub-sector. As a spillover effect, buyer–supplier links with other industries, as well as the exhaustion of labour reserves in West Peninsular Malaysia, led to similar developments in the electrical machinery and apparatus sub-sector. The work organisation of electronics component firms began to change strongly from the 1980s (see Rasiah 1995). Especially in semiconductor production—where product cycles have become increasingly shorter and prices have fallen sharply—firms began to introduce rapid changes in work organisation. Most high-technology firms began to introduce flexible production systems, superimposing cellular manufacturing onto state-of-the-art human resource techniques such as total quality management (TQM) (Rasiah 1987; 1994). From the late 1980s, the larger electrical machinery and apparatus firms, irrespective of ownership, began introducing flexible production techniques, integrating innovative capacity with execution throughout the division of labour, thereby reducing hierarchies and making them interlock in the process. The sharp fall in labour reserves from the late 1980s led even electrical apparatus manufacturers to turn to flexible production strategies. Much of this change appeared to be embodied in capital and labour—rather than in disembodied technical progress—as the emphasis on automated machinery and skilled labour increased following spiralling wages and other production costs. The generally negative TFPG rates recorded by all size categories in the period 1988–94 could be the result of falling profit margins (see Table 6.1). Increasing investment and rising numbers of start-ups also explain the relative stagnation in TFP levels in this period.

Offshore production involving electronics multinationals in Malaysia has transformed from a transient offshore activity (Lim 1978; Rasiah 1987) to a deep-rooted regional operation (Rasiah 1987; 1988). The growth of product and process customisation within the rapidly growing Asia-Pacific market further enhanced such a development. These developments—particularly those enabling flexible specialisation in production—have provided a strong impetus for proximate local electrical machinery and equipment sourcing and the intensification of employee training, both in-house and externally. Currency fluctuations have also been a significant factor here, as the yen appreciated to almost double its value from 1985 to 1993. Interestingly, the appreciation of the ringgit after 1992 reversed the exchange rate advantage until the financial crisis struck in 1997.

Focusing on the use of direct and indirect (cutting-edge process techniques) proxies such as quality control circles (QCCs), small group activities, just-in-time (JIT), quick changeover and multi-product lines, total quality management (TQM), total preventive maintenance (TPM) and statistical process control (SPC), we see that the timing of the application of flexible production techniques in production in the electrical industrial machinery and apparatus industry can be traced from the late 1980s. However, much of the application of these techniques took place in the early 1990s. Unlike production demands that required semiconductor firms to introduce such production methods from the early 1980s (see Rasiah 1994; 1995),[18] it was growing tightness in the labour market and export market demand that stimulated the early absorption of these techniques in electrical industrial machinery and apparatus firms. The infusion of cutting edge process technologies and the learning experience—reflected in input saving or labour saving technologies—helped improve TFPG in all size categories in the 1990s. Small firms achieved the highest TFPG in the periods of 1991–93 and 1993–95. Micro firms—facing the typical problems associated with the entry and exit of new inexperienced firms and the graduation of successful firms to higher categories—have recorded negative TFPG throughout. The number of micro firms expanded by 15.4, 53.3 and 483.3 per cent respectively in the periods 1989–91 1991–93 and 1993–95. The negative TFPG rates of small (100 per cent in 1988–91), medium (100 per cent 1988–91 and 38.9 per cent in 1991–93) and large (600 per cent in 1988–91 and 28.8 per cent 1993–95) were also affected by the large-scale entry of new firms. Nevertheless, the TFP contribution to the value-added of micro firms has been impressive when compared with other size categories.

Conclusion

This chapter has examined the regulatory environment of manufacturing in general and the electrical industrial machinery and apparatus firms in particular in Malaysia, as well as the growth and performance of the latter based on firm size. Political and economic factors skewed government policy support towards medium and large firms over micro and small firms. Incentives have shown a strong bias towards large firms. Despite micro and small firms dominating the number of establishments, medium and large firms continue to lead in terms of employment, investment and value-added. Assuming that the problems inherent in the measurement of TFPG and TFP levels cancel out without seriously affecting the results, the productivity trends of the electrical industrial machinery and apparatus industry do not demonstrate a clear orientation towards a particular firm size. Despite dominating the value-added and factor utilisation results, medium and large firms have not performed better than micro and small firms. Micro and small firms show the highest TFP levels in the years 1989 and 1995, and 1991 and 1993 respectively, and small firms the highest TFPG rates in 1991–93 and 1993–95. Micro and small firms have performance relatively well despite policy biases favouring medium and large firms.

Given the relative infancy of the industry in Malaysia, all size categories have experienced a rapid increase in new entrants, which has affected the TFP levels and TFPG rates: capacity building superseding production efforts. Despite these biases, the growth and performance of electrical industrial machinery and apparatus micro and small firms in Malaysia have not fallen short of those of their bigger counterparts.

The results demonstrate that micro and small firms can perform well in the electrical industrial machinery and apparatus firms. However, a more rigorous individual firm level assessment focusing on the same firms historically is essential for more definite conclusions. Also, the scope and flexibility offered by smallness may still be relevant if it can be established that these firms have graduated to larger categories over time.

Overall, the electrical industrial machinery and apparatus industry does not demonstrate any consensus on the significance of size in Malaysia's manufacturing success, which could be a result of the different production functions facing each of the size categories and further differentiation within them. Nevertheless, the commendable performance of micro and small firms, despite encountering negative policy biases, suggests that industrial policy could do much to enhance Malaysia's industrial competitiveness if these size categories were targeted effectively for promotion. Also, in the face of rising deregulation pressures imposed by global and regional trading arrangements, such as the World Trade Organisation (WTO) and the ASEAN Free Trade Area (AFTA), it might be worth extending effective policy support to micro and small firms to sustain rapid growth.

Endnotes

[1] Data compiled by the Malaysian Statistics Department and comments from an anonymous referee are gratefully acknowledged. The usual disclaimer applies.

[2] Unpublished Malaysian Industrial Development Authority (MIDA) data.

[3] See Chee (1986) and Chee et al. (1981) for a historical account of the evolution of SMIs in Malaysia.

[4]   Manufacturing firms with a paid up capital over 250,000 ringgit and more than 25 employees had to seek mandatory registration. Firms seeking registration were often required to meet New Economic policy conditions that included 30 per cent *bumiputera* equity participation.

[5]   See Rasiah (1994; 1995; 1999) for a detailed account of the additional benefits enjoyed by large export-oriented firms.

[6]   Being small they have faced considerable information and 'perceived capability' asymmetry when compared with medium and large firms.

[7]   The PDC is the economic development parastatal of Penang.

[8]   Interview by author carried out in 1999.

[9]   The NEP when launched in 1971 with the Second Malaysia Plan (1971-75) aimed at alleviating poverty and redressing economic inequality (both regionally and ethnically). Its strategies, among other things, included expanding *bumiputera* share of corporate assets to 30 per cent. Under the ICA of 1975, the Minister of Trade and Industry often emphasised the *bumiputera* share ownership and ethnic employment quotas (the latter less emphasised) (see Rasiah and Ishak 2001).

[10]   The NDP replaced the NEP in 1990.

[11]   Anchor companies act like parent firms, fostering the growth of supplier firms. Their activities in reality are the same as those of the umbrella firms used in the country.

[12]   TFP growth was computed using the growth accounting method, and TFP levels were computed using the translog production function derived from $Y = \propto f(I^\beta, L^\lambda, K^\delta)$ where the variables Y, I, L and K refer to value-added, gross material inputs, labour and capital respectively. The superscripts β, λ and δ refer to the growth rates of I, L and K respectively. The term $\propto$, the intercept, refers to total factor productivity growth.

[13]   Kaldor (1979) raised the issue of technical progress embodied in labour and capital. Embodied technical change is not measured by the typical Solow growth accounting TFP framework. Even endogenous growth theorists working on quantitative models have hardly drawn this issue for relevant policy conclusions (see Lucas 1988; Helpman and Krugman 1989).

[14]   Given the difficulty associated with obtaining firm level interviews, these interviews were conducted on a purposive basis. Past contacts were utilised to obtain responses.

[15]   Interviews by author involving six firms in 1999.

[16]   Interviews by author in 1999.

[17]   Data from Statistics Department, Malaysia.

[18]   Semiconductor firms were forced to initiate the introduction of flexible production techniques in assembly to meet the demands of rapid miniaturisation and product customisation.

References

Alt, J. E. and K. A. Chrystal (1983), *Politic Economics*, Berkeley: University of California Press.

Audretsch, D. B. (2000), 'The economic role of small- and medium-sized enterprises: The United States', paper presented at the World Bank Workshop on Small and Medium Enterprises, Chiang Mai.

Best, M. (1990), *The New Competition*, Cambridge: Harvard University Press.

—— (2001), *The New Competitive Advantage*, Oxford: Oxford University Press.

Chandler, A. (1985*)*, *The Visible Hand: The Managerial Revolution in American Business*, Harvard: Belknap Press.

Chee, P. L. (1986), *Small and Medium Industries in Malaysia*, Kuala Lumpur: Forum Press.

Chee, P. L., D. Lee and R. T. Foo (1981), 'The case of labour intensive industry in Malaysia', in R. Amjad (ed)., *The Development of Labour Intensive Industry in ASEAN Countries*, Bangkok: International Labour Organisation.

Coase, R. H. (1937), 'The nature of the firm', *Economica*, 16 (4), 386–405.

Doner, R. (1991), 'Approaches to the politics of economic growth in Southeast Asia', *Journal of Asian Studies*, 50 (4), 818–849.

Evans, P. (1992), 'The state as problem and solution: Predation, embedded autonomy, and structural change', in S. Haggard and R. R. Kaufman (eds), *The Politics of Economic Adjustment*, Princeton: Princeton University Press.

Haggard, S. (1990), *Pathways from the Periphery: The Politics of Growth in the Newly Industrialising Countries*, Ithaca: Cornell University Press.

Helpman, E. and P. R. Krugman (1989), *Trade Policy and Market Structure*, Cambridge: MIT Press.

Hirst, P. and J. Zeitlin (1991), 'Flexible specialisation versus post-fordism theory: Evidence and policy implications', *Economy and Society*, 20 (1).

Hua, W. Y. (1983), *Class and Communal Politics in Malaysia*, London: Zed Press.

Jomo, K. S. (1986), *A Question of Class*, Kuala Lumpur: Oxford University Press.

Kaldor, N. (1979), 'Equilibrium theory and growth theory', in M. J. Boskin (ed.), *Economics of Human Welfare: Essays in Honour of Tibor Scitovsky*, New York: Academic Press, pp. 271–291.

Kamal, S. and M. L. Young (1985), 'Penang's industrialisation: Where do we go from here', paper presented at the 'Future of Penang Conference', Penang.

Khan, M. (1989), 'Corruption, Clientelism and the Capitalist State', unpublished doctoral thesis, Cambridge: Cambridge University.

Khong, S. M. (1991), 'The Service Sector in Malaysia: Structure and Change', unpublished doctoral thesis, Cambridge: Cambridge University.

Lim, L. Y. C. (1978), 'Multinational Firms and Manufacturing for Export in Less Developed Countries: The Case of the Electronics Industry in Malaysia and Singapore', unpublished doctoral thesis, Ann Arbor: Michigan University.

Lucas, R. E. (1988), 'On the mechanics of economic development', *Journal of Monetary Economics*, 22, 3–22.

Malaysia (1971), *The Second Malaysia Plan 1971–1975*, Kuala Lumpur: Government Printers.

—— (1976), *The Third Malaysia Plan 1976–1980*, Kuala Lumpur: Government Printers.

—— (1994), *Ministry of International Trade and Industry Report*: Kuala Lumpur: Government Printers.

MIDA (1988), *Investment in the Manufacturing Sector: Policies, Incentives and Procedures*, Kuala Lumpur: Malaysian Industrial Development Authority.

Mardon, R. (1990), 'The state and effective control of foreign capital: The case of South Korea', *World Politics*, 43 (1), 111–138.

Munro (1964), 'Untitled mimeo' Penang.

North, D. C. and R. P. Thomas (1970), 'An economic theory of the growth of the Western world', *The Economic History Review*, 22 (1), 1–17.

PDC (1971), *Annual Report*, Penang: Penang Development Corporation.

Pratten, C. (1971), *Economics of Scale in Manufacturing Industry*, Cambridge: Cambridge University Press.

Rasiah, R. (1987), *International Division of Labour* (translated from Malay), master's thesis, Universiti Sains Malaysia (Published in 1993 by Malaysian Social Science Association).

—— (1988), 'The semiconductor industry in Penang: Implications for NIDL theories', *Journal of Contemporary Asia*, 18 (2).

—— (1993), *Pembahagian Kerja Antarabangsa: Industri Semikonduktor di Pulau Pinang*, Kuala Lumpur: Malaysian Social Science Association.

—— (1994), 'Flexible production systems and local machine tool subcontracting: Electronics component multinationals in Malaysia', *Cambridge Journal of Economics*, 18 (3), 279–298.

—— (1995), *Foreign Capital and Industrialisation in Malaysia*, New York and London: St Martin's and Macmillan.

—— (1996), 'Industrialisation as engine of growth and industrial policy in Malaysia', *Managerial Finance*, 9 (2).

—— (1997), 'Class, ethnicity and economic development in Malaysia', in G. Rodan, K. Hewisen and R. Robison (eds), *Political Economy of South-East Asia*, Melbourne: Oxford University Press.

—— (1999), 'From a backyard workshop to a modern machine tool factory: Eng hardware', in K. S. Jomo, G. Felker and R. Rasiah (eds), *Industry Technology Development in Malaysia*, London: Routledge.

—— (1999), From backyard workshop to modern factory:

—— (2000a), 'Politics, institutions and flexibility: Microelectronics transnationals and local machine tool linkages', R. Doner and F. Deyo (eds), *Flexible Specialisation in Asia*, New York: Little and Rowland.

—— (2000b), 'SMIs, transnationals and linkages in the electronics industry', in I. Farukh and S. Urata (eds), *SMIs and Economic Development*, World Bank Discussion Paper.

Rasiah, R. and S. Ishak (2001), 'Market, government and Malaysia's new economic policy', *Cambridge Journal of Economics*, 25 (1), 57–78.

Richardson, G. B. (1960), *Information and Investment*, Oxford: Oxford University Press.

—— (1972), 'The organisation of industry', *Economic Journal*, 82 (3), 883–896.

Sabel, C. (1986), 'Changing models of economic efficiency and their implications for industrialisation in the Third World', in C. F. D. Alejandro et al. (eds), *Development, Democracy and the Art of Trespassing*, Notre Dame: Notre Dame University Press.

Saham, J. (1980), *British Industrial Investment in Malaysia 1963–1971*, Kuala Lumpur: Oxford University Press.

Scherer, F. M. (1980), *Industrial Market Structure and Economic Performance*, Boston: Houghton Mifflin.

Sengenberger, W. and F. Pyke (1991), 'Small firm industrial districts and local economic regeneration: Research and policy issues', *Labour and Society*, 16 (1).

Sheperd, G. (1980), 'Policies to promote industrial development', in K. Young, W. C. F. Bussink and P. Hasan (eds), *Malaysia: Growth and Equity in a Multiracial Society*, Baltimore: John Hopkins University Press, pp. 182–210.

Vijaya Letchumy (1993), 'SMI development programmes', paper presented at MITI/MIDA/FMM seminar, 'Domestic Investment in the Manufacturing Sector', Penang.

Wilkinson, F. and J. I. You (1992), 'Competition and cooperation: Towards an understanding of the industrial district', Small Business Research Centre, Working Paper No. 88, Cambridge: Cambridge University.

Williamson, O. E. (1985), *Markets, Hierarchies and Relational Contracting*, New York: The Free Press.
World Bank (1993), *The East Asian Miracle*, New York: Oxford University Press.

7

Sustaining the growth effects of foreign investment: The case of multinational subsidiaries in Malaysia

Ron Edwards, Adlina Ahmad and Simon Moss

Introduction

Malaysia's economic growth over recent decades has been underpinned by investment from abroad. Approximately half the finance for her gleaming cities and bustling manufacturing sector has been funded by foreign direct investment (FDI) (Doraisami 1996; UNCTAD 1998). The investment was encouraged by the Malaysian government's offering multinational corporations (MNCs) a range of incentives designed to encourage the establishment of subsidiaries. These incentives primarily entail taxation allowances and more liberal ownership rights for investments in particular industries, such as manufacturing and high technology, or in particular geographic locations, such as the Multimedia Super Corridor and the Eastern Corridor. Moreover, they are directed towards investments that offer significant learning opportunities, such as from research and development, or have particular strategic roles, such as operational headquarters and international procurement centres (Government of Malaysia 1999; Tan Ser Kiat 1999).

Investment incentives are justified in Malaysia and elsewhere by the range of benefits that such investment provides. In addition to the boost to economic growth provided by financial capital, Malaysia benefits from the enhancement to human capital in the form of superior management, marketing and technological expertise (BIE 1993; Dunning 1993; Government of Malaysia 1999; Parry 1983; UNCTAD 1998; Vachani 1999). However, the international business literature suggests that the extent to which such benefits flow to the host economy depends on the characteristics of the subsidiary, in particular the degree to which local management participates in developing the corporate strategy and has opportunities to expand the business. Highly centralised organisational structures where subsidiaries are simply channels for headquarter decision making and possibly goods offer the least for host economies (Allen Consulting Group 1994; Langdale 1992; Rugman and Douglas 1996).

This chapter concentrates on the manner in which the structure and strategy of multinational corporations that have invested in Malaysia affect the autonomy of local management and, by implication, the benefits that flow to the host economy. The factors that determine the level of autonomy afforded by MNCs to their subsidiaries in Malaysia will be analysed, we survey the academic literature on MNC strategy and structure and the associated range of subsidiary roles, and describe our methodology, and analyse survey data collected from multinational corporations in Malaysia. Finally we offer some conclusions and discuss policy implications.

International business strategy and structure

In the first major study of organisational structures of international firms, Stopford and Wells (1972) found that similar organisational designs were used across quite different industries. With a survey of 187 large US manufacturing firms each having manufacturing facilities in at least six foreign countries, they observed organisational structures evolving through distinct stages over time.

According to their observations, in their first venture into the international market place, firms established relatively autonomous foreign subsidiaries. Subsequently, the MNC created an international business division, located within the parent firm but separate from domestic operations, that controlled and coordinated the expanding international activities. In the third stage, the MNC established either one of two structures, a worldwide product division or a regional division. A worldwide product division assumes global responsibility for a particular line of products. Regional divisions involve a regional headquarters being responsible for all a company's activities within its geographic area (Egelhoff 1988; Martinez and Jarillo 1991).

From the perspective of the 'centralised–decentralised' continuum, these structures can have different implications for the host country. The early form of relatively autonomous subsidiaries, with some capacity to adapt processes and products to meet the different needs of local markets, and considerable scope to source inputs from local suppliers, fits clearly into the 'decentralised' end of the spectrum. On the other hand, an MNC organised on a worldwide product basis, where the senior product manager controls all production and sales from the parent, is an example of a centralised organisational arrangement. A regional structure is the intermediate case because regional managers, being closer to customers, are in a better position to adapt production processes and products on a regional, if not national, basis. To the extent that political and economic conditions within an area are more similar than they are between areas, this structure leads to a greater autonomy and capacity to respond to local conditions than a worldwide product division (Egelhoff 1988; Vachani 1999).

Associated with the notion of regional headquarters is the notion of a regional sales mandate. A regional sales or product mandate (RPM) subsidiary is defined as one that has full responsibility for the development, manufacturing and marketing, including export marketing, of one or more product lines for sale in a defined region (Birkinshaw 1995; Bonin and Peron 1986; Crookell 1986; Roth and Morrison 1992; Rugman and Douglas 1996). As a result of possessing such a mandate, the subsidiary gains access to parent expertise but retains a degree of managerial autonomy (Pearce

1989). This arrangement has the subsidiary playing a role much more like that of an equal partner of the MNC than a subordinate entity. It ensures that high value-adding activities are undertaken in the sub-unit and provides management with the opportunity to develop the mandate over time. The subsidiary has considerable control over the fundamental technological thrusts that will sustain its development. It makes decisions on the timing and direction of product development. Furthermore, it is substantially involved in making decisions on production facilities, marketing and distribution (Birkinshaw 1995). The subsidiary has the primary responsibility to act as a product champion in corporate decision-making processes, especially those involving resource allocation.

Emerging in the mid-1980s, the 'process school' of research in international management criticised Stopford and Well's (1972) portrayal of organisational structure as being too architectural and deterministic (Bartlett and Ghoshal 1989a; 1989b; Doz and Prahalad 1984). Instead of the MNC being a series of headquarters–subsidiary relationships, with headquarters possessing the greater part of the authority and initiative, this school interprets the MNC as a complicated system with reciprocal interdependencies between units in different countries (Forsgren, et al. 1999). Rather than a hierarchy with subsidiaries controlled strictly from above, this school characterises the MNC as a heterarchical institution where informal coordination mechanisms such as corporate values and patterns of communication replace hierarchical control. In other words, the various parts of the MNC are conceived as a network rather than a formally-structured hierarchy. The main driving forces for change are environmental, with strategy and structure adapting to the opportunities offered in each market (Doz 1986; Martinez and Jarillo 1991). This interpretation allows for multiple centres of expertise around the world, each loosely coupled to the others and to external entities (Birkinshaw 1995; Forsgren and Pahlberg 1992). Such systems are perceived to offer the greater flexibility required to cope with the complexity of the multi-plant, multi-product MNCs that emerged in the 1980s (Vachani 1999).

The 'process school' sees managers as acting on behalf of firms and constantly facing the competing imperatives of cost reduction and the need to accommodate the differing demands of governments and customers in individual national markets. 'Cost reduction' is best achieved through rationalisation of global operations, controlled at the centre; 'accommodation of local demands' is fulfilled by giving a degree of autonomy to subsidiary managers. No unique structure provides a solution to this dilemma. Instead, MNCs are thought to develop multifocal strategies where responsiveness and integration needs are weighed against each other for each separate decision. Also, the various subsidiaries might adopt different stances on the integration versus localisation dilemma. In support of this perception, researchers have found that subsidiary autonomy varies with the decision area (Hedlund 1981; Vachani 1999). Headquarters is likely to have better information about strategic issues, such as global objectives, but subsidiary management is likely to have better information about operational issues with a significant local character, especially where the subsidiary supplies a specialised product into a niche market.

In summary, the literature on organisational structures of MNCs has demonstrated the existence of both centrally controlled, hierarchical structures and more devolved, decentralised, fluid structures. Such diversity implies scope for a range of different subsidiary roles, with implications for the level of autonomy enjoyed by local management. To analyse these relationships, the proposed hypotheses will be tested with reference to survey data collected from subsidiaries of multinational corporations in Malaysia.

Hypotheses

> The process school's emphasis on flexibility leads to the expectation that, for decisions requiring significant local knowledge, especially where the local environment is markedly different from that of the parent and where the local environment is volatile, subsidiary management will have greater say in operational decisions than in the development of strategy (Marginson 1992).

Hypothesis 1: subsidiary autonomy will be higher for operational decisions than for strategic decisions.

Stopford and Well's categories of administrative structures suggest that multinational corporations that adopt a centralised rather than devolved administrative structure will grant less autonomy to subsidiaries.

Hypothesis 2: the more centralised the organisational structure of the multinational corporation the less the autonomy of the subsidiary.

Egelhoff's and Vachani's analysis of regionally structured multinationals suggests that subsidiaries of MNCs with regional divisions will have greater autonomy than subsidiaries in firms with product divisions.

Hypothesis 3: subsidiaries categorised as being part of MNCs with regional divisions enjoy more autonomy than subsidiaries that are part of MNCs organised into product divisions.

Subsidiaries that are more thoroughly integrated into the network of sub-units that form the multinational corporation—in the sense that they purchase and/or sell a relatively large share of the purchases/sales from/to the parent and/or other subsidiaries—might be expected to enjoy less autonomy. Tight control may be essential in order to ensure that the value adding activities of the various sub-units are capable of being brought together to form the finished product.

Hypothesis 4: the more integrated the subsidiary in the operations of the multinational corporation the less the subsidiary's autonomy.

The process school's interpretation of decision making being apportioned so as to achieve the best balance of cost effectiveness and local responsiveness suggests that firms that sell specialised products into niche markets, competing on the basis of their responsiveness to local market conditions, will enjoy greater autonomy than subsidiaries selling into commodity markets.

Hypothesis 5: the more specialised the subsidiary's product the greater the subsidiary's autonomy.

Methodology

A search of the literature, summarised in the previous section, allowed the production of a seven page questionnaire. The questions were designed to ascertain the demographic characteristics of subsidiaries (age, location of ownership, industry, nature of business), the initial and current mode of entry, the reasons for choosing the Malaysian location and the current view as to why the subsidiary remains there, the structure of the MNC, the level of autonomy enjoyed by local management, and whether any special co-ordinating or marketing roles were granted to the subsidiary. The preliminary instrument was evaluated using interviews with three multinational subsidiaries and then revised. The final version of the questionnaire was mailed to the chief executive officers of 527 subsidiaries of foreign MNCs in Malaysia. Following a second mailing, 71 subsidiaries responded. Discriminate function analysis, logistic regression, canonical correlation, multiple regression and ANOVA were used to expose relationships between individual variables and sets of variables.

Results

Characteristics of the respondents

Table 7.1 specifies the frequency of participating organisations in various industry categories. The frequency is similar to that displayed by aggregate foreign direct investment (FDI) in Malaysia (Government of Malaysia 1999).

Table 7.1: Profile of industry categories of the sample

Category	Frequency	Percentage
Manufacturing	21	30
Primary production	5	7
Transport and communication	5	7
Commercial services	12	17
Hotel, travel, and entertainment	2	3
Trading	9	13
Building and public works	1	1
Other industries	15	21

Table 7.2 presents the profile of organisational size as measured by workforce size in the sample. This shows a reasonable representation of all categories of subsidiary—small, medium and large.

About 55 per cent of the organisations were organised according to regional divisions, 27 per cent according to a global matrix, and 12 per cent according to product divisions. The questionnaire asked respondents to rate, on a 5-point scale, the importance of various location advantages to the MNC both when it first invested in Malaysia and at the present time. The responses indicate that the most important reasons for choosing Malaysia as

Table 7.2: Profile of organisational size of the sample

Number of employees	Frequency	Percentage
Less than 25	12	18
25–99	12	18
100–299	12	18
300–999	15	22
1,000–1,999	8	12
More than 2,000	9	13

the site for their activities were, in order of importance, Malaysia's political stability, economic stability, access to Malaysian markets and Malaysia's skilled workforce. Experience appears to have confirmed the importance of these factors as, when asked to weight current location factors, these four factors retained prime importance. Indeed, the mean weighting of each increased. Interestingly, the ability to use Malaysia as a base for exports to regional and world markets was relatively unimportant, and financial assistance from the Malaysian government was ranked the least important factor in both time periods.

Autonomy

The first issue here relates to whether the autonomy enjoyed by Malaysian subsidiary managers varies with the type of managerial decision-making involved. Respondents were presented with a list of 17 business activities and asked to rate the degree to which decisions pertaining to each activity are undertaken by the subsidiary or the parent company. Each activity was rated on a five-point Likert scale, where one represented decisions undertaken entirely by the subsidiary, and five represented decisions undertaken entirely by the parent company. Table 7.3 displays the results of the respondents' answers. This shows that the level of autonomy varies with the area of decision making concerned. In general, parents control financial decisions relating to major projects, international marketing and new product development, whereas subsidiaries have major authority for approving finance for minor projects, implementing industrial relations policy, setting wage rates and domestic marketing. This finding supports Hedlund's (1981) and Vachani's (1999) contention that rigid divisions of decision making are avoided by multinational corporations. Decisions that relate to achieving economies of scale are taken centrally and those that offer the best returns in local responsiveness are taken by the subsidiary. Thus, the first hypothesis was supported: Malaysian subsidiaries have more autonomy over operational than over strategic decisions. Interestingly, no decision area was seen as falling exclusively within the jurisdiction of either the parent or the subsidiary. Rather, all decision making involved a degree of collaboration, with both parent and subsidiary management having input.

Responses to the questions relating to autonomy were scaled to determine whether they could be categorised into groups. Four scales were generated. The items and levels of internal consistency associated with each

Table 7.3: Mean and standard deviation of the ratings associated with the level at which decisions were made for various activities

Activity	Mean	Std
Approving finance for major projects	4.13	0.96
International marketing	3.77	1.38
Developing new products	3.54	1.34
Regional coordination	3.29	1.09
Selecting production technology	3.21	1.28
Regional marketing	3.10	1.25
Designing packaging	3.03	1.47
Developing public relations policy	2.64	1.32
Monitoring and controlling quality	2.44	1.14
Setting prices	2.32	1.40
Implementing public relations policy	2.15	1.18
Developing industrial relations policy	1.97	1.07
Determining the number of employees	1.96	1.07
Approving finance for minor projects	1.95	1.19
Implementing industrial relations policy	1.73	0.96
Domestic marketing	1.67	1.19
Setting wage rates	1.64	1.00

Note that 1 denotes subsidiary only and 5 denotes parent only.

scale are provided in Table 7.4. For all four scales, Cronbach's alpha either exceeded or approached 0.7. Nevertheless, the two scales in which internal consistency is less than 0.7 must be considered with caution, especially in relation to non-significant results. The first scale concerns items that pertain to marketing, such as designing packaging, domestic marketing and so forth. The second scale comprises items that relate to product strategy, such as developing new products and selecting production technology. The third scale includes price setting, wage setting and determining workforce size, and is titled 'local financing'. The final scale entails items that correspond to relations, both public and industrial. The scaling supports the expectation that various areas of decision making are perceived by multinational management to be alike. For example, industrial and public relations, both involving interaction with local stakeholders, are addressed with similar mixes of central and local managerial authority.

This section assesses the determinants of autonomy. The first issue is whether or not autonomy is contingent upon the type of structure operated by the MNC—centralised or decentralised (Hypothesis 2). Respondents were presented with the three types of organisation: decentralised federations, coordinated federations or centralised hubs (Bartlett and Ghoshall 1989b). A decentralised federation is defined as an organisation where each subsidiary has a high degree of autonomy. A coordinated federation is where the subsidiary is more dependent on the parent company than in the case of a decentralised federation and is subject to more control. A centralised hub is where the parent pursues a global strategy and is involved in most of the subsidiary's decision making. Fifty per cent of

Table 7.4: Items and level of Cronbach's alpha associated with each scale pertaining to autonomy

1. Marketing	2. Product strategy	3. Local financing	4. Relations
• Designing packaging • Domestic marketing • Regional marketing • International marketing	• Selecting production technology • Developing new products • Regional coordination	• Setting prices • Setting wage rates • Determining the number of employees	• Developing public relations policy • Implementing public relations policy • Developing industrial relations policy • Implementing industrial relations policy
Alpha = 0.76	Alpha = 0.67	Alpha = 0.67	Alpha = 0.79

respondents categorised their subsidiaries as decentralised federations, 27 per cent as coordinated federations and 23 per cent as centralised hubs.

A discriminate function analysis was conducted to ascertain whether or not the four elements of autonomy differed for subsidiaries that were classified as either part of a decentralised federation, coordinated federation or centralised hub. Only the first discriminant function attained significance, Wilks $\lambda = 0.76$, $\chi^2 (8) = 16.72$, $p < 0.05$. To identify the aspects of autonomy that were responsible for these effects, Table 7.5 presents the rotated structure matrix associated with the first dimension. According to this output, marketing and product strategy were the principal elements of autonomy that varied across the three types of organisation. Specifically, the scores on this scale were lowest for decentralised federations (mean = 1.60), indicating greater autonomy. The scores were higher for coordinated federations, and higher still for centralised organisations, reflecting their greater parental control. In short, subsidiaries associated with centralised hubs tend to have less autonomy in relation to marketing and product strategy. Other types of decision do not vary with the level of centralisation. Therefore, the second hypothesis is partly confirmed: the more decentralised the organisational structure, the greater the autonomy of the subsidiary in regard to marketing and product strategy.

Table 7.5: Rotated structure matrix associated with the first discriminant function

Marketing	0.63
Product strategy	0.57
Local financing	−0.41
Relations	0.14

The second issue concerns whether or not autonomy is contingent upon the organisational structure of the MNC (Hypothesis 3). A one-way MANOVA was conducted to ascertain whether or not the measures of autonomy varied across the structures of MNCs. In particular, three structures were compared: regional divisions, product divisions and global matrices. The sample size for other structures was not sufficient to include them in the analysis. Pillais' trace was used to accommodate the possibility of heterogeneous covariance matrices. This analysis, however, revealed that MNC structure did not influence autonomy, $F(8, 106) = 1.46$, $p > 0.05$. Therefore, the third hypothesis was not supported: subsidiaries categorised as being part of MNCs having regional structures were no more autonomous than those that were part of MNCs with product divisions or matrix structures.

The third issue concerns whether or not autonomy is contingent upon the degree to which the organisation is integrated with the parent and other non-Malaysian subsidiaries (Hypothesis 4). Integration was assessed according to the degree to which the subsidiary purchased from, and sold to, the parent company and other subsidiaries. To investigate this relationship, a canonical correlation analysis was undertaken. Autonomy in marketing, production strategy, wage, price and employment setting and relations constituted the first set of variables. The second set entailed four variables: the percentage of purchases derived from the parent company, the percentage of purchases derived from non-Malaysian subsidiaries, the percentage of total sales dedicated to the parent company and the percentage of total sales dedicated to other subsidiaries.

The first canonical correlation attained significance, $r(16) = 0.582$, $p < 0.01$. None of the remaining coefficients, however, reached significance. Table 7.6 shows that subsidiaries that sell a high proportion of products to their parent company tend to be granted less autonomy in relation to marketing and, to a lesser extent, public and industrial relations. Integration with non-Malaysian subsidiaries, by contrast, did not seem to be appreciably related to autonomy. This is consistent with the literature dealing with the 'rationalised integrated' subsidiary form (Birkinshaw 1996), and confirms the fourth hypothesis. Subsidiaries in this form of MNC organisation may specialise in production of particular components or may perform a complete stage in a vertically integrated production process on behalf of their parent. Such activities must be sufficiently controlled by the parent to ensure that the output of the subsidiary is compatible with that of other elements in the production chain. Individual subsidiaries may have no marketing function, their output being taken up by other subsidiaries or the parent for further value-adding. The last entity in the value chain is more likely to have the external marketing function.

Table 7.6: Cross loadings pertaining to the first canonical correlation

Autonomy	Cross-loadings	Integration	Cross-loadings
Marketing	0.62	Purchases—parent	0.17
Product strategy	−0.04	Purchases—other	0.48
Local financing	0.01	Sales—parent	0.92
Relations	0.37	Sales—other	−0.15

The next issue is whether or not autonomy relates to specificity of products (Hypothesis 5). To put it differently, greater autonomy may be granted to subsidiaries that sell specialised products into niche markets, as opposed to subsidiaries that sell commodities into competitive markets. Products sold into competitive markets are subject to relatively greater cost pressure, suggesting that parent organisations will assume greater central control so as to maximise economies of scale. Those sold into niche markets possess greater product differentiation and reduced price elasticity and may therefore be expected to be subject to less cost pressure than subsidiaries supplying commodities. They must be responsive to consumer demands. Subsidiaries selling niche products may therefore be expected to enjoy more autonomy than those that sell commodities.

To assess this dimension, respondents rated the degree of specificity on a five-point Likert scale, where one represented highly specialised products and five represented commodity products. A multiple regression was then undertaken, where degree of specialisation constituted the criterion variable and autonomy in marketing, production strategy, wage, price and employment setting, and relations constituted the predictors. Table 7.7 presents the output that emerged from this regression analysis. None of the four elements of autonomy related to specialisation. Therefore the fifth hypothesis is not supported by the analysis.

Table 7.7: Output associated with the multiple regressions that relate product specialisation to autonomy

Variables	B	SE	T
Constant	2.14	0.74	2.9*
Marketing	0.16	0.23	0.72
Product strategy	0.08	0.25	0.31
Local financing	0.09	0.26	0.37
Relations	0.01	0.22	0.04

* $p < 0.05$

To recapitulate, autonomy was influenced by the degree of integration of the subsidiary with its parent's operations and whether the MNC had a centralised structure. However, subsidiaries responsible for coordinating regional subsidiaries, producing products designed for niche markets and those that were part of MNCs structured into regional divisions were no more autonomous than others.

Conclusion

In the years since 1957, when it became independent, Malaysia has successfully transformed a commodity-based economy to a manufacturing one. Much of the economic success has been facilitated by foreign direct investment. Foreign investment has been encouraged by the Malaysian government, eager to receive the associated boost to both physical and human capital. Various incentives are available to international companies. These incentives are targeted towards those that invest in manufacturing and high-technology companies, undertake certain specified activities such as research and development, have important strategic roles such as regional coordination, or locate in certain geographic areas such as the Multimedia Super Corridor. The rationale of these policies is that investments differ in the benefits they confer the host economy.

This chapter has examined the academic literature pertaining to how the organisational structure of MNCs affects the autonomy of their subsidiaries and thus gives us insights into the potential contribution of subsidiaries to the Malaysia economy. Multinational corporations that share corporate know-how, particularly management and marketing expertise, and devolve administrative authority to subsidiaries, offer host countries more opportunities to benefit from a sustained growth effect of the investment.

Various organisational structures have been identified, some with strong central control being applied by the parent, others with degrees of autonomy being granted to individual subsidiaries. Subsidiary roles therefore vary, ranging from production-only branch plants through to quasi-autonomous operations with worldwide innovation, manufacturing and marketing rights. The structural roles of subsidiaries will affect their impact on Malaysia, particularly in regard to local management's opportunity to participate in high level decision making. Such participation implies a degree of autonomy for local management. Slavishly following head office edicts generates few opportunities for local management to innovate, pursue new markets or grow in managerial capacity.

Survey results of multinational subsidiaries in Malaysia demonstrate that subsidiary autonomy is determined by a complex array of factors. No rigid rule applies to the division of authority over decision making. Some issues, primarily the strategic ones, fall mainly into the realm of parent management and others, mainly operational, are the responsibility of subsidiary managers. This division of responsibility is not unique to Malaysia but is standard practice in MNCs (Marginson 1992). However, it is worth noting that managers in Malaysian subsidiaries have input into all areas, even the most strategic decisions. Therefore there is no evidence that managers in Malaysian subsidiaries are merely puppets following instructions from above.

The results also confirm that subsidiary autonomy does in fact vary according to the management structure of their parents' international activities. Subsidiaries of MNCs whose international operations were described as decentralised federations enjoyed more autonomy. However, this additional autonomy was limited, relating mainly to marketing and product strategy. Subsidiaries in MNCs that could be classified as decentralised federations enjoyed no greater autonomy in other aspects of management than did those that were part of centralised hubs.

Regionalised organisational structures are perceived as an attempt by MNCs to respond more effectively and therefore more competitively to the varying demands of customers and other stakeholders in each market, the regional structure being seen as a compromise between giving full autonomy to each subsidiary and having centralised control. The survey found that most subsidiaries in Malaysia are part of regionally organised MNCs. However, the survey did not reveal any greater level of autonomy for these subsidiaries compared with those in other structures. Subsidiaries with responsibilities as regional headquarters have greater autonomy, but individual subsidiaries do not.

The level of integration of the MNC's component parts clearly impacts on the level of autonomy enjoyed by subsidiaries. The more integrated the MNC's global operations, the more controlled the subsidiary. This result suggests the presence of subsidiaries that conform to the rationalised–producer model. Such subsidiaries must be subject to central control to ensure that their output can be integrated successfully into the subsequent value-adding activity of the parent or other subsidiaries.

In conclusion, to sustain the benefits of foreign direct investment, Malaysian managers' knowledge and expertise need to be strengthened by links with their associated companies overseas, and they need sufficient autonomy to develop and implement management and marketing strategies. Survey results indicate that Malaysian subsidiaries do indeed enjoy a degree of autonomy. Autonomy is greatest in operational matters, especially in decentralised organisations, but least in subsidiaries forming part of integrated global concerns.

References

Allen Consulting Group (1994), *The Benefits of Regional Headquarters and Factors Influencing their Location in Australia*, Melbourne: Allen Consulting.

Bartlett, C. and S. Ghoshal (1989a), *Managing Across Borders: The Transnational Solution*, Boston: Harvard Business School Press.

—— (1989b), 'Global strategic management: Impact on the new frontiers of strategy research, *Strategic Management Journal*, 12, Summer, 5–16.

Birkinshaw, J. (1995), 'How multinational subsidiary mandates are gained and lost', *European International Business Academy Conference*, Urbino, Italy.

—— (1996), 'How multinational subsidiary mandates are gained and lost', *Journal of International Business Studies*, 27 (3), 467–496.

Bonin, B. and B. Peron (1986), 'World product mandates and firms operating in Quebec', in H. Etemad and L. Sanguin Dulude (eds), *Managing the Multinational Subsidiary*, London: Croom Helm.

Bureau of Industry Economics (BIE) (1993), *Multinationals and Governments: Issues and implications for Australia*, Canberra: Australian Government Publishing Service.

Crookell, H. H. (1986), 'Specialisation and international competitiveness', in H. Etemad and L. S. Dulude (eds), *Managing the Multinational Subsidiary*, London: Croom-Helm.

Doraisami, A. (1996), 'Malaysia', in R. Edwards and M. Skully (eds), *ASEAN Business, Trade and Development: An Australian Perspective*, Sydney: Butterworth Heinemann, Sydney.

Doz, Y. (1986), *Strategic Management in Multinational Companies*, Oxford: Pergamon.

Doz, Y. and C. K. Prahalad (1984), 'Patterns of strategic control within multinational corporations', *Journal of International Business Studies* 15, 55–72.

Dunning, J. (1993), *Multinational Enterprises and the Global Economy*, Wokingham: Addison-Wesley.

Egelhoff, W. G. (1988), 'Strategy and structure in multinational corporations: A revision of the Stopford and Wells model', *Strategic Management Journal*, 9, 1–14.

Forsgren, M. and C. Pahlberg (1992), 'Subsidiary influence and autonomy in international firms', *Scandinavian International Business Review*, 1, 41–51.

Forsgren, M., T. Pedersen and N. Foss (1999), 'Accounting for the strengths of MNC subsidiaries: The case of foreign-owned firms in Denmark', *International Business Review*, 8, 181–196.

Government of Malaysia (1999), *Malaysia Investment in the Manufacturing Sector Policies, Incentives and Facilities*, file.

Hedlund, G. (1981), 'Autonomy of subsidiaries and formalisation of headquarters–subsidiary relationships in Swedish MNCs', in L. Otterbeck (ed.), *The Management of Headquarter–Subsidiary Relationships in Multinational Corporations*, Aldershot: Gower.

Langdale, J. V. (1992), 'Regional administrative headquarters and telecommunications hubs: Australia and the Asia–Pacific region', Canberra: Department of Industry Science and Technology.

Marginson, P. (1992), 'European integration and transnational management–union relations in the enterprise', *British Journal of Industrial Relations*, 30 (4), 529–545.

Martinez, J. and J. Jarillo (1991), 'Coordination demands of international strategies', *Journal of International Business Studies*, 3, 429–444.

Parry, T.G. (1983), 'Arguments for and against foreign investment in Australia', *Economic Papers*, 2 (4), 28–40.

Pearce, R. (1989), *The Internationalisation of Research and Development by Multinational Enterprises*, London: Macmillan.

Roth, K. and A. J. Morrison (1992), 'Implementing global strategy: characteristics of global subsidiary mandates', *Journal of International Business Studies*, 23 (4), 715–735.

Rugman, A. M. and S. Douglas (1996), 'The strategic management of multinationals and world product mandating', in A. Rugman, *The Theory of Multinational Enterprises: The Selected Scientific Papers of Alan R. Rugman*, Brookfield: Elgar.

Stopford, J. and L. T. Wells (1972), *Managing the Multinational Enterprise*, New York: Basic Books.

Tan Ser Kiat (1999), *Malaysia: Foreign Investment Policy*, www.malaysianlaw.com.

United Nations Conference on Trade and Development (UNCTAD) (1998), *World Investment Report 1998: Trends and Determinants*, New York: United Nations.

Vachani, S. (1999), 'Global diversification's effect on multinational subsidiaries' autonomy', *International Business Review*, 8, 535–560.

8

Market performance and the speed of the invisible hand: The case of Malaysian manufacturing

Mita Bhattacharya and Koi Nyen Wong[1]

Introduction

Market performance measures the benefits to consumers in an economy. In a perfectly competitive market, the invisible-hand process ensures prices come close to marginal cost. In the real world, many industries depart considerably from perfect competition. The less competition a firm (or an industry) faces, the greater its market power (that is, the firm can charge a price higher than marginal cost). Competition within firms is a major source of increasing productivity and efficiency in an economy.

Since the mid-1980s, the Malaysian economy has undergone significant changes through various policy reform programmes. The manufacturing sector plays a key role in the economy. Analysis of dynamics of profit (a measure of performance) in manufacturing and determination of its speed of adjustment is timely.[2] This will indicate the effectiveness of competition and various reform programs on the economy.

Mueller's (1977) widely acclaimed paper has discussed the industry–profit adjustment process and led to a considerable amount of research in industrial organisation area. But these studies are mainly based on developed countries such as the USA, UK, Japan and Germany. Literature in this area for developing countries is nearly non-existent.[3]

In this chapter, we specify a long-run equilibrium (steady-state) model of profit with some structural determinants. This model is analysed with the help of data from Malaysian manufacturing for 1996. The extension of the model includes a dynamic version, where significant factors in determining the profit adjustment process are considered over a decade (between 1986 and 1996). Dynamic analysis of profit adjustment may indicate the time lags associated with different reform programs.

This chapter provides an overview of manufacturing within the Malaysian industrialisation programme, summarises the literature, describes the model and data set, presents the empirical findings and analyses our findings from a policy perspective. The concluding section summarises the study.

Industrialisation and Malaysian manufacturing

The manufacturing sector contributes a significant part of gross domestic product (GDP) and is a major source of employment in the Malaysian economy. The rate of growth in manufacturing output has been rapid since independence in 1957. In the 1950s and 1960s, the manufacturing sector started to become significant. Import substitution industries targeted local markets. Impressive growth was recorded for food, beverages and tobacco, printing and publishing and construction materials. To promote such industries, the government directly and indirectly subsidised the establishment of new firms and protected the domestic market. Annual growth of the sector was 10 per cent during the 1960s.

The import substitution phase generated little new employment and soon became saturated in the small domestic market. By the mid-1960s, the inherent weaknesses of this phase were becoming clear. Since 1965, the Federal Industrial Development Authority (FIDA) with the help of the Raja Mohar Committee encouraged the expansion of manufactured exports through various reform programmes including changes in the labour market.

The switch to an export-oriented industrialisation strategy in the late 1960s boosted the export sector. The manufacturing sector shifted its direction of growth from import-substitution industries to focus on resource-based (mainly rubber, tin, palm oil and timber) processing and labour-intensive industries.

Since the 1970s, non-resource-based (mainly electrical and electronic components) export industries have developed. The share of manufactured exports increased rapidly from 11.9 per cent in 1970 to 21.4 per cent in 1975. New Free Trade Zones (FTZs) and Export Processing Zones (EPZs) were introduced to expand exports using imported equipment and material. During this period the government intervened heavily in the market in the form of public sector ownership in industries like food, chemicals, iron and steel, petroleum, cement, transport, tyres and tubes, and wood products.

In the early 1980s, there was a major push for heavy industries. This included the Malaysian car project, a sponge iron and steel billet plant, a petroleum refining and petrochemical project, three motorcycle plants, two new cement factories and a paper mill. Most of these involved expensive foreign technology and caused a large amount of government borrowing. Due to economic liberalisation, there was an increase in foreign direct investment and private ownership.

The global economic crisis had a major impact on the economy and private investment in manufacturing fell. In the mid-1980s, Malaysia's terms of trade fell sharply; the economy was in crisis.[4] Since 1987, the economy has been through the fifth phase of the industrialisation programme. Two Industrial Master Plans (IMP) along with the Seventh Malaysian Plan (7MP) recognise the problems and provide recommendations to improve the efficiency, productivity and competitiveness of the manufacturing sector.[5]

The manufacturing sector still contributes a large share of GDP, employment and exports in the economy. The share of manufacturing in total gross domestic product has increased from less than 10 per cent in the late 1950s to 26 per cent in 30 years. Manufacturing employment increased from 8.4 per cent in 1970 to 20.1 per cent in 1999.

Nevertheless, the sector still remains a highly segmented one, consisting of resource-based export-oriented industries, import-competing industries and EPZs. The adequate supply of a skilled workforce, expansion of the technological base and promotion of higher-value-added activities are needed to increase the competitiveness of this sector. Therefore, the future performance of manufacturing lies in how the 'dual structured' industries are interlinked to serve domestic and international markets.

Literature review

According to traditional Structure–Conduct–Performance (SCP) studies, high profit is often explained as market power being exercised by big firms (normally measured by concentration, an index of market structure). Qualls (1974) finds that the profits–concentration relationship can be explained in terms of monopoly power of dominant firms with high barriers to entry even in the long run. Mueller (1977; 1985) with firm level data also finds the persistence of profits above the long-run competitive level. However, Brozen (1970; 1971a; 1971b; 1971c; 1982) argues that a positive profit–concentration relationship is a disequilibrium phenomenon. The differences between profits of high and low concentration industries vanish over time.

Using US panel data, Domowitz et al. (1986) explain the inter-temporal stability of the concentration–margins relationship by considering the influence of macroeconomic fluctuations. Cyclical effects are found to alter the magnitude of the differences between price cost margins of concentrated and non-concentrated industries.

Levy (1987) considers a dynamic profit model with panel data for US manufacturing industries. An incomplete adjustment is considered when past profits differ from future expected profits. The conclusion suggests that the adjustment process is relatively fast.

Other studies with panel data, such as Odagiri and Yamashita (1987) for Japanese manufacturing industries, Neumann et al. (1983) for German manufacturing industries and Prince and Thurik (1994) for Dutch manufacturing industries deal with the persistence of profits and reach varying conclusions.

The profit models and data

A steady-state version

First we consider a steady-state (equilibrium) profit model across industries. In the absence of dynamic adjustments, the industry price-cost margins (an indicator of profits) can be explained by the following equation:

$$GPM^*_t = \beta_0 + \beta_1 CR4_t + \beta_2 K/S_t + \beta_3 RP_t + \beta_4 EXPINT_t + \beta_5 IMPINT_t + \beta_6 FI_t + U_t$$
$$\quad\quad + \quad\quad\; + \quad\quad\; + \quad\quad\; - \quad\quad\quad\; + \quad\quad\; +$$

$$(8.1)$$

The dependent variable GPM^*_t in (8.1), the price–cost margin, is not directly observable, so the gross profit margin (GPM) is used as the dependent variable.[6] Concentration (CR4) is the market share of the top four firms, representing the degree of monopoly power. Therefore, a positive relationship is expected with profits. The capital–sales ratio (K/S) is introduced as the capital-intensive industries are expected to generate higher profits. Also, K/S takes into account the degree to which the gross profit margin misstates the price–cost margin. Relative productivity (RP) is an indicator of the efficiency of large firms and also serves as a proxy for entry barriers. It is measured as average value-added per worker of the leading four firms divided by the industry average value-added per worker. We expect a positive sign on this variable.

The impact of export intensity (EXPINT) on profits depends upon the degree of competitiveness of industry at home and upon whether or not the exporting firms can dump abroad and prevent re-imports. In the case of homogeneous goods, the effect of export intensity depends on cost conditions. For differentiated products, the influence of exports depends on whether profit from abroad is greater or less than domestic profits. The Malaysian manufactured export market is narrowly-based and concentrated on low value-added products.[7] Also exports depend on external demand and prices primarily in developed countries. We expect a negative sign on this variable.

Gross margin will be lower in industries with a greater degree of competition from imports. Thus a negative relationship is expected with import intensity (IMPINT). However, with tariff reduction, manufacturing is becoming competitive in the domestic market. Imported intermediate inputs are also used in the production process. Thus a positive relationship is expected between IMPINT and GPM.

Most of the studies have emphasised the effect of foreign investments (FI) on profits, considering 'outward' rather than 'inward' investment.[8] Like other developing countries, Malaysia has very little outward investment. Most of the foreign subsidiaries are profitable in the domestic market, so a positive relationship is expected between FI and GPM.

Finally, we have included a disturbance term U_t in equation (8.1), which is normally distributed with zero mean and constant variance, and includes all random factors.

Dynamic versions of the profit model

A linear version of the dynamic profit model   A standard partial adjustment model is adopted. The direction of the change in profits is a function of actual profits relative to the steady-state level (GPM*). Unlike standard models, the steady-state profit (GPM*) is a function of the determinants explained in equation (8.1). Any deviation of the actual level of profits from its steady-state level results in an adjustment process that leads to changes in profits. An incomplete adjustment is allowed for in a partial adjustment model given by:

$$\Delta GPM_t = GPM_t - GPM_{t-1} = \mu (GPM^*_t - GPM_{t-1}) \qquad (8.2)$$

where ΔGPM_t is the change in profits (in absolute term) between two periods. For empirical purposes, we assume $t = 1996$ and $t - 1 = 1986$. μ is the rate of adjustment and remains constant. μ takes values between zero and one. GPM^*_t is the equilibrium level of profits in period t and is determined as in (8.1).

Substituting from (8.1) into (8.2) to remove the unobservable equilibrium profits level, GPM^*_t and solving for GPM_t gives the following equation for the dynamic model:

$$GPM_t = \mu(\beta_0 + \beta_1 CR4_t + \beta_2 K/S_t + \beta_3 RP_t + \beta_4 EXPINT_t + \beta_5 IMPINT_t +$$
$$\beta_6 FI_t) + (1 - \mu)GPM_{t-1} \qquad (8.3)$$

When equations in the form of (8.3) are estimated using the ordinary least squares technique, the coefficient of the lagged margin variable GPM_{t-1} gives the estimate of one minus the partial adjustment.[9] The coefficients of the remaining explanatory variables are estimates of the long-run impact multiplied by the partial adjustment. Both equilibrium and linear versions of the dynamic profit models are estimated by the ordinary least squares method.[10]

A non-linear version of the dynamic profit model   Alternatively, a model with partial adjustment that varies across industries is given by

$$\Delta GPM_t = GPM_t - GPM_{t-1} = \mu_i (GPM^*_t - GPM_{t-1}) \qquad (8.4)$$

where μ_i is the partial adjustment for the ith industry. μ_i should be non-negative and less than one for all values of its determinants. μ_i is specified as a function of variables related to the internal and external adjustment process of the industry. We consider μ_i to be a function of lagged concentration, measured by the four-firm concentration in period $(t-1)$

($CR4_{t-1}$), and the entry barriers measured by current K/S and NETENT between period t and (t–1).[11]

High-lagged concentration may cause higher profit in the previous period due to market power or superior performance of the larger firms. In the absence of effective barriers, this may lead to faster adjustment of profits towards equilibrium in period t. However, if entry barriers are very effective, industries with high-lagged concentration may generate higher profit in period t. In this situation, profit adjustment will be slower. The sign of $CR4_{86}$ with μ can be in either direction.

Capital-intensity (K/S) as an entry barrier should be negatively related to the speed of adjustment. Net entry of firms (NETENT) may be considered a proxy for the absence of an entry barrier. The higher the net entry, the faster is the speed of adjustment. A positive sign is expected. If the relationship between the variables of interest and the degree of adjustment is assumed to be linear, we have

$$\mu_i = \alpha_0 + \alpha_1 CR4_{t-1} + \alpha_2 K/S_t + \alpha_3 NETENT_{t,\,t-1} \qquad (8.5)$$
$$+/- \qquad\qquad - \qquad\qquad +$$

The partial adjustment coefficient in (8.5) is not directly observable. However, substituting (8.1) and (8.5) into (8.4) and solving for GPM_{t-1}, gives a non-linear form as follows with all variables observable:

$$GPM_t = (\alpha_0 + \alpha_1 CR4_{t-1} + \alpha_2 K/S_t + \alpha_3 NETENT_{t,\,t-1}) (\beta_0 + \beta_1 CR4_t + \beta_2 K/S_t$$
$$+ \beta_3 RP_t + \beta_4 EXPINT_t + \beta_5 IMPINT_t + \beta_6 FI_t + GPM_{t-1}) + GPM_{t-1} \qquad (8.6)$$

All variables are as described above, with the indicated direction of impact carried over from (8.1) and (8.5). When equations in the form of (8.6) are estimated using non-linear estimating techniques, each coefficient gives a direct estimate of the parameter of the underlying model. The estimated partial adjustment for an industry is then determined indirectly by multiplying the industry value of each of the variables, $CR4_{t-1}$, K/S_t and $NETENT_{t,\,t-1}$, by its estimated coefficient, and then adding the estimated constant, α_0.

The data

The Department of Statistics (West Malaysia, Kuala Lumpur) conducts a survey of manufactures; unpublished data were supplied by the Department for 1986 and 1996. The choice of the time period was dictated by the availability of data. Considering all variables we have ended up with 62 manufacturing industries at the five-digit level. The descriptions of variables with means and standard deviations are given in the Appendix.

Empirical findings

The findings from the steady-state version

First, we explain the findings from the steady-state version of the level of profit, so that we can compare the findings from the dynamic versions later on. Column 1 of Table 8.1 presents the findings from the steady-state model. The ordinary least squares regression is used for estimation. The gross profit margin of 1996 is the dependent variable.

Except CR4 and EXPINT, all other variables have expected signs. K/S and RP are significant at the 1 and 5 per cent levels respectively. Capital-intensity appears to have a significant independent effect on profits. Also, relative-productivity, a measure of the efficiency of workers in top firms as well as a proxy for an entry barrier, seems to have a significant effect on profit. The FI variable is nearly significant at the 10 per cent level. The adjusted R^2 is 0.184.

Table 8.1: Results of the steady-state version and linear dynamic version, when μ is constant across industries
(Ordinary least squares estimation)

Variable	Steady-state model column (1)	Linear dynamic version column (2)
GPM_{96}	–	0.444^a
		(3.740)
CR_4	–0.033	–0.036
	(0.732)	(0.936)
K/S	0.112^a	0.081^a
	(3.156)	(2.509)
RP	0.063^b	0.052^b
	(1.939)	(1.825)
EXPINT	0.006	–0.006
	(0.838)	(0.923)
IMPINT	0.002	0.002
	(0.104)	(0.909)
FI	0.005	0.010^c
	(1.245)	(1.327)
Intercept	0.078	0.020
R^2 (adjusted)	0.184	0.338

Note: GPM_{96} is the dependent variable.

Figures in parentheses are heteroscedastic consistent t ratios.

a. Indicates coefficient is significant at the 0.01 level using a one-tailed t-test.
b. Indicates coefficient is significant at the 0.05 level using a one-tailed t-test.
c. Indicates coefficient is significant at a 0.10 level using a one-tailed t-test.

The findings from the linear version of the dynamic model

Column 2 of Table 8.1 reports the findings of estimates for the linear version of the dynamic model, where the speed of adjustment of profit (μ) is uniform across industries. Here GPM_{96} is considered as the dependent variable, so that the results can be compared with the equilibrium version in Column 1. The coefficient of the lagged gross profit margin in this regression provides an estimate of $(1-\mu)$, the proportion of adjustment that remains to be completed at the end of the sample period.

Each estimated coefficient has the expected sign, except CR4. Like the steady-state version, the K/S and RP variables are significant at the 1 and 5 per cent level. The FI variable is now significant at the 10 per cent level. The adjusted R^2 is 0.338, about 15 per cent higher than in the steady-state version.

The coefficient of the lagged margin is significantly less than one at the 1 per cent level, so the restriction that full adjustment to long-run equilibrium is achieved during the ten-year interval, $\mu = 0$, is clearly rejected. The partial adjustment over ten years is one minus the estimated coefficient of the lagged margin or 0.556, which corresponds to an annual rate of adjustment of about 8 per cent.[12] Therefore, profit adjustment is not instantaneous, but more than half of the adjustment takes place within a decade.[13] Comparing this adjustment with previous studies for OECD countries, the adjustment process is relatively slow.[14]

In summary, the findings support the role of capital-based technology, efficiency of larger firms in terms of improving labour productivity and the importance of foreign subsidiaries in determining industry profits. This is supported in other Malaysian studies like Kalirajan (1993a; 1993b) and Yean (1995), which deal with the manufacturing sector.[15] Our analysis could not establish the importance of top firms in generating monopoly profit in the case of Malaysia.[16] Also, export and import intensities are not significant in determining profits.

The linear version of the dynamic model provides a better explanation in terms of signs and significance level of variables. Overall the explanatory power from this model is approximately 15 per cent higher than the steady-state model.

The findings from the non-linear version of the dynamic model

Table 8.2 shows the results of the non-linear version of the dynamic model, when μ varies across industries. Results are from the maximum likelihood, non-linear estimation technique in SHAZAM.

Column 1 shows the findings of the steady-state portion of the profit equation. All variables have signs like those in the linear version of the dynamic model (in column two of Table 8.1). K/S, RP and IMPINT are significant at the 5, 1 and 10 per cent level respectively. Like the steady-state and linear dynamic versions, CR4 (market share of the top four firms)

Table 8.2: Results of estimation of dynamic non-linear version, when μ varies across industries

(Non–linear maximum likelihood estimation)

Variable	Steady-state coefficients column (1)	Adjustment coefficients column (2)
$CR4_{96}$	−0.621 (1.183)	−
K/S	0.214^b (1.742)	−
RP	1.302^a (2.690)	−
EXPINT	−0.099 (1.207)	−
IMPINT	0.138^c (1.596)	−
FI	0.139 (1.106)	−
$CR4_{86}$	−	−0.046 (0.938)
K/S	−	0.182^a (3.843)
NETENT	−	0.000002 (0.063)
Intercept	2.483	0.132

Note: GPM_{96} is the dependent variable.

Figures in parentheses are t ratios.

a. Indicates coefficient is significant at a 0.01 level using a one-tailed t-test.
b. Indicates coefficient is significant at a 0.05 level using a one-tailed t-test.
c. Indicates coefficient is significant at a 0.10 level using a one-tailed t-test.

has a negative sign and insignificant effect on profits. In the case of Malaysia, the top firms are competing rather than exercising market power, thereby generating lower profit, although the effect is insignificant. In this respect the finding for the profit-concentration relationship here departs from previous studies. One reason for this difference could be the presence of both market power (measured by CR4) and efficiency (measured by RP) indicators in our model. In all three cases (steady-state, linear and non-linear versions of the dynamic model) RP has a significant effect on profit.

Column 2 of Table 8.2 presents the findings for determining the rate of adjustment. Lagged concentration ($CR4_{86}$) has a negative but insignificant effect on the speed of adjustment. NETENT, a proxy for the absence of entry barriers, is also insignificant in influencing profit adjustment. Only

K/S as an entry barrier has the expected positive sign with a strong significant effect at the one per cent level on the adjustment process.

Applying the estimated coefficients to the values of the variables yields estimates of the partial adjustment of profits for each industry, with a standard deviation of 0.047 around the mean of 0.191. Over 60 per cent of industries partial adjustment lies between 0.1 and 0.2, with maximum and minimum values of 0.365 and 0.117 respectively. The annual adjustment rate is around 15 per cent, 7 per cent higher than the linear model. However, we could not establish the superiority of the non-linear version compared to the linear one.[17]

Policy implications of the findings

The manufacturing sector was not very significant in the Malaysian economy during the colonial era, when plantation rubber agriculture, tin and mining dominated the economy. Post-colonial governments have actively sought to promote industrialisation. This study analyses the determinants of profits and the factors affecting the speed of adjustment of profits in Malaysian manufacturing. In this respect, it establishes the annual rates of profit adjustment when profit deviates from the steady-state level.

The steady-state model is developed to explain profits. Capital-based technology, efficiency of the leading firms and foreign ownership are significant in explaining profits. The market share of the leading firms has no positive significant influence on industry profits. This implies big businesses are competitive rather than monopolistic in nature. In most cases, we establish the importance of domestic competition policy (reducing barriers, improving productivity of large firms) over trade policy (import competition, widening exports) in influencing profits in Malaysian manufacturing.

The adjustment process of profit over a period of time is important in determining competitiveness of the manufacturing sector. Therefore we extend the steady-state model to explain if industry profit deviates from the equilibrium level in a particular period how long it takes to adjust. In this respect, the speed of adjustment of profits is considered to be constant as well as variable across industries. For constant speed of adjustment, a linear version of the dynamic model is considered. The annual rate of adjustment is found to be about 8 per cent, which is relatively low compared to that of developed countries such as Australia.[18]

For a variable rate of adjustment across industries, a non-linear version of the profit model is considered. The annual rate of adjustment is found to be 15 per cent. Only capital-intensity is found to be a significant entry barrier into the adjustment process. In summary, although for the variable adjustment model, the speed of adjustment is faster compared to the constant adjustment model, we could not establish the superiority of the non-linear model compared to the linear one.[19]

Findings from this study are interesting in the current policy arena. We find technology-based development is the driving force of the manufacturing sector. In the twenty-first century, with the emergence of a 'new economy', based on information and telecommunications (ITC) industries, Malaysian manufacturing has to implement more innovation, research and development and technology-oriented techniques to compete in both domestic and international markets. Our study also establishes the importance of domestic factors in influencing the performance of Malaysian manufacturing compared to international factors.

Conclusion

This study is a first attempt to explain the dynamics of profit in Malaysian manufacturing. In all cases, our findings establish the efficiency argument (following the 'Chicago school' theorists) of profits. Government through its various reform programmes should continue to improve efficiency, increase the productivity of workers and use more capital intensive techniques in enhancing the competitiveness of this core sector of the economy. In this respect, future research should incorporate the effects of tariff reform, innovation and research and development in explaining the adjustment process of performance of the manufacturing sector.[20]

Appendix 1A: Variables with descriptive statistics

Variables	Definition	(Mean, Std Dev)
GPM_{96}	Value added minus intermediate expenses minus wages divided by sales for 1996.	(0.201, 0.068)
GPM_{86}	Same as GPM_{96} using 1986 data.	(0.208, 0.070)
$CR4_{96}$	Industry sales accounted by the top four firms divided by total industry sales for 1996.	(0.466, 0.225)
K/S	The average of capital expenditure over sales for 1996.	(0.465, 0.262)
RP	Value-added per worker of the top four firms over the value-added per worker for the industry 1996.	(1.215, 0.304)
EXPINT	Export divided by sales for 1996.	(0.810, 1.257)
IMPINT	Import divided by sales plus import minus exports for 1996.	(1.084, 2.066)
FI	Foreign investment is measured by foreign share of output in each industry 1996.	(0.576, 0.975)
$CR4_{86}$	Same as $CR4_{96}$ using 1986 data.	(0.560, 0.248)
NETENT	Change in number of firms between 1986 and 1996 with respect to 1986.	(143.5, 217.7)

Appendix 8.1B: Calculation of annual adjustment rates

1. Linear model

$GPM_t - GPM_{t-1} = \mu(GPM_t^* - GPM_{t-1})$

$GPM_t - GPM_{t-n} = [1 - (1 - \mu)^n] (GPM_t^* - GPM_{t-n})$

$GPM_t = [1 - (1 - \mu)^n] GPM_t^* + (1 - \mu)^n GPM_{t-n}$

Let, $X = (1 - \mu)^n$

Then $\mu = 1 - X^{1/n}$

$n = 10$

Full sample: $X = 0.444$ and $\mu = 0.0779$

2. Non-linear model

$GPM_t - GPM_{t-1} = \mu(GPM_t^* - GPM_{t-1})$

$GPM_t - GPM_{t-n} = [1 - (1 - \mu)^n] (GPM_t^* - GPM_{t-n})$

$GPM_t = [1 - (1 - \mu)^n] GPM_t^* + (1 - \mu)^n GPM_{t-n}$

Let, $Y = (1 - \mu)^n$

Then $\mu = 1 - Y^{1/n}$

$n = 10$

Full sample: $Y = 0.191641$ and $\mu = 0.152287$

Endnotes

[1] We are grateful to the Department of Statistics, Kuala Lumpur, Malaysia for supplying unpublished data set. Financial assistance from a research grant from the Monash University, Sunway Campus, Malaysia is also acknowledged. Helpful comments were received from Harry Bloch, Curtin University, Western Australia. The usual disclaimer applies.

[2] Market performance is measured in terms of profits in the manufacturing sector. This is due to the importance of this sector for the Malaysian economy. Also, detailed data are not available for other sectors.

[3] For overseas literature, see Scherer and Ross (1990, Chapter 11), Shepherd (1997).

[4] For more details see Jomo (1989; 1990; 1993).

[5] Details are in the Malaysian Management Review (1989), Malaysia (1989) and Sieh et al. (1986; 1987).

[6] The price–cost margin is defined as (Price–Marginal Cost)/Price. As marginal cost is not observable we consider here average cost instead and hence the gross price margin.

[7] Major export markets are Singapore, USA, Japan, Germany and UK.

[8]   Foreign ownership, foreign investment and foreign firms are used synonymously and are taken into account as 'foreign intensity'.

[9]   In estimating equations in the form of (8.3), we consider the 'level' of gross margin as the dependent variable instead of using the 'change' in profits like other overseas studies. This will allow us to compare the goodness of fit of equilibrium and dynamic models directly. Also, there could be a spurious relation if we considered the lagged margin as an independent variable in calculating the change in profits as a dependent variable.

[10]   We did not consider a simultaneous model; Kalirajan (1993a) shows simultaneity is not prominent for Malaysian manufacturing industries.

[11]   Since liberalisation, use of capital-intensive techniques and increases in the number of domestic and foreign firms became important. Therefore we consider these barriers. We tried other variables like foreign intensity, export and import intensity, but did not get any significant results.

[12]   Calculations of the compound annual rate of adjustment for both versions are shown in Appendix 8.1B.

[13]   In the case of Australia, Bhattacharya and Bloch (2000) found 70 per cent adjustment takes place within a seven-year period (between 1977 and 1984) for a set of 102 manufacturing industries.

[14]   For example, Levy (1987) concluded that adjustment to abnormal profits is faster in US industries.

[15]   Kalirajan (1993a; 1993b) found that foreign ownership in Malaysian manufacturing is a significant factor in determining the price–cost margin. Yean (1995) reports capital as a major source of growth, contributing 22.4 per cent of growth in Malaysian manufacturing between 1986 and 1991.

[16]   Beng (1978) found that the critical level of four-firm concentration was 55 per cent using 1971 manufacturing data.

[17]   We performed a likelihood ratio test. The log-likelihood ratio is 6.14, which is less than the critical value, $\chi^2_4 = 7.77$, at the 10 per cent level.

[18]   In the case of Australia, Bhattacharya and Bloch (2000) establishes 70 per cent over a seven-year period.

[19]   Most of the industries in our sample are capital-intensive. Adjustment coefficients of the non-linear model vary from 0.11 to 0.36, with standard deviation 0.04. In this respect, the linear version is more appropriate as adjustment of profit does not vary much across industries.

[20]   We could not include these due to lack of data. The Department of Statistics (Kuala Lumpur, Malaysia) supplied all industry data, from the Census of Manufacturing Industries, West Malaysia and Surveys of Manufacturing Industries for the financial years 1986 and 1996.

References

Beng, G. W. (1978), 'The relationship between market concentration and profitability in Malaysian manufacturing industries', *Malayan Economic Review*, 23 (1), 1–11.

Bhattacharya, M. and H. Bloch (2000), 'Adjustment of profits: Evidence from Australian manufacturing', *Empirica*, 27, 157–163.

Brozen, Y. (1970), 'The Antitrust Task Force deconcentration recommendation', *Journal of Law and Economics*, 13 (2), 279–292.

—— (1971a), 'Bain's concentration and rates of return revisited', *Journal of Law and Economics*, 14, 351–369.

—— (1971b), 'Concentration and structural and market disequilibria', *Antitrust Bulletin*, 16, 241–248.

—— (1971c), 'The persistence of "high rates of return" in high-stable concentration industries', *Journal of Law and Economics*, 14, 501–512.

—— (1982), *Concentration, Mergers and Public Policy*, New York: Macmillan.

Domowitz, I., G. Hubbard and B. C. Petersen (1986), 'The intertemporal stability of the concentration–margins relationship', *Journal of Industrial Economics*, 35, 13–34.

Jomo, K. S. (1989), *Beyond 1990: Considerations for a New National Development Strategy*, Institute of Advanced Studies, University of Malaya, Kuala Lumpur.

—— (1990), *Economic Growth and Structural Change in the Malaysian Economy* , London: Macmillan.

—— (ed.) (1993), *Industrialising Malaysia: Policy, Performance, Prospects*, London: Routledge.

Kalirajan, K. P. (1991), 'Government intervention in Malaysian manufacturing industries: a suggested methodology of measurement', *Applied Economics*, 23, 1093–1101.

—— (1993a), 'Simultaneity bias: Is it relevant in the developing countries industrial structure-performance paradigm?', *Journal of Quantitative Economics*, 9 (1), 147–156.

—— (1993b), 'On the simultaneity between market concentration and profitability: The case of a small-open developing country', *International Economic Journal*, 7 (1), 31–48.

Levy, D. (1987), 'The speed of the invisible hand', *International Journal of Industrial Organisation*, 5, 79–92.

Malaysia (1989), *Mid-Term Review of the Fifth Malaysia Plan 1986–1990*, Government Printer, Kuala Lumpur.

Malaysian Management Review (1989), *Special Issue on the New Economic Policy*, 24 (2), August, Kuala Lumpur.

Mueller, D. C. (1977), 'The persistence of profits above the norm', *Economica*, 44, 369–380.

—— (1985), *Profits in the Long Run*, Cambridge: Cambridge University Press.

Neumann, M., Bobel, I. and A. Haid (1983), 'Business cycle and industrial market power: an empirical investigation for West German industries 1965–1977', *Journal of Industrial Economics*, 32, 187–196.

Odagiri, H. and T. Yamashita (1987), 'Price mark-ups, market structure, and business fluctuation in Japanese manufacturing industries', *Journal of Industrial Economics*, 35, 317–331.

Prince, Y. and R. Thurik (1994), 'The intertemporal stability of the concentration-margins relationship in Dutch and US manufacturing', *Review of Industrial Organisation*, 9, 193–209.

Qualls, D. P. (1974), 'Stability and persistence of economic profit margins in highly concentrated industries', *Southern Economic Journal*, 40, 604–612.

Scherer, F. M. and D. Ross (1990), *Industrial Market Structure and Economic Performance* (Third Edition), Boston: Houghton Mifflin Company.

Shepherd, W. G. (1997), *The Economics of Industrial Organisation*, fourth edition, New Jersey: Prentice-Hall.

Sieh-Lee Mei Ling and Susan Tho Lai Mooi (1986), *Malaysia Manufacturing Futures Survey 1986 Report*, Faculty of Economics and Administration, University of Malaya, Kuala Lumpur.

—— (1987), *Malaysia Manufacturing Futures Survey 1987 Report*, Faculty of Economics and Administration, University of Malaya, Kuala Lumpur.

Yean, T. S. (1995), 'Productivity, growth and development in Malaysia', *The Singapore Economic Review*, 40 (1), 41–63.

9

A comparison of business process re-engineering with other management techniques in Malaysia

Stanley Richardson and Khong Kok Wei

Introduction

Since the Industrial Revolution that began in the 1700s and early 1800s in the United Kingdom, the utilisation of management theory has become an increasing force to improve the ways organisations are run. History has shown that many management practices have been contrived in the past 250 years (Hammer and Champy 1993) and some of these practices are still being implemented. Some believe that such practices are the fundamentals of what forms the modern management practices of today (Anon 1997); without them organisations would be very different. In contrast, there are arguments that the management ideas and theories developed by Henry Fayol and Frederick Taylor years ago may not be appropriate in the dynamic, turbulent and competitive environment of today. In other words, there are limitations to the traditional adoption of change management techniques and approaches (Grint and Case 1998). The use of obsolete management practices may lead to the total downfall of organisations. Therefore many contemporary management techniques and approaches are undertaken in search of the best management practices, such as Total Quality Management (TQM), Just In Time (JIT) in full procurement systems and human resource management. One of the best management practices of today, often referred to as managerial common sense (Fisher 1994), is Business Process Re-engineering or BPR. Hammer and Champy (1993, p. 32) define it as 'the fundamental rethinking and radical redesign of the business processes to achieve dramatic improvements in critical contemporary measures of performance such as cost, quality, service and speed'. This is examined in detail later.

According to Cock and Hipkin (1997), BPR has replaced most of the management techniques and even replaced TQM as the 'hottest topic' in the best practice management arena. It has become the principal framework of organisational restructuring (Grint and Case 1998). The history of BPR is short but overwhelming. A survey by Conti and Warner (1994) reveals that 72 per cent of the senior business executives in North America had a BPR programme in their firms and 59 per cent of the organisations in Britain are planning or undertaking BPR (Grint and Willcocks 1995). Peter Drucker claimed that 'Re-engineering is new, and it has to be done' (Hammer and Champy 1993). However, most of the ways organisations are being managed are still derived from concepts of more than a century ago (Hammer and Champy 1993). These concepts catered for the needs and requirements of that era, but to have the concepts still in vogue in the dynamic and turbulent environment of today must be questioned. Thus, a new managing concept or idea has to anticipate the dynamic environment and confront problems in the contested terrain (Edwards 1979). And so BPR was created.

At present, most management techniques and approaches that most organisations adopt emphasise total quality. These techniques and approaches vary according to the respective organisation's context, history, culture, values and beliefs (Peters 1994). Likewise, as the organisation is also constantly challenged in the external environment through change, customers and competitors (Hammer and Champy 1993), it must allocate resources to cope with these challenges. BPR is designed to translate organisational activities: to be more flexible and responsive to customers, efficient and effective (Knights and McCabe 1998), it 'is now established as a modern-day scientific management technique' (Richardson 1995). Grint and Case (1998, p. 560) said there has been 'a sudden departure from safety and security to danger and insecurity linked to the destruction of the staid and predictable environment that allegedly prevailed before the "nasty nineties" arrived'. The management approaches that once prevailed are no longer sufficient to sustain organisational growth, and to continue these techniques in perpetuity would be foolish. In other words, application of the management techniques that do not suit the corporation would inflict more damage than good (Richardson 1991). In recent years, private sector enterprises have been undertaking counter measures to maintain a competitive edge (Ascari et al. 1995; Drew 1994) within the environment and, even more importantly, to ensure 'business survival' (Hammer 1994).

The aim of this chapter is to compare BPR with other management techniques in Malaysia. This chapter is a progress report concerning an ongoing research project.

The many faces of BPR

The four core words of Hammer and Champy's (1993) definition are fundamental, radical, dramatic and process.

Fundamental

The key word 'fundamental' is defined as the rudimentary state in which something exists. Fundamentals of an organisation represent the base and framework that build the organisation as a whole. Re-engineering rethinks the fundamentals by asking basic questions such as 'Why are we doing what we are doing?' Questions like this often lead to answers that reflect the incapability of the fundamentals once laid upon the organisation when it first started operation. Re-engineering is like 'starting over' (Champy 1995): a new company with no rules and assumptions (Hammer and Champy 1993). BPR determines the objectives once again and figures out the best way to achieve them.

Radical

Radical comes from the Latin word 'radix' which means root. With reference to Hammer and Champy's (1993) definition, 'radical redesign' suggests redoing the whole 'thing' right from the roots. BPR is not activities such as modifications, improvements and alterations in the business activities. It is changing to something that is totally new, that will effectively and efficiently accomplish the desired objectives. In fact, this feature is the most distinctive one in any BPR programme (Dixon et al. 1994; Hill and Wilkinson 1995).

Dramatic

The key word 'dramatic' in the context of re–engineering means 'demanding substantial results'. BPR is often used when enterprises do not favour gradual improvements, as in TQM (Browning 1993). Re-engineering does not believe in continuous or marginal improvements that will lead an organisation slowly to its desired objective. Re-engineering is designed to achieve substantial improvements in critical contemporary measures of performance such as cost, quality, service and speed (Hammer and Champy 1993).

Process

Hammer and Champy (1993) define process as a collection of activities that take one or more kinds of input and create an output that is of value to the customer. Process is perhaps the most challenging element of all the key words in re-engineering. Task-oriented people are only interested in completing the task rather than perceiving the process as a whole (Hammer 1996). Whether the overall process succeeds in the end has little concern for task-oriented people. On the contrary, process-oriented people in the organisation go through each process and see that the desired end result can be accomplished. This improves the enterprises' performance, whereas inefficient, 'bureaucratic' departments, and other non-performing departments do not (Davenport 1993; Hammer and Champy 1993).

BPR as a technique in a new era

Terry Finerty, partner at Arthur Andersen, says that intense challenges posed by their competitors in the global market compel Arthur Andersen to constantly reposition its company strategies (Anon 1997). Like Hammer (1996), Finerty stressed that the fundamental processes in the organisation should be questioned to explore the possibilities of further enhancing their efficiency and effectiveness. Besides, he believes that BPR aims at quantum changes in performance, unlike the traditionally much preferred continuous improvements.

The traditional business practice often breaks jobs and tasks into functional specialities, then connects each of these specialities through a hierarchy. In contrast, BPR labels this practice as obsolete and replaces it with networked, self-managed and motivated teams and multidimensional jobs (Hammer and Champy 1993). Earl and Khan (1994, p. 29) describe BPR as seeking radical, transformational performance improvements, and embracing information technology. Knights and McCabe (1998, p. 168) define BPR as 'an amalgam of recent innovative initiatives brought together and integrated through the radical use of information technology'.

These views have a certain common stance. The characteristics of BPR that are being constantly mentioned are radical changes (Hammer 1994; Hammer and Champy 1993; Dixon et al. 1994; Hill and Wilkinson 1995) and fundamental rethinking (Hammer 1994; Hammer and Champy 1993; Champy 1995). These two characteristics distinguish BPR from any other business practices in the business management field.

Methodology

A questionnaire was designed and criticised by seven practising managers. The improved questionnaire was sent to 75 people from 28 firms in different industries with IT departments, within the Klang Valley. The questionnaires were sent via e-mail directly to individual internet mailboxes. It was believed that using e-mail would be more effective than a postal survey in terms of cost and time. From the 75 questionnaires successfully mailed, 36 from 28 firms were returned: a 48 per cent response rate. The questionnaire was to gather information on how companies conduct their business using their existing management techniques and approaches. Detailed results follow. All 36 respondents were of managerial status, approximately 6 per cent were managing directors and 28 per cent were IT department managers, 40 per cent were line managers and 26 per cent were functional managers (sales, human resources, finance and operations). From the 36 respondents, 83 per cent were males while 17 per cent were females.

The sample of 28 firms was randomly selected from those listed on the web. They were telephoned to obtain the e-mail addresses of at least two likely respondents in each firm.

Results

Data analysis

A series of tests was carried out to determine the need of BPR in private enterprises in the Klang Valley.
The tests were: Reliability Analysis, Factor Analysis and Cronbach's Alpha Reliability Test (see Sekaran 1992) and Pearson Product Moment Correlation Coefficient Test.

Reliability analysis

Reliability analysis was carried out to give consistent data results before further analysis could be conducted. The reliability analysis was tested on the 18 variables of the three constructs defined namely Communications, Contribution to the enterprise and Factors needed in implementation (see Table 9.1).

Table 9.1: Determinants of management techniques' effectiveness

Construct	Description
Communications	How management techniques are communicated to others
Contribution to the enterprise	How management techniques contribute to the enterprise
Factors needed in implementation	What factors are needed to ensure a successful management technique implementation

This computation will determine that all variables share a common core (Aczel 1991) in making a construct. Item-to-total correlation score was used to determine which variable is to be retained for further analysis. Item-to-total correlation was used to measure the relationship of the variable with the rest of the variables in this research. In this research, the cut-off point score of accepting a variable was an item-to-total correlation score of 0.28 or above (an arbitrary choice). Referring to Table 9.2, variable labels 32, 35 and 52 were omitted from the research as the scores were negative in order to improve reliability.

Factor analysis

After improving the reliabilities of variables, factor analysis was carried out to reduce the many variables to a more manageable set of factors (Aaker et al. 1995). The factor analysis was done according to the recommended process provided by the SPSS base 8.0 Application Guide (Anon 1998).
The steps were:

Table 9.2: Reliability analysis of determinants of management techniques' effectiveness

Construct and variables	Variable label	Corrected item-total correlation scores	
Communications			
Verbally informally	32	**−0.0664**	*Variable deleted from analysis*
Verbally formally	33	0.2863	
Written instructions	34	0.3162	
Internet and Intranet	35	**−0.0671**	*Variable deleted from analysis*
Audio/visual equipment	36	0.4082	
In-house magazines and newsletter	37	0.4082	
Contribution to the enterprise			
Gathering useful data for decision making	47	0.3170	
Understanding the process	48	0.3156	
Committing resources	49	0.3426	
Using data to change behaviours	50	0.2852	
Using data to change process	51	0.6940	
Others	**52**	**−0.0893**	*Variable deleted from analysis*
Factors needed in implementation			
Top management support and commitment	53	0.3744	
Other managers support and commitment	54	0.7879	
Non-managers support and commitment	55	0.6822	
Well-managed implementation of techniques	56	0.8117	
Enterprise culture	57	0.6547	
Appropriate techniques	58	0.6673	

- The extraction of factors to represent the data.
- The rotation of factor loadings using the varimax method to make loadings more interpretable.
- The calculation of factor scores for further analysis.

Table 9.3 shows the result of the factor analysis. Five factors were extracted from the 15 variables. These five factors were again tested on their internal reliabilities using Cronbach's Alpha. In this research, Cronbach's Alpha scores of 0.5 and above were accepted. From Table 9.3, Factor

Contribution2 has been omitted from further analysis because the Alpha value was less than 0.5.

Table 9.3: Factor analysis of the three determinants after reliability analysis

Constructs and variables	Total variables	Variables retained	Alpha value
Communications	4	33, 34, 36 and 37	0.5012
Contribution to the enterprise			
Contribution1	3	49, 50 and 51	0.6426
Contribution2	2	**47 and 48**	**0.4298** ***Variable deleted***
Factors employed in implementation			
Implementation1	6	53, 54, 55, 56, 57 and 58	0.8669

Note: Factor analysis accepts a reliability score of 0.5 and above.

Correlation test

From the factors determined and extracted in factor analysis a correlation test was used to test the relationship between these factors and the effectiveness of management techniques. The *Pearson* Product Moment Correlation Coefficient was used. Its range is from –1 to +1 (Aaker et al. 1995). A positive value means that these factors have a positive relationship with the effectiveness of management techniques, while a negative value means the opposite.

Table 9.4 portrays the Significance Level and Correlation Coefficient of management technique effectiveness and the three constructs.

Findings displayed graphically

These findings represent the results of an interim survey that is part of an ongoing research project. Figure 9.1 shows the companies with IT departments from which the 36 respondents came, representing their 28 firms.

Figures 9.2a and 9.2b show which techniques among TQM, ISO 9000, Management by Objectives (MBO), Material Requirement Planning (MRP), Manufacturing Resource Planning (MRPII), SPT Strategic Planning Tools (SPT), BPR and others are being used.

Figures 9.3a and 9.3b show how effective these techniques are.

Table 9.4: Determining the effectiveness of management techniques correlation analysis of management techniques' effectiveness and the three constructs

Determinants	Significance level/Correlation coefficient		
Management techniques' effectiveness	Communications	Contribution to the enterprise	Factors needed in implementation
Total Quality Management (TQM)	0.025 / 0.330*	0.423 / 0.033	0.230 / 0.205
ISO 9000	0.029 / 0.346*	0.008 / 0.395**	0.836 / 0.036
Management by Objectives (MBO)	0.309 / 0.086	0.048 / –0.281	0.573 / 0.097
Material Requirement Planning (MRP)	0.286 / –0.097	0.320 / 0.081	0.425 / 0.137
Manufacturing Resource Planning (MRPII)	0.286 / –0.097	0.320 / 0.081	0.425 / 0.137
Strategic Planning Tools (SPT)	0.004 / 0.443**	0.292 / 0.094	0.008 / 0.436**
Business Process Re-engineering (BPR)	**0.056 / 0.269**	**0.030 / 0.318***	**0.210 / 0.214**
Others	0.332 / 0.075	0.261 / 0.110	0.173 / –0.232

*   Significant at 0.05 significance level
** Significant at 0.01 significance level

Figure 9.1: Companies with IT departments

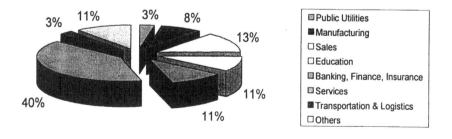

Figure 9.2a: Management techniques used by enterprises

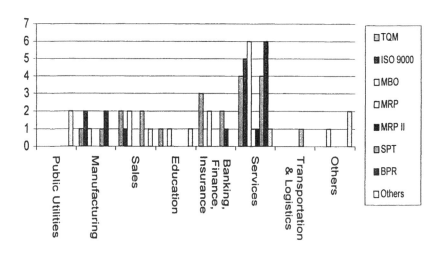

Figure 9.2b: Management techniques used by enterprises

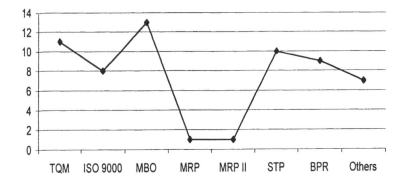

Figure 9.3a: Effectiveness of management techniques used

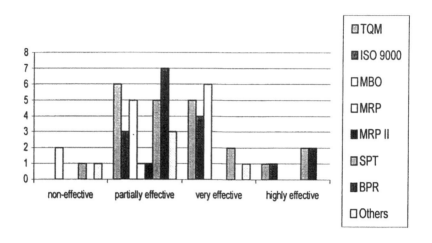

Figure 9.3b: Effectiveness of management techniques used

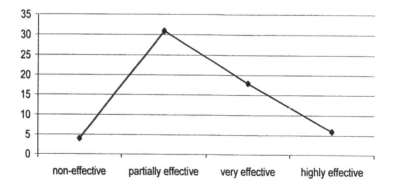

Figure 9.4 shows what techniques the respondents think should be used but are not.

Figure 9.4: Techniques that should be used which are not

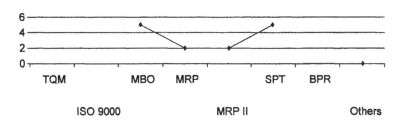

Figure 9.5 shows how management techniques used are communicated within the enterprise.

Figure 9.5: Ways of how management techniques are communicated to each other

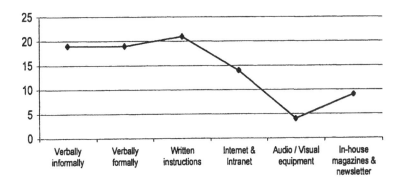

Figure 9.6 shows the emphasis placed on the various management techniques by the enterprise using them.

Figures 9.7a and 9.7b show how the techniques contribute to the enterprise.

Figure 9.8 portrays the critical success factors in implementing management techniques.

Figure 9.9 demonstrates how often the implementation of management techniques used is evaluated within the enterprise.

Figure 9.6: Emphasis of each management technique used

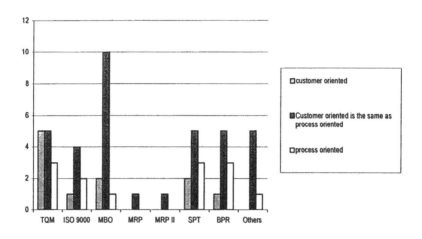

Figure 9.7a: How management techniques contribute to the enterprise

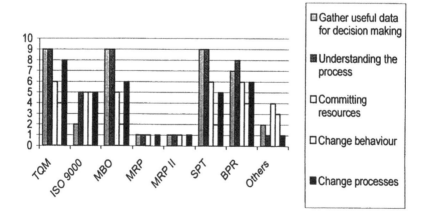

Figure 9.7b: How management techniques contribute to the enterprise

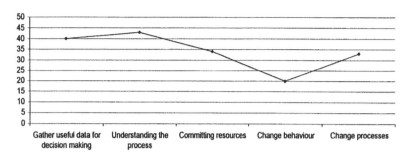

Figure 9.8: Factors needed in implementing management techniques

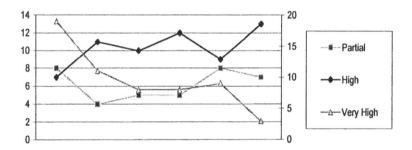

Figure 9.9: Evaluation of management techniques

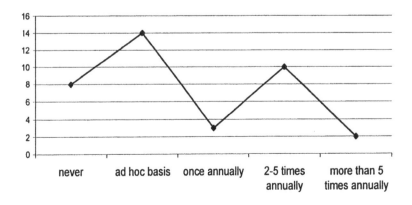

These results are from the 36 respondents drawn from 28 enterprises.

Discussion

It was found that the effectiveness of management techniques is attributable to a combination of variables (see Table 9.3 and Figures 9.3a onwards).

Table 9.5: The variables influencing the management techniques' effectiveness

Construct	Variables
Communications	Verbally formally
	Written instructions
	Audio/visual equipment
	In-house magazines and newsletter
Contribution to the enterprise	Gathering useful data for decision making
	Understanding the process
	Committing resources
	Using data to change behaviour
	Using data to change process
Factors needed in implementation	Top management support and commitment
	Other managers' support and commitment
	Non-managers' support and commitment
	Well-managed implementation of techniques
	Enterprise culture
	Appropriate techniques

From Table 9.5, the factors in the three constructs generate relationships with management technique effectiveness when a certain management technique is used. Based on results in Table 9.4, Table 9.6 below is based on the correlation between the constructs and management technique effectiveness.

Based on Table 9.6, when SPT is implemented it has the best overall ranking between the three constructs and management techniques' effectiveness. BPR effectiveness ranks second. The rest of the management technique effectiveness has mediocre or low ranks. The new emerging techniques (SPT and BPR—see Table 9.6) have better rankings than the rest of the techniques.

Of the three constructs, Contribution to the enterprise portrays how the management technique contributes. Table 9.7 depicts this construct against each management technique (based on the correlation between contribution to the enterprise and management technique effectiveness). BPR ranks second after ISO 9000. TQM as a quality management technique failed to impress the authors after being ranked fifth, although many texts suggest otherwise.

If the sample is representative of the population that is drawn, Malaysian enterprises should re-examine their operations management to ensure

Table 9.6: The ranking of each management technique based on the correlation between the constructs and management technique effectiveness

Determinants	Ranking			
Management technique effectiveness	Communications	Contribution to the enterprise	Factors needed in implementation	
Total Quality Management (TQM)	3	5	3	⎫ Quality Management Techniques
ISO 9000	2	1	7	⎭
Management by Objectives (MBO)	5	8	6	⎫
Material Requirement Planning (MRP)	7	6	4	Old Techniques
Manufacturing Resource Planning (MRPII)	7	6	4	⎭
Strategic Planning Tools (SPT)	1	4	1	⎫
Business Process Reengineering (BPR)	**4**	**2**	**2**	New Emerging Techniques
Others	6	3	8	⎭

Note: Numbers 1 to 8 represent ranks with '1 = best' and '8 = worst'

competitive advantage by placing greater emphasis on BPR. With AFTA imminent in 2005, local industries such as automobile and telecommunication will be gravely affected by the liberalisation of the global markets. The intensity of competition will increase rapidly in Malaysian markets.

In 2005 local companies in Malaysia will not only compete within its geographical limitations but also face the threats of entry of giant companies from abroad. Change is therefore essential. The question is how much change is sufficient to remain competitive in this emerging 'new era'. BPR, in its essence, offers radical changes to organisations. These changes are

Table 9.7: The ranking of each management technique based on the correlation between contribution to the enterprise and management technique effectiveness

Determinants Management technique effectiveness	Ranking Contribution to the enterprise
ISO 9000	1
BPR	2
Others	3
SPT	4
TQM	5
MRP	6
MRPII	6
MBO	8

Note: Numbers 1 to 8 represents ranks with '1 = best' and '8 = worst'

destined to produce 'quantum leaps' in productivity and profitability if made appropriately (Champy 1995).

Embarking on BPR is no easy task. According to Hammer and Champy (1993), 70 per cent of companies that initiated re-engineering failed to achieve what was expected. There are several reasons. One given by Michael Hammer is 'BPR at heart but not in practice'. This problem often arises in many enterprises in Malaysia, where enterprises like the idea of re-engineering but perceive its practice as burdensome. Perhaps Malaysia's cultural entity presents this unique form of BPR rejection. Cultural elements such as politeness get in the way when managers are too soft and polite to tell others there is a vital need to buck up or leave. Champy (1995) says that re-engineering is a painful process because the whole set of values and beliefs in the enterprise are being challenged.

Sometimes one wonders how many Malaysian enterprises are prepared to make the necessary radical changes, especially in view of the apparent end of the economic downturn of 1997–99. With government intervention rescuing various companies from financial catastrophe, many troubled local companies were merely financially restructured rather than reengineered. This demonstrates enterprises' reluctance to switch from their 'bricks and mortar' management techniques since their survival is almost guaranteed by the Malaysian government. However, the recent total revamp of the financial sector and the expansive adoption of e-commerce of companies signifies an interesting awareness of re-engineering in Malaysia.

Conclusions

As has been stressed, this is a progress report for the first phase of an ongoing research project. The responses to the questionnaire came from a small sample of practising managers from 28 enterprises with IT departments in the Klang Valley, although not all the respondents are employed in IT departments. Because of the small sample confined to the Klang Valley no attempt is made here to generalise the results. This will have to wait until the research is completed, probably with an improved questionnaire. Nevertheless, for the sample, the following tentative results appear:

The respondents, although a small sample, represent a broad span of activities (see Figure 9.2).

The three most popular techniques were MBO, TQM and SPT (in that order) with BPR coming fourth (see Figure 9.2).

The effectiveness of BPR is rated as highly as that of SPT and more 'partially effective' than any other technique used (see Figure 9.3).

In answer to the question 'What techniques should be used which are not?' ISO 9000 was most desired followed closely by BPR (see Figure 9.4).

In all techniques used, except MBO, customer emphasis equalling process emphasis was the strongest (see Figure 9.6).

Not surprisingly 'top management support' was considered the most important success factor in implementing management techniques (see Figure 9.8). This may or may not mean that currently there is insufficient top management support in the respondents' enterprises.

Figure 9.9 suggests that management techniques are not evaluated sufficiently frequently.

In the questionnaire the term 'strategic planning tools' was not defined, so it may have been variously interpreted by the respondents. Therefore its significance at $p < 0.01$ must be treated with caution.

Based on Table 9.6, SPT has the best overall ranking between the three constructs and management techniques' effectiveness. BPR effectiveness ranks second. The rest of the management techniques' effectiveness either have mediocre or low ranking with the factors.

BPR is ranked second best in contributing to the enterprise after ISO 9000 (see Table 9.7).

Many of these tentative results would probably be clarified by interviews with respondents. Few 'write-in responses' were obtained, suggesting that the questionnaire is reasonably comprehensive. One respondent did, however, suggest that the management technique used in his firm was 'management by fear'—by its nature this is difficult to research, but an attempt has been made. The literature appears to be silent on this technique, although Kohn (1993) in his book *Punished by Rewards* argues the case against carrots and sticks (management by fear?).

Management research commonly includes an examination of communication within enterprises. Figure 9.5 suggests that management techniques are inadequately communicated to those affected—verbal communication seems quite inadequate. 'Communication efficiency is a subset of productivity; the first must contribute to the second' (Richardson 1990).

With the small amount of data obtained it is dangerous to draw further conclusions from them. However it is concluded that the questionnaire used is an effective instrument that can be improved by, for example, encouraging more 'write-in' responses. Interviewing respondents would produce more data and an improved questionnaire could include the question 'Would you be happy to be interviewed to amplify your answers?' But such questions would result in the loss of anonymity. Another tactic would be to persuade some top managers of firms with IT departments to be interviewed independently of the questionnaire.

It is also concluded that administering questionnaires such as this by e-mail is not only quicker than using 'snail mail' but also gives a higher return rate (in this case 48 per cent) than conventional postal surveys, for which response rates over 20 per cent are rare. The authors are encouraged by the modest success of their efforts and intend to pursue their research so that more robust conclusions about BPR in Malaysia may be reached.

References

Aaker, D. A., V. Kumar, and G. S. Day (1995), *Marketing Research*, fifth edition, New York: John Wiley and Sons Inc.

Aczel, A. D. (1991), *Complete Business Statistics*, Tokyo: Toppan Company Ltd.

Anon (1997), *University of Leicester Learning Module 607, Business Policy*, tenth edition, Leicester: Learning Resources Centre.

—— (1998), *SPSS Base 8.0 Application Guide*, US: SPSS Inc.

Ascari, A., M. Rock, and S. Dutta (1995), 'Re-engineering and organisational change: lessons from a comparative analysis of company experiences', *European Management Journal*, 13 (1), 1–30.

Browning, J. (1993), 'The power of process redesign', *The McKinsey Quarterly*, 1, 47–58.

Champy, J. (1995), *Re-engineering Management: The Mandate for New Leadership*, New York: Harper Business.

Cock, D. E. and I. Hipkin (1997), 'TQM and BPR: Beyond the beyond myth', *Journal of Management Studies*, 34 (5), 659–676.

Conti, R. F. and M. Warner (1994), 'Taylorism, teams and technology in "re-engineering" work-organisation', *New Technology, Work, and Employment*, 9, 93–102.

Davenport, T. H. (1993), *Process Innovation: Re-engineering Work through Information Technology*, Boston MA: Harvard Business Process School Press.

Dixon, J., P. Arnold, J. Heineke, J. S. Kim and P. Mulligan (1994), 'Business process re-engineering improving in new strategic directions', *California Management Review*, Summer, 93–108.

Drew, S. (1994), 'BPR in financial services: factors for success', *Long Range Planning*, 25 (5), 25–41.

Earl, M. and B. Khan (1994), 'How new is business process redesign?', *European Management Journal*, 12, 20–30.

Edwards, R. C. (1979), *Contested Terrain*, New York: Basic Books.

Fisher, L. (1994), 'Total quality: hit or myth?', *Journal of Accountancy*, 3, 50–51.

Gay, L. R. and P. L. Diehl (1996), *Research Methods for Business and Management* (International edition), Singapore: Prentice Hall International Inc.

Grint, K. and P. Case (1998), 'The violent rhetoric of re-engineering: Management consultancy on the offensive', *Journal of Management Studies*, 35 (5), 557–578.

Grint, K. and L. Willcocks (1995), 'Business process re-engineering in theory and practice: business paradise regained?', *New Technology, Work and Employment*, 10, 99–109.

Hammer, M. (1994), 'Re-engineering is not hocus-pocus', *Across the Board*, 45–47.

Hammer, M. (1996), 'The Time 25: Time's most influential Americans', *Time*, 145 (25), 73.

Hammer, M. and J. Champy (1993), *Re-engineering the Corporation: A Manifesto for Business Revolution*, London: Nicholas Brealey.

Hill, S. and A. Wilkinson (1995), 'In search of TQM', *Employee Relations*, 17 (3), 8–25.

Knights, D. and D. McCabe (1998), 'What happens when the phone goes wild: Staff, stress and spaces for escape in a BPR telephone banking work regime', *Journal of Management Studies*, 35 (2), 163–194.

Kohn, A. (1993), *Punished by Rewards*, Boston: Houghton Mifflin.

Limkokwing (1998), *Hidden Agenda*, Kuala Lumpur: Limkokwing Integrated Sdn. Bhd.

Nickels, B., H. McHugh and S. McHugh (1998), *Understanding Business*, New York: The McGraw-Hill Companies, Inc.

Peters, J. (1994), 'Operationalizing total quality: A business process approach', *The TQM Magazine*, 6 (4), 29–33.

Richardson, B. (1995), 'How to manage your organisation scientifically', *The TQM Magazine*, 7 (4).

Richardson, S. (1990), 'Empowering managers with proper questioning techniques', *The Management Development Journal of Singapore*, 2 (1), 14–18.

Richardson, S. (1991), *Southeast Asian Management: Cases and Concepts*, Singapore: Singapore University Press.

Sekaran, U. (1992), *Research Methods for Business: A Skill Building Approach*, second edition, USA: John Wiley and Sons Inc.

10

Tour guide training: Lessons for Malaysia about what works and what's needed

Betty Weiler and Sam H. Ham[1]

Introduction

Ecotourism is increasing throughout the world, particularly in species-rich tropical countries where it is often promoted in association with the management of protected areas and where it is seen as a tool for conservation and for development that is economically and ecologically sustainable. Ecotourism, for our purposes here, is a special form of nature-based tourism; special in that it endeavours not only to provide an enjoyable experience for the visitor, but also to do so in a way that is ecologically and culturally responsible. One of the key strategies for achieving these lofty ideals is ecotourism's frequent reliance on specialised interpretive guides to inform, educate and inspire visitors. The rationale underpinning this approach is that accurate and compelling interpretation of sites and features and modelling appropriate environmental and cultural behaviour will assist the positive impacts of tourism to be maximised and its negative impacts to be minimised, both in the short and the long term (Sweeting et al. 1999).

Malaysia is described in the ecotourism literature as an emerging destination with significant growth potential. If it wants to mature as a destination both for its ASEAN neighbours and in the wider tourism marketplace, it will need to devote more attention and resources to developing the quality of its human capital. For nature-based tourism, the most important factor is its interpretive guides, people who hold the key to educating and inspiring visitors while protecting the natural and cultural resources upon which Malaysia's future depends.

Background

Ecotourism strives to engender an intellectual, emotional and even spiritual connection between people and places as much as a physical experience with land and water, and interpretation is the means by which such links are established. Originally defined by Tilden (1957), interpretation is an educational activity aimed at revealing meanings and relationships to people about the places they visit and the things they see and do there. As we have argued elsewhere, interpretation lies at the heart and soul of what ecotourism is and what ecotour guides can and should be doing (Weiler and Ham 2000; Ham and Weiler 1999).

Clearly, tour guides have a number of responsibilities as providers of tourism experiences, such as: a duty of care for the health and safety of the visitor; managing the itinerary and tour logistics; providing courteous and quality customer service; responding to the needs and expectations of visitors from other cultures and those with special needs; managing interactions within and between client groups; delivering the tour cost-effectively; providing high-quality, informative and entertaining commentary; meeting the legal obligations and expectations of various stakeholders.

In addition, ecotour guides shoulder responsibility for providing a high-quality interpretation of natural and heritage resources and a model of appropriate environmental and cultural behaviour. They are accountable to many masters, including their employers and other players in the tourism industry, protected area managers, host communities and of course the visitors themselves. To be able do their job competently, guides need training, often extensive training, to provide them with necessary knowledge and skills.

This chapter reports on an ongoing research project that is monitoring the development, delivery and outcomes of training programmes for interpretive guides in both developed and developing tropical countries, particularly those with an emerging global economic presence, such as Malaysia. It presents the findings of this first phase of the research in the form of lessons learned from the interpretive guiding component of a six-week training programme conducted in April–May 1999 in Panama. Some of the principles that informed the development of the course are presented first, followed by the methods used to assess the training. The findings are then presented in the form of five lessons and their possible implications for guide training in Malaysia.

Nature tourism and guiding in Malaysia

Several indicators suggest that nature-based tourism and the demand for trained professional guides in Malaysia will increase significantly in the coming years. As a foreign exchange generator, tourism is one of the most important segments of the Malaysian economy and, not surprisingly, this is reflected in the financial resources Malaysia allocates to tourism. The nation's most recent five-year plan, for example, earmarks a particularly generous allocation of funds mainly for the development of tourism facilities and infrastructure (Khalifah and Tahir 1997). In addition to development funds, the Malaysian government has spent considerable sums on tourism marketing and promotion. Since 1996, Malaysia has spent more than US$1.1 million per year on tourism advertising, placing it among the top 25 countries in the world in terms of money spent on tourism promotion (Bridges 1999). Tourism is clearly a priority in Malaysia's economic plans and, because of the international fame of its natural attractions, nature-based tourism is expected to grow in importance well into the twenty-first century. Capitalising on what some (for example, Weaver 1998) describe as the significant growth potential in Malaysia's ecotourism market, attention to tourism training and human resource development has also emerged as a priority within the Comprehensive National Ecotourism Plan developed by the Ministry of Culture, Art and Tourism (MOCAT). In the last decade, MOCAT, the Malaysian Department of Wildlife and National Parks, the University of Putra-Malaysia and PATA (a regional tourism coordinating body) have begun specialised training and licensing of ecotourism guides. Since 1999, a curriculum involving multiple guide certification levels has been in existence. According to Dr Zaaba Zainol Abidin, who has helped lead these developments for the Department of Wildlife and National Parks, demand for professional guide training courses in Malaysia is high, especially for localised nature guides at the community level (Abidin 2000).

As they were in most of South-East Asia, foreign arrivals to Malaysia were down in 1997-98, due both to the 1997–98 economic crisis and the dense haze created by Indonesian forest fires during the same period. Since then, however, Malaysia's tourism industry has shown signs of significant recovery. The return of clean air and better economic times promises to re-establish the tourism growth trends that characterised the region throughout most of the 1990s. Most indicators point to a 1–2 per cent economic growth rate in 1999, with even greater growth in 2000 (Bridges 1999). Indeed, all indications are that Malaysia's tourism industry is following suit. According to PATA (1999), for example, first quarter inbound tourism to Malaysia was up 41 per cent compared to 1998. And even during 1997–98, when the economic crisis, political unrest and Indonesian fires combined to slow international tourism in Malaysia, tourism continued to advance as an economic player. According to Malaysian government statistics, during this time the number of lodging establishments in the country grew by 4 per cent and the number of rooms grew by 10 per cent. The average number of nights spent in lodging establishments also grew, rising 6 per cent from 1997 to 1998. Barring serious economic setbacks and political unrest, these figures suggest a bright future for Malaysia's tourism industry and, along with it, a growing need for education and training, including that of professional guides.

Guiding, as an important sector of Malaysia's tourism industry, stands to grow in the coming years. A primary factor underlying this growth will be the country's myriad natural tourism attractions. Guided tours to Malaysia promise to put visitors in close proximity to an amazing array of plant and animal life. Situated in the western half of the Indo-Malayan archipelago, Malaysia is located in the heart of Sundaland, identified by biologists as one of the world's few 'Mega Biodiversity Hotspots' (Mittermeier et al. 1999). More than two-thirds of the country is jungle, and expanses of mangrove-lined beaches remain intact, especially along the west coast and in Borneo. To protect these resources, a well-managed national protected area system has grown up, which now includes some 39 national parks and wildlife reserves covering a land area of about 700,000 hectares, or nearly 6 per cent of Peninsular Malaysia (Elagupillay 2000; Cochrane

1993). Contained in these protected areas are some of Asia's most spectacular landscapes and biological attractions. Recent tourist guide books (such as Cheam and Cheam 1998) promise tourists opportunities to see staggering plant diversity, including more than 8,000 species of flowering plants, 2,000 species of trees, 200 palms and 800 species of orchids. Likewise, thousands of wildlife species, many endemic or unique to the region, inhabit the jungles and coastlines of Malaysia (Cheam and Cheam 1998; Mittermeier et al. 1999). Protected in some of Malaysia's wildest and most remote areas are more than 200 species of mammals, including tigers, elephants and the endangered rhinoceros, along with tapirs, wild cats, bears, deer and, of course, many species of gibbons and monkeys, all of world-wide appeal to tourists (Cheam and Cheam 1998). Since many tourists will not venture, or do not know how to venture, into such wild areas alone, skilled and knowledgeable guides for them will be in high demand.

Despite these outstanding natural assets, however, many of Malaysia's biological features and natural attractions are very similar to those of its neighbouring countries and, as a relative latecomer to the international tourism scene, the country is having to work very hard to compete in the international marketplace (Khalifah and Tahir 1997). High-quality interpretive guides represent an important marketing advantage to individual operators and destinations aiming to tap into this highly competitive yet highly lucrative market segment. Little doubt remains that the demand for nature-based tourism experiences is growing significantly worldwide, and that guides are playing an increasingly important role in facilitating quality experiences, particularly for visitors from comparatively wealthy countries who are unfamiliar with tropical environments.

Course context

It is important to note that the Panamanian interpretive guide training programme, upon which this research is based, was initiated by a local commercial tourism developer/operator, the Gamboa Tropical Rainforest Resort. The resort owners approached the authors for advice on the development of a staff training programme and invited them to participate as trainers. Given the lack of precedence for such training in Central America, the resort sought and was able to obtain the financial support of a number of public organisations that made it possible to open the course to the wider community. The US Agency for International Development (USAID) through its global Environmental Education and Communication Project (GreenCOM), the University of Idaho, RMIT University, the Smithsonian Tropical Research Institute (STRI), several Government of Panama institutions and a number of private tour operators contributed direct funding, sponsorship of individual trainees, or in-kind support such as donated teaching time, training facilities, accommodation for trainees and training materials. Despite the wide range of external donors, however, the course was a host-country initiative and ownership of the course remained with the Panamanian organisations previously listed. The authors worked with a planning team that included representatives of many of these organisations, providing expert advice where it was sought.

The authors were able to draw on their combined backgrounds in tourism planning, management and environmental interpretation as well as their international experience as researchers and educators that included training in 15 other developing countries. The course content was also informed by a review of the literature pertaining to tourism, training and environmental interpretation, with particular attention given to training in developing countries and adult learning theory (see, for example, Weaver 1998; Rios 1998; Kaye and Jacobson 1995; Huszczo 1990; Ham et al. 1993; Ham and Sutherland 1992; Ham et al. 1989). A related body of literature used was that of competency-based training and, in particular, the work of industry bodies in Australia and Canada that identifies the occupational (competency) standards deemed to be necessary for interpretive tour-guiding (CTHRC 1996; TTA 1999). In summary, every attempt was made to develop the course based on methods and objectives that were educationally sound and industry-relevant.

The final curriculum was a six-week full-time course of study consisting of two broad substantive areas: (1) knowledge about the natural and cultural heritage of the destination country and (2) interpretive guiding skills. In-country experts from STRI and other organisations assumed responsibility for component 1 and the authors were largely responsible for delivering training on interpretive tour guiding (component 2).

Methods

Although stories of success and failure abound in international development circles, a body of theory and research related to guide training has yet to accumulate. Few systematic attempts have been made to evaluate or assess training aimed at local guides, probably because those responsible for delivering training have little understanding of or interest in research or training evaluation. The literature on training evaluation (Kirkpatrick 1983) was useful in providing a framework and identifying potential research tools for assessing this training program. Kirkpatrick links evaluation to levels of learning and notes the importance of measuring outcomes appropriate to what is being evaluated: trainees' reactions (level one), trainees' learning (level two), trainees' behaviour (level three) and organisational results (level four). Others (Gardner 1993; Moore 1993) note the need to use a combination of qualitative and quantitative methods and measures when assessing training outcomes.

Three main assessment methods informed the data collection. The first was a pre- and post-training self-assessment questionnaire that was administered to each trainee. The statements in the questionnaire were carefully worded competency statements that corresponded to the course's learning objectives. These aimed to measure learning at Kirkpatrick's level two evaluation. Trainees were asked to rate themselves as 'not competent', 'somewhat competent', or 'competent' on 41 statements that covered learning outcomes related to: introduction to ecotourism and the role of an ecotour guide; visitor profiles, motivations and expectations; communication and interpretation; customer service; leadership; intercultural communication and special groups; group management; minimal impact.

Trainees completed the questionnaires independently, although some trainees with limited literacy were allowed to respond to the questions orally. The pre-training questionnaires were completed in two parts during class time prior to covering the subject material; the post-training questionnaires were completed during class time on the last day of the course.

The second data collection method sought to measure trainees' reactions to the training (Kirkpatrick's level one evaluation) via verbal and written feedback and, in particular, a trainee-completed reflective journal. Each trainee was given a notebook and carbon paper and was invited to write or draw on a regular basis in this journal. The purpose of the journal was explained verbally and was also printed on the inside cover of the trainee's notebook. Trainees were told that the journal was meant to help them understand and apply what was being taught in the course. We stressed that the purpose was not to test their ability as learners, but that it would help us to see where we were doing a good job and where we could do a better job as teachers. On some days, particularly early in the course, trainees were given specific suggestions as to what to draw or write in their journal, for example to draw themselves as a learner, or to describe the most useful thing they had learned that day.

While journal-writing initially created some anxiety for some trainees (notably the less literate trainees), it proved to be a significant creative outlet for most of them. Unlike reflective journals in university classes (which are regarded as very private musings often done with a considerable degree of self-consciousness and embarrassment), at the guides' insistence, these journals became the subject of classroom discussion and sharing which led to cohesiveness and bonding among many of the trainees.

The third method was our own and others' (non-trainees) observations of the trainees (Kirkpatrick's level three evaluation). After each full day of training, Weiler and Ham debriefed each other about observations made during the day and made written notes of these so that they could be considered in aggregate form following the course. In addition, the intensity of the training programme meant that there was considerable opportunity for informal discussion. Because trainees had only to attend and participate, rather than be formally assessed and graded as an outcome of the course, there was a greater willingness to discuss difficulties and successes openly with the trainers and with other course observers. Trainees were observed applying what they had learned in individual talks and guided walks, and were videotaped and informally assessed by some of the training sponsors at the end of the six weeks.

Findings: Five lessons learned

The Panama guides course was seen as the first of a series of courses of its type that will be offered in Panama and elsewhere in the Latin American and Asian tropics in the next five years. As a prototype effort, the course therefore represented an important opportunity to begin to document lessons about the effective training of local interpretive guides.

Five lessons stand out among the many that were learned in delivering this course.

Lesson one: Recruiting and selecting trainees was critical to success

The course planning team put considerable thought into how the trainees were recruited and selected, with a focus on providing training opportunities for local and indigenous Panamanians, regardless of formal education background or language ability. Of the 34 participants, about half were indigenous, from three different cultural groups, most with fewer than six years of formal education. The range of educational level is indicative of the diversity of the group: from functionally illiterate to university-educated. About one-third had mid to low literacy, while about half had high school education. The group also showed diversity in language skills. The course was taught in Spanish, sometimes with the aid of simultaneous translation. Several trainees spoke limited Spanish and needed translation into their indigenous languages, while half a dozen were bilingual (English and Spanish). Trainees were both male (two-thirds) and female and ranged widely in age (17 to about 50). A number had some experience as guides; about five had extensive tour guiding experience.

Many of the trainees, especially those with little or no formal education, felt a measure of trepidation at being in a classroom, even though the teaching facilities and classroom layout were very carefully chosen to minimise this reaction. Most of the first day of the course was spent in activities and discussions designed specifically to reduce these anxieties. It was obvious from verbal and written feedback from the trainees on days two and three of the course that this was appreciated, and was also very evident in the change in atmosphere in the classroom that, by the end of day three, was very relaxed and inviting. This was so noticeable that several of the guest speakers and course sponsors who dropped in to observe the course commented on how positively charged the classroom felt.

Very early in the course, the diversity of the trainees became a strength upon which the trainers and trainees could draw. The trainees mentioned this frequently, both verbally and in their journal entries. One trainee wrote, for example, 'Learning to me means taking advantage of the experiences of my classmates' (Janett). And another revealed that, 'my classmates are experts in their own area. They help me learn about biology and environmental interpretation' (Aris).

Lesson two: Collaborative teaching and learning were necessary in this course

Turning a large and diverse group of trainees with variable learning styles and needs from a liability to a strength was made possible by making extensive use of collaborative teaching methods. Throughout the course, short lectures of 30 minutes or less were used, interspersed with individual, two-person and small-group exercises and activities. With the trainers taking extra care in how individuals were allocated to work groups, even assigned reading exercises could be undertaken collaboratively.

It was important to continually vary the work groups in both size and membership, as this was a residential training programme and there was certainly potential for conflict and intolerance. The common living quarters were used as a tool to facilitate out-of-classroom learning and various tasks were assigned, usually as group assignments, to reinforce the classroom learning and make the most of time spent away from family and kinship groups, a difficult experience for some.

Work groups provided an important opportunity for trainees to observe the learning of others and to help their peers learn, but this had to be managed skilfully so as to make it a constructive rather than destructive experience. As Marciel, one of the indigenous participants, wrote in his journal, 'We must criticise each other but only in a constructive way.' Sometimes trainees wrote about the learning of others, indicating how this had enhanced their own learning, for example: 'I'm worried about my other classmates—they don't have the knowledge to understand. We must have patience and tolerance' (Luis). The tone and expectations set by the trainers were critical factors for nurturing a collaborative rather than a competitive learning environment. We believe that establishing this atmosphere was centrally important in the success of the course.

Lesson three: Trainees must be encouraged to learn and perform at their own levels

Class exercises, discussions and assigned activities such as reading and reflective journal writing were always preceded by a statement about the standards and performance expectations of the trainers. The message was consistent: trainees were expected to put in their best effort, participate in all learning activities and reflect on their learning and progress in the context of their knowledge and skills at the beginning of the course. Trainees were actively discouraged from comparing their progress to other trainees.

A variety of training methods were used to ensure that those who felt uncomfortable or unable to learn from one teaching/learning style (such as overhead transparencies, or questions-and-answers) would benefit from other styles (Gutloff 1996; Gardner 1993). Wherever possible, individual learning objectives were addressed with multiple methods in the classroom, including small group discussions, written exercises, debates, role-playing, skits, chalkboard activities and practical exercises to demonstrate competencies (for example, presenting talks and guided tours around the local environs). Trainees were invited to comment at the end of each day, or write in their journals, about which learning activities they found beneficial and what they had learned. This was always encouraged in the spirit of 'we are all here to learn and improve' and resulted in frequent feedback on how much they enjoyed and learned from the various hands-on classroom activities. Several trainees indicated that they were nervous or felt shy about some of these activities, but acknowledged that these were important barriers to overcome in becoming a professional interpretive guide: 'I was nervous because I didn't know anyone. Then I was happy because I developed good relations with my classmates' (Cirelda). 'I really liked sharing experiences with my classmates—makes me a better guide' (Michael). 'It's important to put into practice what you hear' (Azalia).

Individual responses as well as mean scores on the pre- and post-training questionnaires were examined to identify the extent to which trainees felt they were competent and to explore whether particular teaching techniques and activities were associated with 'better' results with respect to competencies. The results proved useful in providing some indicators of trainees' perceptions of themselves and their competencies.

As a group, respondents' post-training scores were better (mean = 2.8 on a scale of one to three) than their pre-training scores (mean = 2.1). Examination of trainees' pre-training self-assessments revealed that some of the indigenous participants had very low opinions of themselves prior to the training, although a few also rated themselves as competent on several of the statements. Not surprisingly, a few of the experienced guides had fairly high opinions of their pre-training skills. Our research did not include objective assessments of actual pre- and post-training competencies, only the trainees' self-assessments of their own competencies.

Examination of the post-training scores revealed the trainees' self-evaluations as a group, as well as some individual differences. For example, 10 out of the 25 trainees who completed the post-training questionnaire rated themselves as 'competent' (a mean score of 3.0 on the 41 items) after the training. This compares to no trainees (out of the 26 who completed the pre-training questionnaire) rating themselves as 'competent' before the training.

The statements on which the trainees consistently rated themselves as most competent overall were three associated with interpretation and communication, two associated with leadership, one associated with intercultural communication and one associated with minimal impact. Our notes and observations indicated that these competencies correspond to those that were reinforced through collaborative activities in the classroom and practical exercises requiring the trainee to apply the knowledge being taught. The statements on which the trainees rated themselves as 'least competent' overall were those that were entirely lecture-based.

These results, taken together with the journal entries and verbal feedback to the trainers, suggest that collaborative learning together with participatory training techniques were largely responsible for the success of the course, as measured by the trainees' satisfaction with the course and their self-ratings of competencies. As Rosalba wrote, 'The experience of sharing with people so different, learning a way of communication that most probably will help us on the road of becoming better each day, makes me feel happy and satisfied for being here'. And Crecencio added, 'After these three weeks, the course for me is incredible because we have learned so many new things that I would not be able to count them. I feel very happy with the talks and explanations by the teachers and scientists—very professional.'

Lesson four: Delivering cost–effective guide training is an important sustainable development strategy

One of the real challenges of interpretive guide training is making it affordable to those who have the most to gain from it. Besides the actual cost of the training, which is certainly high, there is the opportunity cost of attending a six-week residential course: many just cannot afford to be away from family and a regular income for that long. The costs to the participants must be reduced, but without sacrificing the quality of the training.

In the short term, courses such as the Panama guides course, which was largely subsidised by aid agencies and non-profit organisations, will continue to rely on funds from wealthy developed countries. If these courses can concentrate on the development of standardised but adaptable curricula, teaching methods and training materials and on training in-country trainers, then the long-term costs of training can be greatly reduced.

Lesson five: Training in-country trainers is essential for ensuring that ecotourism is of benefit to host economies

The benefits of a train-the-trainer approach are obvious: many countries (whether developed or developing) cannot continually fund outsiders to deliver training, particularly when we consider that guide training is not a one-shot effort but a lifelong undertaking. In addition to careful selection of trainees who are able, willing and motivated to become 'multipliers', the training approach needs to incorporate techniques that develop and nurture the individual from being able to deliver one-on-one training on the job, to small group training, to classroom-based teaching. There needs to be infrastructure and support to assist in-country trainers to develop their own training materials, to access up-to-date information and resources and to continually upgrade their skills and sustain their enthusiasm for training.

Conclusion

This chapter has reported the findings of the first phase of an on-going research project that is monitoring the development, delivery and outcomes of training programmes for interpretive guides in both developed and developing tropical countries. This research is particularly important and timely for countries such as Malaysia that are relative latecomers to ecotourism. Malaysia has long been rich in natural and cultural resources, but both its national and state parks and tourism authorities are now taking a more proactive role in marketing and managing nature-based tourism in a way that is both economically and ecologically sustainable. Well-trained guides are an essential element of this strategy, and well-researched training programmes are critical to producing and nurturing good quality guides. Building on the lessons learned from the training initiatives of other developing countries is an important means to achieving both high-quality training programmes and high-quality ecotour guides.

The Panama guides course was a short-term success from many perspectives, including the trainees' satisfaction with the course and their self-assessments of their own competencies. The sponsors of the course and those who observed the guides in their final practical exercises also describe the course as a resounding accomplishment. But what is most important is not that this initial course enjoyed some measure of success. More significant is that we are beginning to achieve a systematically derived understanding of why, which of course is critical for drawing lessons for Malaysia. The long-term outcomes of this type of training are still unclear, both with respect to the trainees in the course and the multiplier effects of the course. This will be the focus of our continued research on guide training in Latin America, the Caribbean, Asia and the Pacific in the coming years. This will include the development and systematic testing of instructional aids and curricula that have potential for standardisation and other cost-saving training strategies.

As a final note, we wish to acknowledge that our research did not assess the actual pre- and post-training competencies of the trainees, only the trainees' self-assessments of their own competencies. There is a great need for more extensive and long-term research on whether trained guides are actually able to deliver the promise of ecotourism, that is, to provide accurate and compelling interpretation of sites and features and model appropriate environmental and cultural behaviour (Kirkpatrick's level three evaluation), and whether this leads to maximising the positive and minimising the negative impacts of tourism (Kirkpatrick's level four evaluation). Only if we work towards measuring the extent to which they are able to achieve these lofty goals can we reach our goal of assessing the guide's contribution to a sustainable future. In the meantime, documenting the lessons of the training of interpretive guides is an important step towards sustainability, and this is the spirit in which these lessons are offered to Malaysia.

Endnotes

[1] Funding for this project was provided by the Academy for Educational Development, Washington, DC, through its worldwide Environmental Education and Communication (GreenCOM) Project, which is jointly funded and managed by the Centre for Environment, Centre for Human Capacity Development, and the Office for Women in Development of the Bureau of Global Programs, Field Support and Research of the US Agency for International Development (USAID), and a buy-in from USAID/Panama. Co-funding from the Gamboa Tropical Rainforest Resort, Panama and the Smithsonian Tropical Research Institute (STRI) is also gratefully acknowledged. In addition, the authors want to express their gratitude to the many organisations that sponsored scholarships for the Panama guides course including Special Expeditions, Inc., the Organisation of American States (OAS), USAID/Panama and USAID's Central America Regional Natural Resources Project (PROARCA/CAPAS) that is managed by International Resources Group (IRG), Washington, DC. Opinions expressed in this chapter are the authors' alone and do not necessarily represent the views of any of the above listed organisations.

References

Abidin, Z. Z. (2000), Personal communication, February 11.
Bridges, T. (ed.) (1999), *Travel Industry World Yearbook (Volume 42) 1998–99*, New York: Travel Industry Publishing Company.
Canadian Tourism Human Resource Council (CTHRC) (1996), *National Occupational Standards for the Canadian Tourism Industry: Heritage Interpreter*, Ottawa.
Cochrane, J. (1993), 'Tourism and conservation in Indonesia and Malaysia', in M. Hitchcock, V. King and G. Parnwell (eds), *Tourism in South-East Asia*, London: Routledge, pp. 317–326.
Cheam, J. and G. J. Cheam (1998), *Malaysia*, London: APA Publications.
Elagupillay, S. (2000), 'Some issues on the management of gazetted protected areas in Peninsular Malaysia', paper presented at the *Workshop on Project Proposal and LFA Development INTAN*, Bukit Kiara, Kuala Lumpur, January, 25–27.
Gardner, H. (1993), *Multiple Intelligences: The Theory in Practice*, New York: Basic Books.
Gutloff, K. (1996), *Multiple Intelligences*, West Haven, CT: National Education Association.
Ham, S. and D. Sutherland (1992), 'Crossing borders and rethinking a craft: Interpretation in developing countries', in G. Machlis and D. Field (eds), *On Interpretation: Sociology for Interpreters of Natural and Cultural History* (Revised Edition), Corvallis: Oregon State University Press, pp. 251–274.
Ham, S., D. Sutherland and J. Barborak (1989), 'Role of protected areas in environmental education in Central America', *Journal of Interpretation*, 13 (5), 1–7.
Ham, S., D. Sutherland and R. Meganck (1993), 'Applying environmental interpretation in protected areas in developing countries', *Environmental Conservation*, 20 (3), 232–242.
Ham, S. and B. Weiler (1999), 'Capacitación de Guías Ecoturísticas en Centroamérica: Lecciones Aprendidas y sus Implicaciones para la Capacitación Regional de Guías', in *Proceedings of Las Tecnologías Más Limpias y La Gestión Ambiental: Herramientas para la Competividad del Turismo en Centroamérica*, Washington, DC: Environmental Export Council/Concurrent Technologies Corporation, pp. 56–57.
Huszczo, G. (1990), 'Training for team building', *Training & Development Journal*, 44 (2), 37–43.
Kaye, B. and B. Jacobson (1995), 'Mentoring: A group guide', *Training & Development Journal*, 49 (4), 23–26.
Khalifah, Z. and S. Tahir (1997), 'Malaysia: Tourism in perspective', in Frank M. Go and Carson L. Jenkins (eds.), *Tourism and Economic Development in Asia and Australasia*, pp. 176–196.
Kirkpatrick, D. (1983), 'Four steps to measuring training effectiveness', *Personnel Administrator*, November, 19–25.
Mittermeier, R. A., N. Myers and C. G. Mittermeier (1999), *Hotspots: Earth's Biologically Richest and Most Endangered Terrestrial Ecoregions*, Washington, DC: Conservation International.
Moore, A. (1993), *Capacitación de Capacitadores*, Washington, DC: US National Park Service, Office of International Affairs.
PATA (Pacific Asia Travel Association) (1999), *Annual Statistical Report of Pacific Asia Travel Association*, San Francisco: PATA.

Rios, H. (1998), 'Team building with hispanic groups: some considerations', *International Journal for the Advancement of Counselling*, 20, 123–129.

Sweeting, J., A. Bruner and A. Rosenfeld, (1999), *The Green Host Effect: An Integrated Approach to Sustainable Tourism and Resort Development*, Washington, DC: Conservation International.

Tilden, F. (1957), *Interpreting Our Heritage*, Chapel Hill, NC: University of North Carolina Press.

Tourism Training Australia (1999), TTA web site: www.tourismtraining.com.au.

Weaver, D. (1998), *Ecotourism in the Less Developed World*, New York: Cab International.

Weiler, B. and S. Ham. (2000), 'Tour guides and interpretation in ecotourism', in D. Weaver, (ed.), *The Encyclopaedia of Ecotourism*, Wallingford, UK: CABI Publishing.

11

Economic growth, international competitiveness and public service moral values: A study of Penang Island Municipal Council officers

Ali Haidar, Len Pullin and Lim Hong Hai with
Owen Hughes

Introduction

This study is concerned with the potential impact of public service moral values on Malaysia's economic growth and international competitiveness. The Malaysian case is significant because in Malaysia the government plays a leading role in both social and economic development. This effectively leads to a highly discretionary style of public administration where the moral orientations of public servants are a crucial factor in achieving the country's social and economic goals.

It is critical for any country to develop an understanding of its public service moral values, but even more so for a country like Malaysia, which relies heavily on this the public sector for social and economic success because of the nature of its development policies. Therefore the aim of our research has been to develop a greater understanding of the moral orientations of Malaysian civil servants. To achieve this, an empirical study was conducted on the moral values of higher level officers of the Penang Island Municipal Council (MPPP). Our respondents included heads and deputy heads of departments. To support this, and to broaden the findings, we have utilised anecdotal and other secondary data on civil servant value orientations at the state and federal levels.

The chapter identifies and discusses the empirical framework used in this study, then outlines the research methodology, reports on the questionnaire survey results and finally discusses the findings and their implications. But first we will consider the role of the public service in Malaysia's economic development and international competitiveness in greater detail.

The role of the state in economic development and international competitiveness

Since Malaysia gained independence, its economic performance has been exceptionally high compared with that of many other Asian countries (Means 1991, p. 279; Crouch 1993, p. 141. A key factor in this development is the country's political stability (Means 1991, p. 283). Unlike some other countries in Asia, Malaysia has not experienced any military coups since independence and as a result has maintained constitutional continuity. In the view of Crouch (1993, p. 153) Malaysian society is a socially harmonious one compared to many other multicultural societies.

It is important to note that governments play a key role in establishing and maintaining the social, economic and legal framework of institutions and the general social environment in their countries. In the context of Malaysia, Mahathir Mohammad, the current Prime Minister and the architect of modern Malaysia, clearly supports this notion in identifying that:

> The state cannot of course retreat totally from the economic life of Malaysia. It will not abdicate its responsibility for overseeing and providing legal and regulatory framework for rapid economic and social development. The government will be pro-active to ensure healthy fiscal and monetary management and smooth functioning of the Malaysian economy. It will escalate the development of the necessary physical infrastructure and the most conducive business environment-consistent with the social priorities (Karim 1992, p. 32).

However, this role is not at the expense of private sector involvement. The state in Malaysia under various policies including 'Malaysia Incorporated'[1] has formalised a symbiotic relationship between the public and the private sectors.

> The private sector was expected to be the primary engine of growth for national development. This meant that the public sector is to play the supportive role of providing services to facilitate, assist, advise, coordinate and ensure that the activities of the private sector are consistent with national objectives and national interests (Karim 1992, p. 49).

Whilst one can identify that the state and the private sector both have a role in the economic, political and social success of a country, it is more difficult, if not impossible, to indicate who contributes what, and in what proportion. However, within a politico-administrative system, the development and maintenance of a healthy and understanding relationship between politicians and bureaucrats plays an important role in the maintenance of political stability and, thus, economic success and social harmony. A key factor in this relationship is the moral values exhibited by civil servants and the underpinning ethos or moral framework that supports them.

In terms of Malaysia, the Malaysia Incorporated policy contains elements that emphasise the significance of creating appropriate moral values among civil servants (Taib and Mat 1992, p. 432). Given that this was achieved, and Malaysia's strong economic growth, political stability and social harmony are a testimony to this (see Means 1991, p. 283), then it is important that Malaysia continues to maintain and support these values. However, surprisingly enough, there has been very little systematic empirical research on civil servant moral values in Malaysia.

Conceptual framework

In the Malaysian context, the only discernible study on Malaysian public servant managerial values was conducted by Puthucheary (1978) on federal government employees in the late-1970s. A more recent trend in Malaysian studies in this area is for researchers to examine the moral values of private rather than public sector managers (Westwood and Everett 1995; Zabid and Alsagoff 1993; Gupta and Sulaiman 1996). Besides concentrating on the private sector, these studies focus on such issues as bribery, falsifying reports, expense accounts, and the degree of career orientation, which are outside the focus of the present study.

In this study we examine what Quinlan (1993, p. 542) has termed the 'ethics of role'. The focus is on the moral values that guide civil servants in their relationships with their superiors, who are usually politicians in office, and the civil servants' relationship to the general public. Moral values are concerned with the performance of one's duties. In this context, they are observable in the 'ethical environment of everyday bureaucratic discretion in public policy, in which public officials translate government policy into effective programs through the endless acts of advice, amendment, implementation, promotion and evaluation of public policies' (Uhr 1988, p. 110).

Following Durkheim, with the aim of situating the research in 'current practice', we focus on the actual moral orientations of public managers rather than the preachings of public management 'moral philosophers' (Durkheim 1953, p. 76). In other words, the focus of the research is on 'descriptive' rather than 'normative' ethics where the descriptive ethics focus examines 'the ethical beliefs and practices of given societies or people...They tell us what *is* in different cultures...[whereas]...moral philosophy is distinctly normative rather than descriptive. It is about ideal behaviour about what should be...' (Pojman 1989, p. 4).

This study is not concerned with what Uhr (1988, p. 109) called the 'orthodox approach to public service ethics' that deals with 'conflict of interest, especially bribery and illicit financial gain...'. The terms morality and ethics are used interchangeably in concert with Thompson (1985), on the grounds that 'Historically both terms refer to fairly much the same thing..."ethics" is of Greek origin and "morality" is of Latin origin' (Uhr 1988, p. 113).

It can be safely stated that the one question in public management that has never been satisfactorily resolved is, 'whom should public servants be serving'? At least three broad claims on public service loyalty can be identified.[2] One tradition suggests that politicians are partisan while public servants are non-partisan. As a result, the latter should be overlooking the activities of politicians in order to serve the public interest. Public managers, remaining above partisan politics, follow a 'service ethic'. Jackson (1987; 1988), for example, advises that public servants are obligated to work for 'public interests'.

Constitutionalists in the UK and Australia and other Commonwealth countries have consistently advised public servants engaged in providing independent advice to remain independent of the duly elected representatives of the people and follow the neutrality ethic (Armstrong 1989; Quinlan 1993). In contrast, there has recently emerged a very strong vocal group who argue that public servants should be responsive rather than independent. They should be responsive to the ideologies of their political masters and their role should remain confined to the implementation of policies formulated by their political masters (Rourke 1992; Aberbach and Rockman 1994).

In order to conduct an empirical study on the moral orientations of civil servants we isolate conceptually distinct elements on which these moral types vary. Three elements have been conceptualised which can be considered as dimensions of PMM. They are object of obedience, degree of anonymity, and degree of partisanship (see Table 11.1).

Table 11.1: Public management morality (PMM): Dimensions and patterns

Dimensions	Moral Pattern Continuum		
	Service	Neutrality	Responsive
Object of Obedience	Public Interest	Law/Public Interest/ Superordinate	Superordinate
Degree of Partisanship	Partisan for Public Interest	Non–Partisan	Partisan for Superordinate
Degree of Anonymity	Conditional (Public Interest)	Anonymous	Non–anonymous

These dimensions are used to formulate a continuum of three moral ideal types: the service type, the neutrality type, and the responsive type.

Neutrality ethic

The neutrality ethic appeared with the emergence of the modern public service and is usually associated with it (Heclo 1975). The notion of neutrality is not new and has been the subject of extensive discussions. Neutral managers are obedient to the law, not to individuals (Aucion 1997; Caiden 1996; Wright 1977). They only obey lawful instructions and if they need to complain about unlawful commands they do so by utilising proper channels, processes and available procedures (Armstrong 1989). Neutral managers serve the elected representatives from a broad spectrum of political affiliations with equal loyalty (IMM 1995, D2; Williams 1985) and do not show bias or partiality to any political party or to any political agenda or view (Aberbach et al. 1994; Armstrong 1989). Neutral managers are anonymous, they do not comment publicly on public policy issues without proper authorisation and do not disclose official secrets (Armstrong 1989; IMM 1995; Williams 1985).

Service pattern

Service-oriented managers serve the public interest. It is 'unethical for a public servant to be indifferent to the public interest' (Jackson 1988, p. 249). The service ethic demands that public managers serve their superiors so long as the latter work in the public interests (Jackson 1988, p. 247). Therefore they implement only those policies that they believed to be in the public interest. Service-oriented managers, in their advice, are only concerned about 'public interest' and not about the interests of their superiors at all.

The service ethic requires managers to resist and obstruct policies that are against the public interest. Their resistance includes, but is not limited to, engaging in secret white-anting from within if necessary, and even leaking information. 'There are occasions when leaking serves the public interest. Leaking may always be illegal but it is not always unethical or immoral' (Jackson 1988, p. 248).

Responsive pattern

Responsive managers are loyal to the wishes of their superiors and their programs (Aberbach and Rockman 1994, p. 465). They implement any policy determined by their superiors (Aberbach and Rockman 1994, pp. 462–463). These managers are not obedient 'to the letter and spirit of existing law or considered advice, but committed believers who would go about doing whatever was necessary to achieve [their superiors'] policy goals' (Aberbach and Rockman 1994, p. 466). Responsive managers, while advising, provide information that supports superordinates' ideology, suppress information that goes against it, and fabricate data in order to support the policies of their superiors. They slant conclusions drawn from information and provide advice that bolsters superiors' ideology or policy commitment (Rourke 1992, p. 545). It follows then that responsive managers would not hesitate to make public comment and disclose information with the intention of helping to gathering support in favour of the policies of their superiors.

These three patterns are utilised as a basis for the comparison and analysis of the managers' actual pattern of moral values. They are analytical rather than normative constructs and, in reality, the actual moral orientations of managers may combine characteristics of one or more of these patterns.

Research methodology

The empirical data was collected from local government council officers in the state of Penang, Malaysia. The Penang local council was established in the British tradition in 1913 (Norris 1980, p. 10). There are currently two local government units in the state of Penang: Majlis Perbandaran Pulau Pinang (MPPP)—the Penang Island Municipal Council and Majlis Perbandaran Seberang Perai—the Seberang Perai Municipal Council.

This research concentrated on senior MPPP council officers, heads and deputy heads of departments, who are directly appointed by the council. In a statutory sense, these senior officers have secure employment, as the council can only dismiss them from office, impose penalties on them, or have their ranks and/or salaries reduced with the 'prior approval of the state Authority' (Local Government Act 1976, ss. 16 and 17).

The survey questionnaires were hand-delivered to the 21 heads and deputy heads of all the departments of MPPP and a 100 per cent response rate was achieved. The majority of respondents were male and possessed postgraduate qualifications. They came from many different policy and functional areas of the council, including corporate affairs, human resource management, customer service, strategic planning, budget and finance and community services. The study is also well represented in terms of the levels of managerial position held by senior officers but is limited to those officers who deal directly with councillors. Hult suggests that the inclusion of such diversity strengthens the inferences that can be drawn from the observation of similar outcomes. If similar results are reported despite these differences, then the validity of the results is enhanced (cited in Felts and Schumann 1997, p. 364).

The authors are aware of inherent limitations in the study regarding the small number of respondents ($n = 21$), the reliability of self reporting, potential social desirability bias in the responses, respondents' interpretation of value terms and the general lack of reference to a specific problem or decision or moral dilemma (Frederick and Weber 1990, p. 128). As the respondents are from the one workplace, this may have the potential to limit the diversity of their views in some aspects.

Results

The responses in Table 11.2 indicate that the object of obedience of most of the MPPP officers is the law or legal framework (Q2.1 and Q2.2 = 76 per cent support for lawful orders). Interestingly enough, there was a significant proportion (Q2.3 = 52 per cent) that identified their loyalty as being directed towards the public interest.

Table 11.2: Object of obedience (n = 21)

	Agree %	Not sure %	Disagree %
Q2.1. I implement all orders of my councillors even if they are not lawful or are against public interest	9.52	14.28	76.19
Q2.2. I carry out only lawful orders of the councillors	76.19	9.52	14.28
Q2.3. I only implement orders which, in my view, are in the public interest.	52.38	33.33	14.28

The findings confirm that many officers are not necessarily responsive to the councillors' wishes. They are more likely to implement policies that are lawful, and those that promote the public interest. The findings indicate that MPPP officers combine the neutrality and the service ethic in this dimension.

In terms of the degree of partisanship (Table 11.3), it is clear that all of the respondents (Q3.2 = 100 per cent) adhere to rules and regulations while they implement policies. A significant majority (Q3.3 = 91 per cent), state that when they implement policies they also endeavour to make them as consistent as possible with the public interest.

A strong identification with the public interest is also demonstrated in that a significant majority (Q3.5 = 86 per cent) state that they take into consideration both the preferences of the councillors and the public interest. Furthermore, a sizeable majority (Q3.6 = 67 per cent) also identify their primary consideration as the promotion of public interest issues when they give advice to councillors. In contrast, none of the officers stated that they only consider the preferences of the councillors in their advice (Q3.4). However a small percentage (Q3.1 = 14 per cent) endeavour to promote the interests and preferences of the councillors while implementing policies. Therefore, we conclude that MPPP officers in their role as advisers to the councillors also combine the neutrality and service ethical patterns.

Unlike the above two dimensions, the MPPP officers were extremely categorical in their responses to the question on anonymity (Table 11.4). All of them were completely neutral rather than responsive or service-oriented.

Table 11.3: Degree of partisanship (n = 21)

	Agree %	Not sure %	Disagree %
Q3.1. I promote the interest of the councillors and the ruling party while implementing policies	14.28	28.57	57.14
Q3.2. I implement policies impartially and in accordance with rules and regulations	100.00	0.00	0.00
Q3.3. While implementing policies I make them as consistent as possible with the public interest	90.47	4.76	4.76
Q3.4. While advising I only consider the preferences of my superior and nothing else.	0.00	23.80	76.19
Q3.5. While advising I consider both the preferences of councillors and the public interest	85.71	4.76	9.52
Q3.6. While advising my primary consideration is to promote public interest	66.66	19.04	14.28

Table 11.4: Degree of anonymity (n = 20)

	Agree %	Not sure %	Disagree %
Q4.1. I make public comments and disclose information to promote public support for the councillors	5.00	20.00	75.00
Q4.2. I never make public comments or disclose information without proper authorisation	100.00	0.00	0.00
Q4.3. I comment publicly and disclose information even without authorisation on policies that are against public interest.	0.00	10.00	90.00

None of them would make public comment without proper authorisation (Q4.2 = 100 per cent). They stated that they do not make public comments, nor do they disclose information even if they feel that a certain policy they are implementing is against the public interest (Q4.3 = 0 per cent). This is a curious situation because a large majority of officers have indicated that they identify with the public interest when they advise and implement policies. However, they remain completely silent and act as anonymous implementers, even if they feel that a certain policy is against the public interest. There was virtually no support for the possibility that officers make public comment in any form (Q4.1 = 5 per cent).

In summary, there is a clear indication in the responses of MPPP officers that they exhibit aspects of both the neutrality and the service patterns in terms of their object of loyalty and degree of partisanship. In general, they tend to emphasise the public interest in advising councillors and in implementing council policies. The officers appear to believe that it is their duty to look after the interests of the community. However, in contrast to this, they would not leak confidential information or make public comments even if they believed the public interest to be threatened. Interestingly, a small minority of officers displayed a responsive orientation in terms of object of loyalty and degree of partisanship. These officers were loyal to the preferences and wishes of councillors and were ready to interpret information to the requirements of councillors.

Discussion

The data indicate that MPPP officers have a tendency towards both the neutrality and the service ethical patterns. However, having said this, we see that the neutrality ethic is the most dominant ethic and MPPP officers are not alone in the Malaysian civil service regarding this trait. One top level federal civil servant has stated:

> Malaysian civil servants closely adhere to the concept of civil service neutrality. The change in State Governments, either from an opposition party to the National Front or vice versa, as has happened in the states of Trengganu, Penang, Sabah, and Kelantan, did not in the least impair the efficiency and dedication of the Civil Service to the party in power (Omar 1980, p. 255).

The study has shown that MPPP managers are non-partisan in their advice to councillors and in their implementation of council policies. They do not tailor their advice to suit the political ideologies of councillors. The MPPP officers believe in complete anonymity and they do not want to have a public face. Federal level officers also seek to maintain similar values. Consider this statement from one of the chief secretaries to the Government of Malaysia:

We must continue to maintain and uphold our intellectual honesty in
the exercise of our responsibilities. Our honesty in providing advice
and opinions to the Government on matters of policy, programme and
projects, in an objective manner must be maintained at all times. The
practice of this intellectual honesty must also be clearly demonstrated
in the production of reports and research for the Government (Sarji
1993, p. 46).

Sarji adds that intellectual honesty in terms of honest advice to
politicians helps to establish and maintain a healthy relationship between
politicians and civil servants, which is essential for the stability of the
political system. As he says:

There are a number of very practical reasons why integrity is so
important as you move up the hierarchy. If you are going to trust a
person with increased responsibilities, you have to be able to count on
him. This presupposes your trust and belief in him. Honesty is one of
the most important facets of personal integrity because the
Government wants to be able to trust your advice and judgment (Sarji
1993, p. 47).

In this respect MPPP officers and federal level Malaysian officers
demonstrate remarkable similarity to their local government counterparts in
Victoria, Australia (Haidar and Pullin 1999), to their local government
counterparts in South Carolina, USA (Felts and Schumann 1997) and to
their federal-level counterparts in the USA (Maranto and Skelley 1992).

We can identify several reasons for the prevalence of the neutrality ethic
among this group of managers. The most important factor seems to be a
managerial belief in a division of labour between managers and councillors.
Most of the officers (76 per cent) believe that the councillors have the right
to decide on policies. While most of the officers believe that they have a
role in the policy process, they also believe that their role is confined to
providing advice and to implementing council policies. This deference to
politicians stems from the democratic values underpinning the Malaysian
civil service, as exemplified by the following statement:

What all these conditions mean is that civil servants should serve the
will of the people as articulated through the authority of the executive
and the legislature. Policy matters and decisions thereof should rest
ultimately with the elected representatives of the people, and all
decisions made by civil servants must be within the parameters of
defined mandates and delegated authority (Sarji 1993, p. 69).

This belief in neutrality is nothing new to Malaysian civil servants. In
fact, it seems to have been present among Malaysian civil servants since
independence. Milne, a long time observer of Malaysian political
development, noted in the 1960s that a 'Western'-type democracy prevailed
in Malaysia, where civil servants took a subordinate position to politicians
because the latter were elected (Milne 1967, p. 157). It is interesting to note

that the policy administration dichotomy, as it has been applied to American local government, holds that managers have 'no role in shaping policies' (Svara 1998, p. 51). However, our data indicate that managers do not see their role as dichotomous. They consider that they do have a role in policy formulation but it is confined to the provision of policy advice.

The enduring nature of the neutrality ethic also stems from the fact that it is a prudent principle for public managers' own self-interest. In many employment situations, the manager with a neutrality orientation will find it easier to maintain job continuity than a manager motivated by service or responsive values. The neutral manager can continue working for many political groups, while a responsive or a service-oriented manager may find it difficult to work for a political group that does not agree with his or her views and attitudes. Neutrality as an ideal is 'more understandable and functional for career executives than other ideals such as "public service" or "public interest"' (Maranto and Skelley 1992, p. 184). The neutral managers, by distancing themselves from ready identification with any particular group and from political intrigues, can 'preserve their reputation for indispensable competence and fairness' (Caiden 1996, p. 21).

Having identified and established some plausible motivations for the strong MPPP emphasis on neutrality in Malaysia, it is important to determine why a significant proportion of MPPP managers also believe in the service ethic in terms of the object of loyalty and the degree of partisanship. We believe this is related to their attitude towards councillors. Most of the officers (76 per cent) identify that they are more objective and able to determine the public interest clearly than councillors. Only 14 per cent of officers disagreed with the statement that 'Councillors often fail to see the public interest because they are too concerned with narrow interest'. Only 5 per cent of officers disagreed with the statement that 'Councillors interfere with implementation to serve their own interests rather than the legitimate interests of the public'. These findings indicate that officers adopt service ethic values because they believe councillors are guided by narrow self-interest.

However, MPPP officers are distinctly different in their emphasis on the service ethic when compared to local government officers in the USA and Australia. As such, the officers seem to be undertaking a role supposed to be performed by councillors (Report of the Royal Commission of Enquiry to Investigate into the Workings of Local Authorities in West Malaysia 1970, s. 793). These findings show similarity with those of federal and state level public servants in the USA, where public managers were found to give lower importance to monetary incentives and higher importance to work that is worthwhile to society (Posner and Schimdt 1996, p. 281).[3]

In this situation, officers see themselves as the legitimate representatives of community concerns and believe it is one of their duties to look after the public interest. The belief among officers that councillors do not represent community interests can also be related to the fact that MPPP councillors in particular and councillors in Peninsular Malaysia in general, are not democratically elected. State governments (Local Government Act 1976, s. 10) appoint them. Thus the relationship is not one between an 'elected' representative and an appointed official; rather, both have been appointed. It follows then that officers are less likely to believe that these 'councillors' are in touch with people and know where the public interest lies. Based on this, we can hypothesise that at the federal and state levels, where ministers are elected, civil servants are less likely to display a service orientation such as this.

Another significant finding of this study is that a small proportion of MPPP officers demonstrated responsive ethical values. In the responsive pattern, such respondents implement policies and advise councillors by keeping the latter's preferences and interests in mind. A possible explanation for this may be related to the nature of the MPPP officers' employment relationship, legally enunciated in the Local Government Act 1976 (s. 16). Under this Act, the appointed councillors have an important, and at times decisive, influence over MPPP officer selection, promotion and salary increases. Whilst committees make these human resource decisions, the councillors have significant representation on them. Although it was not tested in this study, some officers may see an advantage in being responsive to the wishes and preference of councillors.

Prior to the mid-1960s, when local government members were elected, the ruling or dominant party was the current opposition party. Since local elections were abolished in the mid-1960s (Local Government Act 1976, s. 10), the same coalition party that has been in continuous control of local government for over 30 years, has also been in continuous control at the Penang state government and the federal level. It should therefore be of no surprise that Penang council officers might evince a slight departure from a strict neutrality ethical pattern. More to the point, however, is the fact that there is so little responsiveness reported. This can be considered indicative of the enduring nature of public sector neutrality in Malaysia.

We can safely say, then, that the actual behaviour of civil servants in this research is a hybrid of all three models/patterns. This is consistent with Morgan and Kass (1993, pp. 179–180), who reported similar findings in an American study. Festinger's (1957) 'cognitive dissonance' theory argues that conflict in behaviour patterns of this nature needs to be managed. It is clear that the respondents manage this conflict by relying more on one model, rather than another, on different occasions or in different situations. As such, the models are sequentially invoked while remaining intact. Thus, a civil servant may veer towards the responsive model and 'give in' to the partisan interests of a politician(s) on an issue that is especially salient to the latter, but then shift to a different model when handling another issue. For example, our respondents, the officers, report frequent interference by councillors in policy implementation and their usual compliance in such instances. The majority of respondents disagreed with the statement: 'Councillors generally do not interfere with the implementation of policy by civil servants' while most agreed with the statement: 'Civil servants generally comply with the requests of councillors during policy implementation'. Such pragmatism can be rationalised as a necessary adaptation to a complex, recalcitrant world.

Another strategy civil servants adopt for managing such conflict is to drop or avoid using the conflicting requirements of two different models that cause them the most dissonance. For example, this would at least explain why both the neutrality and the service ethic are not completely embraced by our respondents. They rely on these models but do not relate to all of the dimensions in each. In each case, the dimension rejected appears to be the one that would be most inconsistent with a combined use of the two models. For example, in order to avoid head-on conflict with ruling politicians, the civil servants embrace all requirements of the service ethic except those concerning public comment and disclosure. They do not expose issues of concern publicly, leak information or blow the whistle on actions that they regard as offensive to the public interest. In some cases these actions would be illegal, and in all cases would be seen as a blatant challenge to their authority that is unlikely to be ignored by politicians in office.

Conclusion

In our introductory comments, we identified that governments play a key role in establishing and maintaining the social, economic and legal framework and environment in their countries. There is no doubt that through good political leadership and good government, Malaysia has experienced significant economic success, political stability and social harmony. A key factor in this socio-economic prosperity is the neutrality ethic, which has underpinned the Malaysian civil service since its inception.

However, there are indications in Penang that the neutrality ethic may be beginning to decline in its appeal and impact. There are clear indications that the values of the 'service' ethic and, to a lesser extent, the 'responsive' ethic, are beginning to be exhibited by senior officers. This decline in neutrality appears to be related to the 'appointment' rather than the 'election' of councillors and the power that these councillors can exert in the senior officer human resource decision-making process. Given that the neutrality ethic has served Malaysia so well in the past, any threat to its continuation might well be cause for concern.

The key question to be answered is whether or not the neutrality ethic should be maintained in this society. A clue to the answer may well rest in another society, in another culture. Malaysia has on many occasions looked towards Japan as a model for its development through its 'Look East' and 'Malaysia Incorporated' policies. In this society, collaborative relationships between government and business are seen as a key feature of national economic development and prosperity. This is supported by the views of Yanaga (1968) that resulted from an extensive study of business-government relationships in Japan during the 1950s to the 1980s. This was the period when Japan experienced a similar growth era to that which Malaysia is currently experiencing. Yanaga (1968, p. vii) stated that: 'Japan's resurgence as one of the great industrial and trading nations of the world,' was, more than anything else, the result 'of close cooperation and collaboration between organised business and the government'.

The experiences of Japan and other developed and developing countries suggest that, among other factors, a country needs to have a trusting relationship between business and government. In many respects the key government relationship is the one between politicians and civil servants.

In our view, the basis of this trust relationship in Malaysia emanates from the historical prevalence of the neutrality ethic among its civil servants. This is because the neutrality ethic assures a mutually accepted role division between politicians and civil servants, where politicians determine policy and civil servants advise on and implement those policies. Given this, every effort should be made to ensure that the neutrality ethic underpinning the Malaysian Civil Service value system is not undermined.

Endnotes

[1] The concept of Malaysia Incorporated was introduced in 1983. It called for cooperation between the public and the private sectors in sharing information and responsibility for the social, economic and administrative development of the country. The concept requires civil servants to trust the private sector. It changed government procedures to facilitate interaction between the public and the private sectors. The concept calls for business participation in the formulation of government policies (Taib and Mat 1992, p. 432).

[2] For a long list of claims on the loyalty of a public manager see Waldo (1985).

[3] Rainey cautioned that 'service motivation'—the duty to serve the public interest—may only be distantly-related to such concepts as motivation, 'reward preferences', 'levels of organisational involvement' or 'organisational commitment', job involvement, professionalism, altruism, or pro-social behaviour. He argued that these concepts might even clash with the concept of public service motivation (1982, pp. 298–99).

References

Aberbach, J. D. and B. A. Rockman (1994), 'Civil servants and policy makers: Neutral or responsive competence', *Governance*, 7 (4), 461–469.

Armstrong, R. (1989), 'The duties and responsibilities of civil servants in relation to ministers', in G. Marshall (ed.), *Ministerial Responsibility*, Oxford, UK: Oxford University Press, 140–153.

Aucion, P. (1997), 'A profession of public administration: A commentary on a strong foundation', *Canadian Public Administration*, 40 (1), 23–39.

Caiden, G. E. (1996), 'The concept of neutrality', in H. K. Asmerom and E. P. Reis (eds), *Democratisation and Bureaucratic Neutrality*, London: Macmillan, pp. 20–44.

Crouch, H. (1993), 'Malaysia: Neither authoritarian nor democratic', in K. Hewison, R. Robinson and G. Rodan (eds), *Southeast Asia in the 1990s: Authoritarianism, democracy and capitalism*, St Leonards: Allen and Unwin, pp.135–157.

De Maria, W. (1995), 'Quarantining dissent: The Queensland public sector ethics movement', *Australian Journal of Public Administration*, 54 (4), 442–454.

Durkheim, E. (1953), *Sociology and Philosophy*, London: Cohen and West.

Felts A. and A. Schumann (1997), 'Local government administrators: A balance wheel breakdown', *American Review of Public Administration*, 27 (4), 362–376.

Festinger, L. A. (1957), *Theory of Cognitive Dissonance*, California: Stanford University Press.

Frederick, W. C. and J. Weber, (1990), 'The values of corporate managers and their critics: An empirical description and normative implications', in W. C. Frederick and L. E. Preston (eds), *Business Ethics: Research Issues and Empirical Studies*, London: JAI, pp. 123–144.

Gupta, J. L. and M. Sulaiman (1996), 'Ethical orientations of Malaysian managers', *Journal of Business Ethics*, 15 (7), 735–748.

Haidar, A. and L Pullin (1999), 'Managing for results but with neutrality: A study of moral values of Gippsland local government managers', paper presented to the Sixth National Conference of the Australian Association for Professional and Applied Ethics hosted by the Centre for Professional and Applied Ethics, Charles Sturt University, Old Parliament House, Canberra, 1–3 October.

Heclo, H. (1975), 'Omb and the presidency—the problem of neutral competence', *Public Interest*, 38, 80–98.

IMM (Institute of Municipal Management) (1995), *Code of Ethics*, December.

Jackson, M. (1987), 'The eye of doubt: Neutrality, responsibility and morality', *Australian Journal of Public Administration*, 46 (3), 280–292.

Jackson, M. (1988), 'The public interest, public service and democracy', *Australian Journal of Public Administration*, 47 (3), 241–251.

Karim, M. R. A. (1992), 'Administrative reform and bureaucratic modernisation in the Malaysian public sector', in *The Changing Role of Government: Administrative Structures and Reforms, Proceedings of a Commonwealth Roundtable held in Sydney Australia*, 24–28 February, London: Commonwealth Secretariat, pp. 25–56.

Local Government Act 1976 (Laws of Malaysia, Act 171).

Malaysia (1970), *Report of the Royal Commission of Enquiry to Investigate into the Workings of Local Authorities in West Malaysia* (Senator Dato' Athy Nahappan, Chairman), Kuala Lumpur: Di-chetak Di-Jabatan Chetak Kerajan Oleh Thor Beng Chong, A. M. N. Penchetak Kerajaan.

Maranto, R. and B. D. Skelley (1992), 'Neutrality: An enduring principle of the Federal Service', *American Review of Public Administration*, 22 (3), 173–187.

Means, G. P. (1991), *Malaysian Politics: The Second Generation*, Singapore: Oxford University Press.

Milne, R. S. (1967), *Government and Politics in Malaysia*, Boston: Houghton Mifflin.

Morgan, D. F. and H. D. Kass (1993), 'The American odyssey of the career public service: The ethical crisis of role reversal', in H. G. Frederickson (ed.), *Ethics and Public Administration*, New York: M. E. Sharpe, 177–190.

Norris, M. W. (1980), *Local Government in Peninsular Malaysia*, England: Gower.

Omar, E. B. (1980), 'The Civil Service systems in Malaysia', in A. Raksasataya and H. Siedentopf (eds), *Asian Civil Services: Developments and Trends*, Kuala Lumpur: Asian and Pacific Development Administration Centre, pp. 249–299.

Pojman, L. P. (ed.) (1989), *Ethical Theory: Classical and Contemporary Readings*, California: Wodsworth.

Posner, B. Z. and W. H. Schmidt (1996), 'The values of business and federal government executives: More different than alike', *Public Personnel Management*, 25 (3), 277–289.

Puthucheary, M. (1978), *The Politics of Administration: The Malaysian Experience*, Kuala Lumpur: Oxford University Press.

Quinlan, M. (1993), 'Ethics in the Public Service', *Governance*, 6 (4), 538–544.

Rainey, H. G. (1982), 'Reward preferences among public and private managers: In search of the service ethic', *American Review of Public Administration*, 16 (4), 288–302.

Rourke, F. E. (1992), 'Responsiveness and neutral competence in American bureaucracy', *Public Administration Review*, 52 (6), 539–546.

Sarji, A. H. A. (1993), *The Changing Civil Service: Malaysia's Competitive Edge*, Malaysia: Pelanduk Publications.

Svara, J. H. (1998), 'The politics–administration dichotomy model as aberration', *Public Administration Review*, 58 (1), 51–58.

Taib, M. B. and J. Mat (1992), 'Administrative reforms in Malaysia: Toward enhancing public service performance', *Governance*, 5 (4), 423–437.

Thompson, D. F. (1985), 'The possibility of administrative ethics', *Public Administration Review*, 45 (5), 555–561.

Uhr, J. (1988), 'Ethics and public service', *Australian Journal of Public Administration*, 47 (2), 109–118.

Waldo, D. (1985), *The Enterprise of Public Administration*, California: Chandler.

Westwood, R. I. and J. E. Everett (1995), 'Comparative managerial values: Malaysia and the West', *Journal of Asia–Pacific Business*, 1 (3), 3–37.

Williams, C. (1985), 'The concept of bureaucratic neutrality', *Australian Journal of Public Administration*, 44 (1), 46–58.

Wright, M. (1977), 'Ministers and civil servants: Relations and responsibilities', *Parliamentary Affairs*, 30 (3), 293–313.

Yanaga, C. (1968), *Big Business and Japanese Politics*, New Haven: Yale University Press.

Zabid, A. R. M. and S. K. Alsagoff (1993), 'Perceived ethical values of Malaysian managers', *Journal of Business Ethics*, 12 (4), 331–337.

12

Globalisation and labour in Malaysia

P. Ramasamy

Introduction

This chapter takes the approach that economic growth in Malaysia over the last two decades has not addressed important social concerns of the working class. More broadly, economic growth subsumed under the term of globalisation has negatively affected the position of women, migrant labour, plantation labour and those in the manufacturing sector. The close accommodation between the interests of the state and global capital is mainly responsible for this state of affairs. Given the absence of legal and other institutional mechanisms, labour has challenged the manner of economic development by resorting to alternative forms of struggle.

Globalisation

There are multiple meanings attached to the concept of globalisation. In a very broad sense, it refers to the cross-national flow of goods, investment, production and technology. For the advocates of the globalisation thesis, it has created a new world order, with new institutions and new configurations of power that have supplanted or replaced the previous structures of international political economy. Apart from the conventional approach to globalisation, present debates about this concept centre on whether globalisation represents a new epoch and whether it can be relied on to bring about progress and prosperity. For the sake of simplicity and clarity, one can identify two broad approaches to globalisation. One approach holds that despite its internal differences globalisation is something new and has the potential to bring economic and social benefits to humanity. The other approach, Marxist in orientation, thinks that globalisation represents a particular phase in the development of global capitalism and does not contribute in any meaningful sense to the progress of human beings (Held et al. 1999; Falk 1999; Wood et al. 1998; Amin 1997).

It is argued in this chapter that globalisation is not a novel phenomenon but merely represents a particular phase in the development of late capitalism. While there are fundamental continuities, the aggressiveness associated with late capitalism has been conditioned by a variety of political, ideological and social factors. More specifically, the articulation of globalisation in the global political economy has been made possible by the collapse of the socialist alternative to capitalism. At the empirical level, the collapse of socialism in the Soviet Union and Eastern Europe and the attempts made by the existing socialist or communist countries to incorporate capitalist elements for modernisation have undermined the search for a new alternative.

Labour studies

The many works on labour in Malaysia can be categorised into two principal groups based on their ideological, political or normative position. The first category consists of historical and contemporary works that accept the inevitably of the capitalist formula. Variations and differences notwithstanding, it is this inevitability that has predisposed this category to conceptualise, theorise and discuss labour issues and problems within the framework of capitalism. These works invariably call upon the state or employers or both to embark on more humane labour policies, or alternatively urge labour unions to take a more vigorous role in defending existing labour rights. Whatever differences these works have with the existing policy of the state or capital cannot be seen from the perspective of conflict in a fundamental sense. The other category consists of works both theoretical and empirical that examine and analyse labour from the perspective of class exploitation in the context of capitalist imperialism. For this category of works, capitalist solutions are really no solution, and complete liberation and emancipation of labour is only possible with the adoption of a socialist alternative. Such a perspective presupposes a vigorous critique of the nature of the capitalist system, the nature of resistance and how national and international alliances can be built to uproot the system.

Labour legislation and policy

There is a popular predilection to explain the stance of the state towards labour by reference to the industrialisation strategy pursued. Kuruvilla and Arudsothy (1993), for instance, argue that when the state pursued the policy of ISI (import substitution industrialisation) it had a tendency to pursue a more liberal or plural policy towards labour. However, its policy changed to one of outright control and domination when the country switched to EOI (export orientated industrialisation) in the late 1970s and onwards. But contrary to this perspective, the state's paternalism to labour was more a reflection of a particular historical condition within the global capitalist system than a function of following a particular development strategy. Such an argument is basically flawed in the sense that severe cases of labour repression go unnoticed. Such a model pays no attention to labour repression undertaken by the colonial and post-colonial state in Malaysia (Ramasamy 1994; Stenson 1980).

Labour legislation was first enacted during the colonial period to regulate the employment of Indian and Chinese labour. It was only after the Second World War that the authorities passed labour laws in the form of the Trade Union Act to provide for registration and settling of labour disputes. This law ensured only unions approved by the government were allowed to register, while Communist Party-affiliated unions were disallowed. During the period of Emergency, this act was utilised to weaken the left-wing unions organised under the umbrella of the Pan Malaya Federation of Unions. After political independence in 1957 labour legislation took the form of the Trade Union Act of 1959 (TUA) and the Industrial Relations Act of 1967 (IRA). The TUA provided registration for unions and at the same time allowed the state to have effective control over the labour movement, including a number of provisions that gave near absolute power to the Minister of Labour. The IRA formalised collective bargaining procedures and provided the state with ultimate authority in giving effect to compulsory arbitration. Over the years these instruments have been amended several times to ensure labour organised within the parameters set by the state (Ayadurai 1993; Arudsothy and Littler 1993).

The utilisation of labour and other legislations to discipline and manage labour relations represented the coercive option of the state, and is not a new phenomenon in association with globalisation and export-orientated industrialisation. Rather, globalisation–labour–repression has become more systematic and severe with existing labour law being strengthened to tighten control over the labour force. With the turn to the EOI strategy in the early 1980s this strengthening of labour law was supplemented by 'soft' programmes that drew on the Look East Policy with the state seeking to popularise Japanese management methods and with labour being urged to prioritise company loyalty, productivity and sound management–labour relations. More significantly, labour was urged to move away from its preoccupation with national unions to in-house or company unions. Additionally, the introduction of the Malaysian Incorporated Policy served to reinforce the notion that the interests of labour and capital are not antithetical and that the two should cooperate and work towards the benefit of the nation. And not least, the establishment of a Code of Conduct for Industrial Harmony and the National Labour Advisory Council allowed the state to impel labour along a 'responsible' path.

Globalisation then has propelled the state to take a more direct interest in development issues, employment generation, and the creation of an investment more attractive to foreign investors. This has had a number of implications for the labour movement.

Plantation labour

It is estimated there are about 50,000–60,000 plantation workers in the country, with the majority of these individuals being migrants from countries like Indonesia, Bangladesh and Thailand. The bulk of these workers labour in the oil palm industry through a third party contract system, and the Indian labour force that formerly worked on rubber plantations has moved to urban areas in search of better prospects and to avoid the low wages, isolation and lack of social benefits that characterise the plantation industry (Ramasamy 2000, p. 7). In comparison with the other sectors, the wage structure of the plantation economy is depressed, with mean monthly income having been exaggerated by the government. This is a situation that has tended to remain relatively constant, with wages for plantation workers registering only a 25 per cent increase 1974–1989, whereas the increase registered for electronic workers was around 225 per cent, while workers such as drivers, conductors and attendants enjoyed wage increases of over 100 per cent. All talk of introducing a monthly wage system is still confined to the realm of propaganda, and discussion of the need to revive the house ownership scheme introduced in the mid-1970s has been basically abandoned (Ramasamy 1994; Selvakumaran 1994; Ramasamy and Anantha Raman 1999; Selvakumaran and Bala 1995).

The state's thinking about the plantation system and plantation labour is based on the belief that it is a 'twilight' industry, which will make way for industrialisation. It is also held that as the majority of plantation workers are foreigners there is no reason to undertake measures to improve their economic and social well-being, and this the more so as plantations provide a convenient place for housing cheap foreign labour that might be needed in the manufacturing sector .

Migrant and foreign labour

It is estimated that there are 1.5–2 million foreign migrant workers in Malaysia. As noted by Yoshimura (2000), data on international migration flows into Malaysia lack a sound statistical base, especially on undocumented foreign workers. Migrant inflow is from places like Sumatra, Kalimantan, Philippines, Southern Thailand and Bangladesh. Indonesians mainly work in the plantation sector (34 per cent), the construction sector (40 per cent) and domestic help (25 per cent). Bengalis are mainly found in manufacturing sector (59 per cent), the construction sector (25 per cent) and the plantation sector (14 per cent). Filipino migrant workers in Peninsular Malaysia are mainly domestic helpers (87 per cent) (Yoshimura 2000, p. 6).

Foreign labour constitutes the most exploited segment of the labour force, often suffering terrible working and living conditions. Maximum overtime hours are frequently exceeded and there are cases where workers have had to work continuously for more than 54 hours. Since the majority of foreign workers are illegal immigrants, they are at a terrible disadvantage and are often subjected to police surveillance and detentions. There have been cases where identification papers of foreign workers have been seized and destroyed to deny their legality. In 1995 50 foreign workers were reported to have died in the detention camps. While the government has sought to legalise the status of foreign workers to safeguard their rights, the living and working conditions of migrants leaves much to be desired and fear of unemployment and hunger militates against them going back to their countries of origins (ICFTU Report 1997).

Contrary to some conventional analysis, foreign labour in Malaysia cannot be assumed to be temporary. This perspective is problematic because it suggests foreign labour will only stay in the country for a short term, an image that provides unjustified comfort to unions and local workers. It also absolves the state and capital from taking responsibility for the economic and social well-being of foreign labour, allows for extreme and cruel manipulation of foreign labour in the service of capital, and induces extreme treatment from the authorities. In reality, a sizeable number of foreign workers in Malaysia have become either permanent residents or citizens. While it is true there is a noticeable inflow and outflow of foreign labour, this movement does not contradict the fact that foreign labour is very integral to the functioning of the economy. Arrests and deportations of foreign labour seem more related to the public relations exercises of the state than anything else. The very fact that the country's economy is predicated to grow on the basis of its cheap labour is based on the assumption foreign labour—both legal and illegal—will be a key aspect of the Malaysian labour market for some time to come.

Labour in manufacturing

In comparison with other sectors, manufacturing labour has been directly affected by globalisation. Since the 1980s it has become common to hear of manufacturing employers preventing workers from forming unions by threatening to move operations, and transferring and firing active unionists. Moreover, changes to production methods have lessened employment security, while down-sizing, use of casual and foreign labour, and the extension of probationary periods have also contributed to this problem (Kuruvilla and Arudsothy 1993). One issue faced by manufacturing workers employed in foreign firms is the lack of labour representation. In the 1970s the Electrical Workers' Union attempted to organise electronic workers in the free trade zones, but this was disallowed by the Registrar of Trade Unions on the grounds that electrical and electronic industries were not similar within the meaning of the Trade Union Act. The general ban on unions in the electronics sector was only partially lifted in 1988, when the Malaysian government, under pressure from the ILO and the America Labour Movement, allowed the formation of in-house unions. According to Grace (1990), the government insisted on company unionism because American multinationals threatened to move their production operations elsewhere if the government allowed national unions. (Rajasegaran 1999; Grace 1990; Kuruvilla and Arudsothy 1993). In 1992 a statement by the Minister of Labour indicated that these companies had put a great deal of pressure on the government and in response the MTUC called on the state not to shelter the MNCs: 'MTUC is of the view that the present dispute arose as a result of Government's desire to please the Multinational Corporations who are anti-Union' (Rajasegaran 1999). Lacking effective labour representation, workers in the electronics industry are only paid one-third of the normal salary paid to workers in Singapore, and the non-union atmosphere has not limited job security with the manufacturing sector, particularly in the state of Penang, recording the highest number of retrenchments. Out of the total number (January 1999–January 2000) of 3,921 workers, 2,970 (75.7 per cent) came from Penang. Of those retrenched, 78.3 per cent came from the manufacturing sector. In 1998 a total of 83,865 workers were retrenched and in 1997 the figure was 18,863 (the number reported in 1997 might be underreported since mandatory reporting took effect only in February 1998) (Ministry of Human Resources 1999–2000).

While there is some attempt to assist workers to acquire skills, the nature of the production system militates against the acquirement of skills that can enhance the quality of work. Such transformation is needed not only to induce higher wages for workers but also to enable Malaysian manufacturing to compete with that in other nations that have moved up in the hierarchy of production. Malaysia, however, still seems to be located at the lowest point of this hierarchy. While political stability and administrative efficiency might provide Malaysia with some lead over other low-cost producers, the country needs to embark on a scheme that will influence companies to upgrade the skills of their workforce. Such measures, if systematically introduced, might attract high-wage production to Malaysia and push the country to a higher level in the production hierarchy.

Women workers

Women make up over 38 per cent of the workforce of eight million (Ariffin 2000, p. 2). The vast majority of women workers are employed in low-skilled, repetitive jobs that have little prospect for upward mobility. Although Malaysia has signed the ILO conventions on discrimination, it has not signed those relating to women, foreign labour and children. The continued practices of locating women in the lowest-paying jobs and denying them the right to join trade unions have prevented them from benefiting from overall socio-economic progress.

For instance, in the electronics industry, women constitute 80 per cent of the labour force, with most being in their early 20s and unmarried. Given the inequality prevailing in the country and the fact that women have a heavier share of household duties, employers take on women workers in the expectation that they will only remain for about three years. Moreover, the government's lack of initiative in providing for more systematic child care facilities is a factor inhibiting women from assuming a bigger role in the labour market (Standing 1993).

Women are increasingly moving into the service sector, but as in other sectors of employment their participation is not equal to that of men. In the early 1990s it was found that 50 per cent of women took up jobs like maids, housekeepers, laundresses, cooks and waitresses. This is not to deny that minimal improvements were also registered in the early 1990s as result of women's entry into wholesale, retail, finance, property and business accounting (Ariffin 2000, p. 5). It seems obvious that education, skills and technical training are lacking among women.

Child labour

The practice of child labour is not a major problem in Malaysia. However, recent studies suggest it remains an issue in rural and small-sector industries. The nature of child labour in certain areas makes it difficult for the existing legislation to have any major impact. A recent study undertaken by the ICFTU puts the number of child labourers at about 75,000, located in small, family-orientated businesses, plantations and in some public entertainment outlets, though the MTUC believes the use of child labour is on the decrease. In 1994, a Japanese firm was fined for the violation of the Children and Young Persons Act (ICFTU Report 1997).

Labour resistance

It must be said that in the Malaysian context legal strikes are practically non-existent. Amendments to the TUA and IR have virtually made it impossible for unions to engage in what are termed as 'legal' strikes. Because of this situation, disputes take the form of spontaneous strikes or demonstrations. These collective forms of action very often are executed primarily to address immediate issues, and once these are resolved, or workers' resistance defeated, the action ceases. At the same time, long-outstanding issues and grievances might be added to the complaints of workers. It has been found that trade unions or the central leadership might not support these actions.

Workers' resistance to capital is ineffective for a variety of reasons. First, the alliance of state and global capital in transforming Malaysia into an industrialised country by virtue of the exploitation of the country's low-cost labour is a paramount factor that works against labour resistance and solidarity. Second, related to the first, is a philosophy shared by state elites with backing from international capital that labour discipline is essential for the country's growth and prosperity. Since labour discipline cannot be taken for granted, the state has been instrumental in subduing and disciplining labour. Third, in Malaysia, the presence of a number of racial and religious groups with their respective exclusive ideologies and politics has served as a major deterrent to the emergence of multi-ethnic, working-class solidarity. Fourth, the leadership of the Malaysian trade union movement is weak and divided (Ramasamy 1987). Fifth, the collapse of socialism and communism identified with certain countries has dimmed the hopes of a socialist alternative for the working class; in this context of sterility and the absence of major debates, improvements of working class conditions is sought within the neo-liberal formula.

Conclusion

The nature of the accommodation between global capital and the state in Malaysia has ensured the compliance of labour. As a consequence, the welfare and interests of labour have been neglected. The absence of effective trade union representation has further denied workers an opportunity to articulate their workers' grievances. However, they cannot be said to be totally subservient. There are signs that workers are resisting with wild-cat strikes and other forms of non-compliance, revealing workers' frustration with the present state of affairs. Economic development and growth are essential for the well-being of Malaysian workers, but where the benefits appear skewed to employers, workers are not happy. More importantly, the Malaysian workers' situation illustrates a fundamental point—economic growth without re-distribution does not serve the overall development process. While Malaysia has paid much attention to economic growth in the last two decades, it is time now to take stock of the situation to ascertain how gaps between classes can be reduced.

References

Amin, S. (1997), *Capitalism in the Age of Globalisation*, London: Zed Books.

Ariffin, R. (2000), 'Globalization and its impact on women workers in Malaysia', paper presented at a recent Seminar on Globalization and Labour in Malaysia, UKM, Bangi, September.

Arudsothy, P. and C. Littler (1993), 'State regulation and union fragmentation in Malaysia', in Stephen Frankel (ed.), *Organised Labour in the Asia–Pacific Region: A Comparative Study of Trade Unionism in Nine Countries*, Ithaca: ILR Press.

Ayadurai, D. (1993), 'Malaysia', in Stephen Deery and Richard Mitchell (eds), *Labour Law and Industrial Relations in Asia*, Melbourne: Longman Chesire.

Falk, R. (1999), *Predatory Globalisation: A Critique*, Cambridge: Polity Press.

Grace, A. (1990), *Short-Circuiting Labour in Malaysia*, Kuala Lumpur: Insan.

Held, D. et al. (1999), *Global Transformations: Politics, Economics and Culture*, Stanford: Stanford University Press.

ICFTU (1997), 'Internationally recognised core labour standards in Malaysia', Report for the WTO General Council Review of Trade Policies of Malaysia, Geneva.

Kuruvilla, S. and P. Arudsothy (1993), 'Economic development strategy: Government labour policy and firm industrial relations practices in Malaysia', paper presented at the International Conference on Industrial in East Asia and Africa Sydney, September 1992.

Ministry of Human Resources, Labour Market Report (January 1999–January 2000).

Petras, J. (1999), 'Globalisation: A Critical Analysis', *Journal of Contemporary Asia*, 29 (1), 3–37.

Rajasegaran, G. (1999), *Electronics Workers: Their 25 Years of Struggle to Establish an Industrial Union*, MTUC 50th Anniversary publication.

Ramasamy, P. (1987), 'Trade union leadership in Malaysia', *Solidarity*, 114, September–October.

Ramasamy, P. (1994), *Plantation Labour, Unions, Capital, and the State in Peninsular Malaysia*, Kuala Lumpur: Oxford University Press.

Ramasamy, P. (2000), 'Globalisation and plantation labour in Malaysia', paper presented at a Seminar on Globalisation and Labour in Malaysia, UKM, Bangi, September.

Ramasamy, P. and G. Anantha Raman (1999), *Estate House Ownership Scheme: A Case-Study of Four Estates in the State of Selangor*, unpublished manuscript.

Selvakumaran, R. (1994), *Indian Plantation Labour in Malaysia*, Kuala Lumpur: Abdul Majeed and Co.

Selvakumara, R. and S. Bala (1995), 'Plight of plantation workers in Malaysia: Defeated by definitions', *Asian Survey*, 35, 394–407.

Standing, G. (1993), 'Labour flexibility in the Malaysian manufacturing sector', in K. S. Jomo (ed.), *Industrialising Malaysia: Policy, Performance, Prospects*, London: Routledge, pp. 40–46.

Stenson, M. (1980), *Class, Race and Colonialism in West Malaysia*, Brisbane: University of Queensland Press.

Wood, E. M. et al. (1998), *Rising from the Ashes: Labour in the Age of 'Global' Capitalism*, New York: Monthly Review Press.

Yoshimura, M. (2000), 'Economic development and foreign workers in Malaysia— migrant workers and labour structure in globalisation', paper presented at the seminar on Globalisation and Labour in Malaysia, UKM, Bangi, September.

13

Islamic identity and work in Malaysia: Islamic work ethics in a Japanese joint venture in Malaysia

Wendy A. Smith, Chris Nyland and Adlina Ahmad

Introduction

A key political and development challenge for Malaysia has been to manage its ethnic diversity. Malaysian society is made up, in approximate proportions, of indigenous Malays (60 per cent), Malaysian Chinese (30 per cent) and Malaysian Indians and others (10 per cent). These groups have cultures and lifestyles that are highly distinct and have traditionally been distinguished by different occupational specialisations and residential patterns: the Chinese being associated with urban commercial activities, the Malays with rural peasant occupations and the Indians with rural plantation labour. After an incident of racial unrest on 13 May 1969, the Malaysian government introduced the New Economic Policy (NEP) which, by combining rural development and an export oriented industrialisation programme, aimed to eradicate poverty, to overcome the identification of ethnic groups with certain sectors of the economy and thereby to reduce racial tension. The NEP set out to achieve these goals by ensuring political stability, providing a disciplined and well-educated labour force to attract foreign investment, providing the rural and urban poor with new opportunities for land ownership and industrial wage labour, and introducing affirmative action policies designed to encourage Malays (or *bumiputera)* to become entrepreneurs and professionals. Under these latter schemes Malay ethnic identity became a gateway to opportunity, and as Malays in Malaysia are Muslims, a major result of the NEP has been the strengthening of the Muslim component of Malay identity and the politicisation of their Muslim identity overall.

A major challenge that Malaysia has had to confront in its drive to sustain economic growth and remain internationally competitive has been to reconcile the ethnic and religious implications of the NEP. This has necessitated efforts by policy makers and the private sector to handle the Islamic identity of employees in the cross-cultural management context resulting from the NEP's heavy reliance on DFI. This meant that the DFI-based rapid economic growth process had to be engineered to preserve guarantees that Muslim employees would be able to make their religious observances, while at the same time ensuring that intolerance for the values of non-Muslim Malaysians and foreign managers did not arise. Given the significance of foreign investment in the NEP strategy, it was also necessary to promote an investment climate where foreign managers were sensitive to the need to reconcile the considerable demands of daily Islamic practice on individual Muslims, as discussed below, with the corporate needs of their organisations.

This chapter looks at a Muslim in a foreign venture. Islamic values are not antithetical to economic development, but Islam does demand that all believers pray five times a day, heed the month of fasting and undertake the pilgrimage to Mecca. Widespread piety in the observance of these practices is a characteristic of Muslims in Malaysia and many Malay employees give precedence to the performance of their religious obligations over other aspects of their daily lives. It is possible that non-Muslim foreign managers may see these requirements as inhibiting job performance. Indeed, this became manifest in 1999 when two senior expatriate managers of a large multinational company were threatened with deportation after allegations that they extended working hours on the basis that Muslims were taking time off work to attend Friday prayers, cut pay by 10 per cent because Muslim workers stopped work to pray, and changed holiday schedules for publicly gazetted religious festivals.[1] While it is uncommon for foreign managers to take such drastic action, the attitudes behind their action are more widespread. Therefore a primary aim of this chapter is to redress misunderstandings about Malay Muslim managers' and workers' attitudes to work.

Indeed, as little has been published on the cross-cultural management of Islamic labour, this chapter also presents primary data and an analysis of how the Islamic work ethic is accommodated when Muslim managers and workers, and non-Muslim managers participate in a Malaysian–Japanese venture whose management style has been transferred from the parent company. Focussing on a Japanese firm is particularly appropriate as Japanese investment has been the most significant contributor of DFI through the NEP period, in terms of both the volume of capital and technology transferred. Other important factors are the popularisation of the Japanese management model in Malaysia's post-1981 Look East Policy era (Smith 2000) and Japan's cultural impact on Malaysian society in the spheres of consumerism and popular culture (Smith 1999). The chapter begins by outlining the nature of the Islamic work ethic and then examines the experience of Islamic employees within the Japanese transplant.

Religion, economy, and labour

Islamic doctrine is based on the *Qur'an*,[2] the word of God revealed to the Prophet, on the *Sunna*, that is, the body of tradition or precedent, and on the *Shari'a* or divine law. Below, we summarise the key points of the doctrine that relate to issues of work and economic activity.

It is held that economic activity cannot be conceptualised as separate from the realm of religion, and Islamic scholars argue that Islam therefore differs from both capitalism and socialism. Thus Bannerman observes:

> 'Islamic economists' believe that though capitalism does provide scope for individual effort, for the fulfilment of ambitions and for economic progress, it breeds selfishness, greed and corrupt practices because of the absence of moral and ethical principle. Socialism is similarly flawed: it subordinates the individual's freedom of economic action to rigid state control, kills the incentive to work harder by removing the incentive of greater personal gain, is dehumanising, and has also led to corruption and nepotism (1988, p. 106).

Naqvi (1994) maintains that the psychological make-up of Muslims includes both an 'individual man' and a 'collective man', which means peoples' individuality highlights their freedom while their collectivity renders them responsible to society. This duality requires that the pursuit of economic self-aggrandisement must be tempered by 'co-operation and moderation in all human pursuits, whether profits or consumption, whether economic or non-economic', in short, that the individual must 'be more than a mere homo-economicus' (Bannerman 1988, p. 106).

Most Islamic literature on work focusses on the place of labour, employment relations and distribution. Egami (1990, p. 72) begins his analysis by describing how the idea of action in Islamic thought is both closely related to human autonomy and 'organically and relatively intertwined with other elements in the community,' there being no distinction between private and social action. Under these conditions 'both family life and economic life are involved in the sphere of religion' and 'labour is just a part of the totality which harmoniously works with other types of actions' (Egami 1990, p. 66).

Likewise, Mehdi Bazargan (1980) argues that work is both a means spiritual growth and an intrinsic means of securing prosperity in the Hereafter. Consequently, Muslims have an obligation to work. As Khalil-ur-Rehman observes, in 'an Islamic society there is no place for an individual who is not prepared to work and does not discharge his economic obligations, or considers various professions which require labour as below his dignity' (Khalil-ur-Rehman 1995, p. 8; Anjum 1995, p. 231). Reminiscent of Marx, Egami (1990) notes that the emphasis capitalism places on the material results of work alienates from the products of production and separates the individual from society. By contrast, in an Islamic world, 'human beings are hardly alienated by labour' (Egami 1990, p. 94) being 'connected to others by an organic and intimate sense of solidarity' (Egami 1990, p. 96). A number of scholars, though, have warned that Western individualism can undermine the intrinsic value Islamic societies place on work (Bazargan 1980; Khalil-ur-Rehmar 1995). Bani-Sadr (1980, p. 51), for example, concludes that the secularisation of Iran under the Shah, 'and the inclination towards the 'great civilised West', resulted in Iranians devoting excessive time to material pleasures that led to the dominance of self-centredness and a rejection of 'communal existence and society' and a just system of distribution (Bani-Sadr 1980, p. 62).

Anjum (1995) holds that we can identify within the *Qur'an* and the *Sunna* an 'Islamic distributional scheme' that seeks to achieve justice and equality of opportunity. He adds that the *Qur'an* accepts that some wage inequality is required for the efficient functioning of society (Anjum 1995, p. 227), a view reinforced by others. Thus Khalil-ur-Rehman (1995, p. 100) suggests that while workers should receive 'equal pay for equal work', without some inequality of income it would be impossible to 'establish the standard of workmanship, skill and quality of work'. Just as inequality is acceptable between workers, it is also acceptable between employer and employee, although the relationship between employer and employee must be based on 'fraternal and mutual co-operation' (Ahmad 1987, p. 305) or a 'brotherhood between worker and master' (Khalil-ur-Rehman 1995, p. 158). Workers are entitled to a share of profits (Ahmad 1987; Faruqi and Banna 1984; Khalil-ur-Rehman 1995) and because trade unions work towards equality and justice, Islam permits their formation. However, while workers are 'permitted to organise unions for securing their just dues' and may engage in strikes to achieve this goal, collective bargaining is incompatible with Islamic thought if it seeks to gain for the worker or employer an inappropriate reward for their contribution according to community standards (Ahmad 1987, p. 309; Khalil-ur-Rehman 1995; Faruqi and Banna 1984). Moreover, in return for the right to strike, employees must heed the instructions of the employer and must not deliberately waste time (Khalil-ur-Rehman 1995, pp. 162–164). In summary, 'Islam has fixed the principle that if a worker takes the responsibility for doing a job, he should work in a way as if it was his own work. If he does not perform the work honestly and to the best of his ability, he will be answerable on the Day of Judgement' (Khalil-ur-Rehman, p. 165).

Obligations also extend to managers. Safi (1995) and Beekun and Badawi (1998) have shown that Islamic managers are expected to provide direction, mobilisation—through the acknowledgement and empowerment of their subordinates—and integration, with organisational unity being maintained through dialogue between leaders and subordinates.

The contribution of these latter scholars is part of the small body of empirical literature on the impact of Islamic thought on employment practices. This research has shown that Islamic workers have a deep sense of commitment to work and a desire to improve community and social welfare, want to be creative and cooperative, and wish to be loyal to their employer and organisation (Ali 1988, 1992; Aba-Saad 1998). On the other side of the equation, Muna (1980) found two-thirds of the Arab executives he surveyed believe employee loyalty is more important than efficiency. And Abu-Saad concluded from his research that in practice within the Islamic workplace 'values about individual effort and obligations are not separated from values about the importance of one's contribution to community and society, and the obligations of the organisation to its employees' (Abu-Saad 1998, p. 379). Likewise, Naim (1988), in his study of Malaysian restaurants, concluded that the Islamic work ethic underpinned the employment relationship, it being accepted that employer–employee relations are based on an equitable and mutually-benefiting relationship between owners and employers, a strong sense of belonging to the organisation and a lack of an 'us' and 'them' mentality.[3]

These studies, however, have focussed on situations where both employer and employee are Muslims. There has been little research on how the Islamic work ethic is affected when the employment relationship involves Muslim workers and a non-Muslim, foreign multi-national employer. It is to this issue we now turn.

Muslim managers and employees under Japanese management

The Japanese joint venture (Iroha (M) Berhad)[4] was established in Kuala Lumpur in the 1960s; some 60 per cent of its employees are Malay Muslims. Top posts are filled by expatriate Japanese but locals are present at all other levels in the organisation including the posts of Production Manager, Engineering Manager, and Personnel Manager. Fifty per cent of local managers are Muslims and the company recognises the need of Muslims to practice their faith in a number of ways:

Daily prayers: A small *surau* (place of prayer) is provided, consisting of a room kept clean and used exclusively for this purpose When it is not possible for workers to leave their posts, they pray close to the machines.

Friday prayers: A longer lunch break is allowed on Fridays throughout Malaysia so male Muslim employees can attend Friday prayers at their local mosque. As production involves a continuous process some staff have to be present at all times, so attendance is on a roster basis. The company provides a bus service between the workplace and the mosque.

Fasting during the month of Ramadan: Fasting involves not eating or drinking from first light until sunset, and non-compliance is prosecutable by the religious authorities. As fasting can slow job performance the Japanese managers consider it a hindrance, but they accept the Muslim employees' need to fulfil their religious obligations.

Pilgrimage to Mecca: It is obligatory for Muslims to make the *haj* once in their lifetime, if they can afford to do so. It takes about one and a half months to carry out all the elements of the pilgrimage. The company has been reluctant to grant leave of absence to its Muslim members for such a long period of time, as it means temporarily promoting subordinates into 'acting' roles to replace supervisors and managers. This issue is vividly illustrated in Case 2 below.

Eating and drinking together: On the whole, social interaction between the Japanese and the local managers is based on formal invitations in the context of company business or the ritual events on the Malaysian cultural calendar. The fact that Malay managers cannot drink alcohol makes social interaction for business reasons complicated. One solution has been to attend a *halal* Chinese restaurant, where non-Malay managers can order beer, and the Chinese food is prepared in a way acceptable to the Muslim dietary rules.

Dress: The company uniform does not pose any problems for Muslim males, for whom it is only mandatory to be clothed from waist to knees. Muslim women must cover themselves from ankles to wrists, and cover their neck and hair. A suitable style of dress has therefore been incorporated into the design of uniforms for the packers.

Religious holidays: All important religious holidays for the major religious groups in Malaysia are gazetted public holidays, so this is not a problem for the Muslim employees. The company conducts its annual shutdown for the repairing and servicing of the machines at the time of the Hari Raya festival, following the Muslim month of fasting. At this time, Malays take about two weeks holiday and return to their villages. The engineering department is mainly composed of Chinese, precisely because they can be available during the Hari Raya period.

Thus we see that organisationally there is a mood of accommodation on the part of the Japanese. However, this is more a result of conforming to wider social norms than an active appreciation of the Islamic lifestyle. Individually, and at an informal level, it could be said that Muslim managers indirectly suffered a slight handicap in their career advancement through factors like not being able to socialise freely with the Japanese, or through having wider community and religious loyalties that conflicted with their loyalty to the company. But the *bumiputera* policies inherent in the NEP counteract this, in the sense that companies have to prioritise Malays in recruitment and promotion in order to fulfil the guidelines of the Industrial Coordination Act.[5]

Case Studies[6]

This section contains case material on four Malay Muslim employees who attained the status of manager through different routes and all of whom were pious Muslims.

Case 1: Sanusi—member of the 'old guard'

Sanusi was recruited in the first batch of supervisory staff in the 1960s. Initially a junior manager on the production side, he became Personnel and General Affairs Manager and a company director. He is a graduate of an English colonial school and his father was an English-educated bureaucrat, giving the family a footing into the old middle class. As is the norm with such families, Sanusi's wife stayed at home and he sent one of his sons overseas for tertiary education. Unlike the new middle class, where it is common for both husband and wife to have professional jobs and be concerned with maximising the interests of the nuclear family, Sanusi's concerns extended more widely. He was careful to fulfil the traditional obligations of rural peasant society, taking care of a wide circle of kin and community members. This is coterminous with the Islamic ethos of not separating work and community roles. Thus, when new employees were needed, the company advertised internally for friends or relatives of existing employees, and Sanusi recruited many relatives and residents of his native village. He was close to most of the veteran workers, in the older village-style patron–client sense, and went out of his way to assist them in various ways. For instance, a Malay worker asked the company, through Sanusi, for a loan to purchase a motorcycle. Sanusi's Japanese superior refused the request so Sanusi made the loan out of his own pocket. This was both to save face personally, and to smooth over relations between workers and the Japanese management. Such loans, based on patron-client ties, were rarely recovered in full.

Though Sanusi displayed managerial skills based on these village-style relationships, he also showed 'Japanese-style' loyalty to the company; as a *bumiputera*, he could have moved to another foreign company quite easily, but did not. Instead, he used the context of the Japanese company, where he had recognition and influence to foster the interests of workers and people from his community of origin. Though not ostentatious in his piety he nevertheless embodied the principles of Islam, making an adequate, comfortable living for himself while helping those around him as much as he could, rather than seeking to maximise his own career interests alone.

Case 2: Rahman—NEP graduate to manager

Rahman, a post-NEP science graduate, was appointed section chief in the technical department in the mid-1970s. He resigned to take up a university tutorship after one year but returned to Iroha (M) Berhad after being persuaded by his relatives not to leave a job with such good promotion prospects. The case of Rahman illustrates a common pattern: it was his relatives' perception of the company as a good long-term economic prospect that caused him to return, rather than intrinsic loyalty to the firm. His loyalty as a member of the new Malay middle class lay elsewhere, particularly towards Islam, as was demonstrated when he asked for two months leave to perform the *haj* after being promoted to production manger. At first the Japanese refused, as this was too long for a key manager to be away. But Rahman insisted and said he would rather risk losing his job than not make the pilgrimage. Finally the Japanese agreed, as it would have become a sensitive political issue. A number of explanations can be offered as to why the parties acted as they did during this episode.

For Rahman, performing the *haj* involved choosing between identity and career. He felt he had to make the pilgrimage because the performance of his religious duties was the most important element of his daily life. Moreover, in doing so he would gain respect from people in his community. As he came from a pious family there would have been pressure on him to perform the *haj* once his income made it possible for him to do so. Family and friends would have questioned his religious devotion had he, for instance, purchased an expensive car before making the pilgrimage. While he showed dedication and a high degree of competence at work, maintaining loyalty to his religious beliefs was a priority. Nevertheless, he still reaped the benefits of the Japanese system in his career, because the Japanese valued his personal qualities, which were, after all, intimately bound up with his religious approach to life.

Case 3: Ridzuan—a manager promoted from the ranks

The case of Ridzuan, who was promoted from the shop floor, is one of the most interesting in the company. In his early days he had been a successful union leader, becoming deputy secretary of the national committee. He stated that at the time he was respected by both his fellow workers and by management, and though he supported the union he was wary of becoming a union official: 'if I come to the union, I may lose my good name. I just want to have a peaceful life, rest, enough food and money. But I didn't see anyone else who could do the job'. This is a typical statement of a Malay of that era, and has overtones of the wish to live a pious life with priority given to one's religious duties. That is, one should accept one's station in life, so long as it is adequate to live with a reasonable degree of comfort and security for the family, and one must accept that one has responsibilities to the wider community.

Following his appointment to the union position Ridzuan was promoted to unit chief level, the lowest rung of management, a practice common in Japanese companies, who value union leaders for their demonstrated leadership potential and understanding of workers. He went on to be a popular junior manager, but in so doing was caught between the generations, a phenomenon common to young Malays in the NEP era. He had respect for the opinions of his family regarding his career, was a pillar of the prayer group in his neighbourhood and tried to avoid work engagements that conflicted with the timing of the after-sunset prayers. At the same time he was touched by the new consumerist values of fast food outlets, shopping complexes and golf clubs. On top of this, he had internalised the Japanese value of hard work in concert with the Islamic value of prospering through one's own efforts (Faridi 1997, p. 87). He usually had no difficulty reconciling the two as there is a high degree of overlap, but when a conflict arose in terms of dedication to the company or to his Islamic obligations, he chose the latter.

Case 4: Aziz—a mid-career recruit

Aziz was a mid-career recruit, rare in the Japanese internal labour-market-type organisation, being recruited to the specialty area of 'security'. The position was hotly contested, with applicants having to sit a written exam, which included such questions as: 'What is your opinion of the function of a security officer of a large firm like ours? Do you feel that problems may arise if the government were to compel our company to allow all our male employees to go for Friday prayers? Do you feel communism is an immediate threat to our country?' These show the central concern of Japanese investors in the 1970s with the political stability of the South-East Asian countries in which they were investing, and their perception of Islam as difficult to cope with yet unavoidable.

Aziz got the job on merit. He was a sincere, honest, hardworking and pious individual whose Islamic principles were his first point of reference, even when working in a modern organisation. At the time, he lived in an old-style wooden house in the compound of family land that had once been their *kampong* allotment. His wife's occupation was recorded as 'home duties' and they had two children. As an urban Malay who had attained a middle-class lifestyle by virtue of his occupation, Aziz's piety and sincere values were overlaid with a concern for financial matters, which he frequently expressed in relation to dissatisfaction with his job. This was not greediness, or desire for ostentatious display, but rather the pressing demands of life in the city, with children to educate and a wife to support. Moreover, Aziz had expected to be employed to handle security issues, but he found that only four of the 25 categories in his job description related to security. Aziz's dissatisfaction that his salary was disproportionate to his actual skills and responsibilities led him to consider taking another job but, as in the cases of Rahman and Ridzuan, family members' opinions influenced his decision. In this case, his mother opposed him taking a better-paid security position as it was far away and his children's education would be jeopardised. He was offered a job at Motorola, a large American company, but worked there for only one day, deciding that, while working for the Japanese had its frustrations, it was less stressful than the organisational rigour of Western companies.

The Malay casualness in social relations and their commitment to ties with friends and relatives, as opposed to work roles, may have gone against Aziz in the eyes of the Japanese. He narrated how once a senior manager had invited him to his house on a Friday evening. But on the day before, some friends of Aziz arrived from Singapore, and in his eagerness to show them a good time, he forgot the invitation. Asked subsequently why he had not come, Aziz apologised, but his lack of a reasonable excuse in Japanese terms left the senior manager with the impression that Aziz was unreliable. In Malay terms, such changes of plan are quite usual. People turn up unexpectedly all the time; the society remains based on pre-telephone patterns of interaction; despite the existence of telephones in the cities, things are slow to change. Once guests arrive, it is one's duty to entertain them no matter how inconvenient. Even if one is about to leave the house, when guests arrive, they must be invited in. The problem arises if your destination is to meet a fixed appointment in the modern organisational sense. This was the meeting of two systems in which Aziz was caught. He would not know the Japanese etiquette of invitations, the supreme honour of being invited to a Japanese person's private home, a thing not customary in Japan itself. The Japanese manager was making a special effort outside his cultural range by inviting local employees to his home. A Malay person would have been disappointed too if he had not turned up to a *kenduri* (religious ritual feast) or other fixed invitation. But the Malay would have understood the guest's last-minute change of plan, as they themselves would have been placed in that position many times.

Aziz's lack of educational qualifications in an era of graduate recruitment gave him little bargaining power. However, he was noticeable in the organisation because of his conscientiousness, piety and honesty, virtues that intersected with Japanese notions of the ideal employee. These qualities brought him a degree of success in the organisation, enough to lead a comfortable lifestyle. Aziz's primary concern, however, was with living a life of principle as a Muslim, performing the daily prayers and other ritual obligations, and he saw the job in the Japanese company as a means to this end. It gave him a stable, predictable daily life, and he chose this option over others that offered more money but which conflicted with his desire to lead the life of a devout Muslim, adequately providing for his family. He nevertheless felt frustrated at what he saw as his inadequate financial recompense.

New graduates recruited to management—work ethics and Islamic identity

As opposed to the 'old guard' managers who did not have much bargaining power with the company owing to deficiencies in their basic qualifications, the new Malay graduates have bargaining power as *bumiputera*. Unlike the first generation of local managers, who knew 'every valve and pump' and every worker personally, these graduates have in many cases been educated in schools committed to Muslim fundamentalism (Shamsul 1995). This background is reflected in their middle-class culture, mixture of fundamentalist piety and consumerist materialism (Smith 1999). Despite being first generation city dwellers themselves, most new graduates have lost the thread of the patron–client village relationships maintained by older-generation Malays like Sanusi. They would return to the village for weddings, funerals, important religious festivals and social visits, perhaps even on a monthly basis if the village is readily accessible by the super-highways now linking much of rural Malaysia with the major cities, but they have become more individualist in their status orientation, demonstrating status with material possessions alone rather than combining this with a show of patronage to those less fortunate than themselves, as is usual in village society. In other words, they have become middle-class in the isolationist sense typical of the Western middle-class. Their success is considered an individual achievement and this gives them a one-dimensional confidence and a degree of pride in being the first members of their families to live as urban professionals.

The new graduates have three roles to fulfil in their lives: (i) their managerial roles in the company; (ii) their technical roles, as science graduates, which are sometimes under-utilised as they are there in a token role as *bumiputera* numbers; and (iii) their social roles as young prosperous *bumiputera* in both the urban community and their rural communities of origin. In their lives it is this latter role that ultimately assumes the most importance and provides the most difficulty, as their behaviour is required to be different in some aspects in the two contexts. The main common point in both the urban and rural social contexts for the young, educated, Malay middle class is their Muslim identity, expressed through the overt symbols of piety in speech, dress and the performance of regular ritual prayers and the pilgrimage. Otherwise there are great paradoxes in the coexistence of the two spheres, such as being expected to attend the weddings and funerals of a large number of distant relatives in the village, while being required to maintain a professional daily schedule of important meetings and appointments. Individuals trying to cope with these two disparate and mutually conflicting worlds often suffer a profound clash in values and it is understandable that Islam, which binds the two together, has come to be embraced so fervently by young middle-class people. Consequently, the Japanese managers were not able to divert their loyalty towards the company and away from their religious and other social representations in the critical community of their families and peers in the Malay middle class.

Work ethics of unionised employees

The unionised Malay Muslim employees are not able to afford trips to Mecca during their early working years, or be in the dilemma experienced by the Malay managers of having to decide whether to drink alcohol with work associates, as they cannot afford it. The expression of conflict between their Islamic identity and their work roles and career ambitions occurs more in relation to their community and kinship relations. Many are first-generation industrial workers who once lived in the village and have deep enduring ties with an extended range of kin. In pre-NEP village society, people could eat off the land and needed cash only for things like cloth. Later, as consumer items filtered into the kampong, they bought radios, batteries and then more and more complex electrical goods as the villages were electrified. Life focussed on daily food production and the annual cycle of religious festivals and life crises. These were conducted as cooperative community events, with people contributing labour, cooking and eating utensils, and the richer relatives contributing cash. When someone married or died, it was almost mandatory to attend the ceremony, or one's loyalty was questioned and one courted lack of cooperation when one's own turn came. This high level of participation in community and family events extends into the urban life of workers, who are expected to attend many weddings and funerals in their villages of origin. In Islam, funerals are conducted on the day of death where possible, so workers need emergency leave to attend them. This is granted in the case of very close relatives, but not for the extent of kin Malay workers must recognise. The Japanese complained that sometimes workers had three or four grandfathers who died.

Frequent absences disrupt production and shift schedules and jeopardise an individual's chances of promotion. Yet for many of the Malay shop floor workers, their obligations to village society are more important than monetary gain. Moreover, some workers have second sources of income as petty-commodity traders, usually in conjunction with a non-waged spouse. In order to run their street stalls, for example, workers would manipulate their shift schedules with the help of workmates and supervisors (Smith 1988). This was possible in the 1970s but later when the company engaged in a productivity drive and at the same time reduced the size of its labour force by natural attrition, such flexibility became more difficult. Unpaid activities after working hours, such as participation in Quality Control circles, which Japanese workers readily accept, are unpopular among Malays because many are engaged in commercial activities in the informal sector. Thus their work ethic followed the Islamic tradition established by the Prophet Mohammed and his first wife, Khatijah, which held that gaining profit from the hard work put into one's own business is commendable.

Conclusion

The work ethic derived from Islam is not incompatible with the work ethic Japanese managers attempted to transfer to the Malaysian venture: honesty, diligence and loyalty. These all have a central place in both systems of thought. However, differences lie in the fact that the Islamic system sees paid labour as merely one way in which human beings express their spirituality, whereas the Japanese work ethic locates an individual's loyalty and efforts within the bounds of the organisation, rather than in the context of a higher spiritual state of existence. The Muslim managerial and union level employees in our case studies were able to fulfil their obligations to God and the community by not giving priority to organisational demands over their identity as Muslims. They participated in a complex set of social relationships, exacerbated by the state of rapid social change being experienced in Malaysia. They fulfilled their traditional kinship and community obligations to varying degrees depending on their generation and, at the same time, the demands of a busy professional working life and middle-class lifestyle. Despite their primary loyalty to their Islamic identity, they nevertheless achieved success in the Japanese organisation precisely because the personal qualities sought by Japanese employers were part of their Muslim personae.

Unlike other parts of Asia where ethnic conflict, often expressed in terms of religious differences, became a major social problem following the onset of the economic crisis of 1997–99, Malaysia experienced little ethnic strife. In the light of this development, it would appear reasonable to conclude that the ethnic elements of the NEP have successfully dealt with the issue of religious differences both between Muslim and non-Muslim Malaysians and between Muslim employees and foreign managers. Not only has the NEP achieved economic growth, and generated the skilled and disciplined workforce Malaysia needs to remain internationally competitive and to attract continued foreign investment, but it has also brought the country to the stage where its social structure and economic stability can withstand the ethnic pressures that all too often are intensified in times of economic crisis. In this sense it may truly be said that Malaysia has entered a new era.

Endnotes

1 See *The Age*, 16 February 1999.
2 Because of the centrality of the belief in Islam that the *Qu'ran* accurately preserves the revealed word of God, there can be little possibility of doctrinal disputes and Islam is comparatively free of these, in contrast with other major world religions. Therefore, it is possible to talk about a monolithic body of 'Islamic work ethics'.
3 Although there are few articles giving empirical details from Malaysia, Islamic doctrines and practices are universally applicable to a high degree. Therefore we feel that the values stated here are applicable to the Malaysian case.
4 Pseudonyms are used for the names of individuals and the company in this chapter. See Smith (1994) for a more detailed examination of the organisation of this company.
5 The ICA of 1974 stipulated that companies must submit the ethnic breakdown of employees at all levels as part of the annual review of their licenses. They were advised to achieve the ethnic percentages at all levels of the company organisation chart, which was a problem as there were few Malays in management in the 1970s; the number only began to increase in the 1980s as Malay science and engineering graduates from the new universities began to be employed in private industry.
6 The following data is derived from the anthropological field notes of Wendy Smith.

References

Abu-Saad, I. (1998), 'Individualism and Islamic work beliefs', *Journal of Cross-Cultural Psychology*, 29 (2), 377–383.

Ahmad, F. (1987), 'Labour welfare in Islamic law', *Islamic & Comparative Law Quarterly*, VII (4), 301–311.

Ali A. J. (1988), 'Scaling an Islamic work ethic', *Journal of Social Psychology*, 128 (5), 575–583.

Ali, A. J. (1992) 'The Islamic work ethic in Arabia', *The Journal of Psychology*, 126 (5), 507–519.

Anjum, M. I. (1995), 'An Islamic scheme of equitable distribution of income and wealth', *The American Journal of Islamic Social Sciences*, 12 (2), 224–239.

Arinze, Francis (1997), 'Social cohesion: Tolerance and policy making in religiously diverse societies', *Migration Action*, XIX, (3), 16–21.

Bani-Sadr, A. (1980), *Work and the Worker in Islam*, translated by H. Mashhadi, Tehran: The Hamdami Foundation.

Bannerman, P. (1988), *Islam in Perspective: A Guide to Islamic Society, Politics and Law*, London: Routledge.

Bazargan, M. (1980), *Work and Islam*, translated by M. Yusefi, A. A. Behzadnia and N. Denny, Houston: Free Islamic Literatures.

Beekun, R. I. and J. Badawi (1999), *Leadership: An Islamic Perspective* (forthcoming).

Egami, T. (1990), *Labour and Action in Islam: Searching for an Outlook on Lost Labour*, Japan: Institute of Middle Eastern Studies.

Faridi, F. R. (ed.) (1997), *Islamic Principles of Business Organisation and Management*, Kuala Lumpur: S. Abdul Majeed & C.

Faruqi, al I and al G. Banna (1984), *Towards Islamic Labour & Unionism*, Cairo: The International Islamic Confederation of Labour.

Khalil-ur-Rehman (1995), *The Concept of Labour in Islam*, Karachi: Arif Publications.

Muna, F. (1980), *The Arab Executive* New York: Macmillan

Naim, Mochtar (1988), 'Islamic work ethic as observed in the management of Minangkabau restaurants in Indonesian cities', *Research Report on Urbanism in Islam, Monograph Series No. 1*, Tokyo: University of Tokyo, Institute of Oriental Culture.

Naqvi, S. N. H. (1994), *Islam, Economics, and Society*, London: Kegan Paul International.

Safi, L. (1995), 'Leadership and subordination: An Islamic perspective', *The American Journal of Islamic Social Sciences*, 12 (2), 204–223.

Shamsul A. B. (1995), 'Invented certainties: the Dakwah persona in Malaysia', in W. James (ed.), *Pursuit of Certainty*, ASA Monograph, London: Routledge, pp. 112–133.

Smith, W. (1988), 'Skill formation in comparative perspective: Malaysia and Japan', *Labour and Industry*, 1 (3), 431–462.

—— (1994), 'A Japanese factory in Malaysia: Ethnicity as a management ideology', in K. S. Jomo (ed.), *Japan and Malaysian Development*, London: Routledge.

—— (1999), 'The contribution of a Japanese firm to the cultural construction of the new rich in Malaysia' in M. Pinches (ed.), *Culture and Privilege in Capitalist Asia*, London: Routledge.

—— (2000), 'Management in Malaysia' in M. Warner (ed.), *Regional Encyclopedia of Business and Management: Management in Asia Pacific*, London: Thomson Business Press.

14

The 1997–98 financial crisis in Malaysia and its social impact: Some lessons

Ishak Shari

Introduction

From July 1997, Malaysia experienced a drastic change in its economic and political landscape as a consequence of the serious financial crisis affecting South-East and East Asia. As the economy plunged into recession in 1998 it was feared that the remarkable achievements in social development during the 27 years before the crisis, which had contributed to political stability in the country, would be significantly eroded. There were concerns that severe recession would lead to higher unemployment and poverty rates and, worse still, trigger racial conflicts and political instability, thus making the country less attractive to foreign investment.

However, as the economy experienced rapid recovery from the crisis in 1999, such concerns appear to have been misplaced. Nevertheless, the crisis has left Malaysia with two interesting questions. First, how is it that Malaysia, with a multi-ethnic society, was able to maintain racial harmony despite her worst economic recession since independence? Second, was the social impact of the 1997–98 financial and economic crisis sufficient to affect the political stability of the country in the long run? This chapter attempts to provide some insights into Malaysia's recent experiences, in a world where the power and authority of national governments are being reconstituted and the states have to adapt and seek coherent strategies of engaging with a globalising world. It is hoped that exploring these issues will contribute to the developing societies' search for appropriate institutional arrangement, developing societies, particularly in the complex relationship between market and state, as they strive for sustainable development.

Economic growth and social progress 1971–97

It is first essential to briefly describe Malaysia's successful development, particularly in tackling their problems of poverty and income inequality during the 1971–97 period. Considering the available evidence, there is no doubt that the country enjoyed high export growth, rapid economic growth, near-full employment and falling poverty levels during the period. For example, the expansion of employment opportunities as a consequence of the sustained high economic growth has contributed to the declining unemployment rate from 7.8 per cent in 1970 to 6.0 per cent in 1990 and 2.5 per cent in 1997. The labour shortage experienced by several sectors of the economy led to the increasing recruitment of foreign migrant workers. The rapid economic growth, together with the deliberate government affirmative measures to improve the position of the *bumiputera* and other disadvantaged groups, has also resulted in a significant decline in the rate of poverty in the country, for example from 52.4 per cent in 1970 to 6.8 per cent in 1997. The number of poor households decreased from 1,100,000 to 346,000 during the same period (Malaysia 1991; 1999, p. 63). This reduction in absolute poverty in Malaysia was accompanied by a reduction in income inequality from the late 1970s until 1990. The Gini ratio for the whole of Peninsular Malaysia fell from 0.529 in 1976 to 0.445 in 1990. The income share for the bottom 40 per cent of households increased from 10.8 per cent in 1976 to 14.5 per cent in 1990 (Ishak 1998; Shireen 1998, p. 60). Furthermore, the ratio of urban mean household income to the rural mean household income also narrowed from 2.14:1 in 1970 to 1.70:1 in 1990, while the Chinese–*bumiputera* disparity ratio was reduced from 2.29:1 to 1.74:1 (Ishak 1998).

During the 1991–97 period, average household income in both rural and urban areas as well as among the major ethnic groups in the country was increasing at a significant rate. However, the differential rates of income growth among income groups and between strata have resulted in widening of income disparities since 1990. The Gini coefficient for the country increased from 0.445 in 1990 to 0.456 in 1993, 0.462 in 1995 and 0.470 in 1997 (Malaysia 1999, p. 69). The urban–rural income disparity ratio increased from 1.70:1 in 1990 to 2.00:1 in 1997. During the same period, the Chinese–*bumiputera* income disparity ratio increased from 1.70:1 to 1.83:1 (Malaysia 1999, p. 69). At the same time, income disparity within each ethnic group, particularly among *bumiputera* households, remained relatively high.

At a superficial glance, the Malaysian development experience seems to confirm the thesis of orthodox neo-classical writers that the country owes its success to liberal, 'market-friendly' regimes and 'open-door' policies towards foreign trade and investment. However, as argued elsewhere (Rasiah and Ishak 1997; Ishak 1998), there is incontrovertible evidence showing that extensive direct state intervention in Malaysia, particularly with the implementation of the New Economic Policy (NEP) since 1971, played a key role in the country's prosperity. While export-oriented manufacturing increased the demand for labour and stimulated the growth in wage employment and the consequent enlargement of household incomes and reduction in poverty and inequality, critical interventions stimulated the necessary investments. Thus, state intervention has made a significant contribution to Malaysia's progress in attaining rapid economic growth and reducing poverty and income disparities.

The financial crisis and its social impact

The sequence of events leading to the worsening of the financial crisis in Malaysia from mid-1997 seemed to involve several important developments at both global and national levels. Some recent works (Montes 1998; Jomo 1998) show that the crisis in Malaysia was due to the fact that previous systems of international and national economic governance were undermined by deregulation and other developments associated with financial liberalisation and globalisation. At the same time, it has been argued that Asian governments were strongly pushed into opening their financial markets by what is referred to as the 'Wall Street–Treasury–IMF complex'. The financial situation in Malaysia was further adversely affected by selective administrative measures, such as declaring all the 100 component stocks of the Composite Index of the KLSE as 'designated securities'. This was ostensibly introduced by the Malaysian government to check 'short-selling', aimed to curb speculation in the currency and stock markets. Such moves may have been motivated by the need to protect politically connected business interests. The various contradictory statements of Malaysia's Prime Minister (including his tough speech at the joint World Bank–IMF annual meeting in Hong Kong on 20 September 1997) also appear to have adversely affected investors' confidence and contributed to a further fall of the ringgit and the share prices at the KLSE.

The combination of these factors had a contaminating effect on Malaysian business where common risk factors were perceived to be present by speculators and genuine investors alike. Furthermore, with the sharp and sudden depreciation of the ringgit, coupled with the reduction of Malaysia's foreign reserves in initial anti-speculation attempts (estimated to be about US$3.5 billion), the burden of debt servicing rose in correspondence to the amount of local currency required for loan repayments. The fact that a rather significant proportion of foreign loans were short-term became an additional problem. This was followed by a sharp increase in foreign investors pulling out their funding, causing reserves to fall further. Therefore despite its relatively stronger economy initially, compared with other regional economies, Malaysia was not spared from the contagious effects of the crisis.

Retrenchment, rising unemployment and falling income

After a lag of several months, the financial crisis began to affect Malaysia's general economy, which began to experience slow growth in the remaining months of 1997 and contracted by 6.7 per cent in 1998. The contraction of the real economy in turn adversely affected the pace of job creation and led to rising unemployment. For example, in contrast to an average increase of 7.7 per cent during the 1996–97 period, employment in the manufacturing sector registered a decline of 3.6 per cent in 1998. The construction sector experienced the largest decline, 16.9 per cent. However, official employment figures documented a decline of about 3.0 per cent and the unemployment rate increased to 3.9 per cent in 1998. Official statistics showed that the number of the unemployed increased from 233,100 in 1997 to 343,200 in 1998. Unemployment increased partly as a result of retrenchment in the major sectors of the economy. According to official statistics, a total of 83,865 workers (about 1 per cent of the total workforce) were retrenched by 4,789 firms in 1998, and 18,863 workers were retrenched in 1997.

However, in a crisis situation, it is difficult to estimate unemployment and retrenchment figures. Allowance, therefore, has to be made for workers unemployed and retrenched but not captured in official figures. Often a significant number of retrenched workers are foreign labourers, and many of them are unregistered (or illegal) workers. This is especially so in the construction sector, where about 80 per cent of the workforce are migrant workers and a significant percentage are unregistered. According to one estimate, there were 1.7 million foreign workers in Malaysia in 1997, out of which 560,000 were unregistered workers (Malaysia 1998a, p. 63). During this crisis, reverse migration took place among foreign workers in Malaysia, most noticeably among illegal foreign workers, both on an organised basis (repatriation and deportation) and on an individual, informal basis. According to official figures, between January and mid-November 1998, at least 383,946 foreign workers and their dependants returned to their countries. In addition, registered foreign workers in the manufacturing industries also faced non-renewal or termination of their contracts during this crisis, and they are not part of the official retrenchment statistics. Retrenchment of locals in the informal sector was also taking place and again their number most probably is not captured in official statistics. Interviews with various focused groups carried out by a rapid assessment study also revealed that there is considerable under-employment, which is probably not captured in official statistics (Ishak and Abdul 1999).

Some firms reacted to the crisis not by laying off their workers but by cutting wages or lowering (and sometimes freezing) pay increases. For example, in the car-assembling industry, workers had to accept a 25 per cent wage cut to avoid retrenchment. But there were some employers who imposed excessive pay cuts of 30 to 50 per cent, even to lower-paid workers. The move by firms to cut wages, together with low or no pay increases agreed upon in collective bargaining negotiations between unions and employers to avoid retrenchment of workers, contributed to the decline in workers' wages during 1998. In addition, a very high percentage of workers in both the private and public sectors could not work overtime.

Some companies also defaulted on or delayed paying wages and Employment Providence Fund (EPF) contributions on behalf of their workers. For example, during the first six months of 1998, a total of 15,560 employers (or 5.4 per cent of the total registered employers) failed to contribute to the EPF, while only 13,143 had done so in the whole of 1997. The default by employers would seriously jeopardise the workers' savings for old age.

This changing situation in the labour market resulted in a big drop in workers' income, causing serious difficulties for many, especially those with vehicle and housing loans. With the retrenchment of workers and the reduction of wages in some sectors of the economy, several indicators showed moderating increases in wage rates. It was estimated that wages were increasing at the rate of 5.6 per cent in 1998, but 10.2 per cent in 1997 (Malaysia 1999b, p. 78). According to one official report, real wages per worker declined by 9.9 per cent during the first seven months of 1998, but had increased by 18.9 per cent during the corresponding period in 1997 (Malaysia 1998b, pp. 73–74). The fall in real wages was more significant in some of the sub-sectors (for example the electrical, electronics and machinery industry) of the manufacturing sector.

Although the urban workforce in the formal sector seemed to be the hardest hit by the crisis, those in the informal sector and some sections of the rural working population were not spared either. For example, the livelihood of taxi drivers was adversely affected, as people tended to be more cautious with their spending and travelling and because of the decline in tourist arrivals. As a result, many taxi drivers had to work long hours, sometimes up to 16 hours per day. The *batik* (traditional textile) cottage industry in Kelantan was also badly affected due to the rising price of imported white linen and a slump in demand. Hawkers and petty traders were not spared the brunt of the crisis, experiencing a big drop in their business. Yet the informal business sector provided some sort of safety net for those who had been retrenched and others seeking more income to make ends meet, although this sector quickly became overcrowded.

Urban–rural remittances also declined as a result of job losses and a decrease in workers' income. Many workers interviewed in the rapid assessment study reported that they either had to stop sending money to their parents altogether, or to reduce the quantum. This could affect the income of rural folk as transfer payments (including remittances from children working in urban areas) form a substantial proportion of their income.

Other impacts on human development

Every section of the community in Malaysia was adversely affected by rising prices of goods and services, including basic essentials, reflecting largely the impact of ringgit depreciation on the prices of imported food. The official consumer price index (CPI) recorded an increase of 5.3 per cent in 1998, of 2.7 per cent in 1997 and 3.5 per cent in 1996. However, the price increase in essential commodities such as rice, flour, sugar, milk and cooking oil was much higher and affected monthly household expenditures. This was reflected in an 8.9 per cent increase for food items in 1998, significant when compared with the 4.1 per cent increase in 1997 and the 5.7 per cent in 1996 (Malaysia 1999, p. 44). The burden of rising prices was heavier among sections of the population that experienced a big decline in their nominal incomes. With increasing unemployment, falling incomes and rising prices, it was not surprising that the crisis had an adverse impact on poverty in the country. According to official estimates, the incidence of poverty in Malaysia increased from 6.7 per cent in 1997 to 8.5 per cent in 1998 (2000 Budget Speech, 25 February). In absolute terms, the number of poor households increased by 22 per cent from 346,000 in 1997 to 448,500 in 1998.

The financial and economic crisis also had a negative impact on household investments in human development, particularly in education, health and nutrition, and fertility, for several reasons. First, although social services were subsidised, households still incurred direct or associated costs in trying to get access to these services. With reduced income and higher prices, including medicines and schooling expenses, the poor and low-income households tended to consume less than what is individually and socially optimal. Second, investment in human capital takes time; however, time had become scarcer as household members worked longer hours to attempt to offset falling incomes. Third, the quality and quantity of certain public services were affected by budget constraints and big shifts of clients from private to public providers. Fourth, as households tried to maintain their levels of consumption, they reduced human capital investment or even depleted their existing stocks. However, due to the limited amount of data available, our discussion of these points is constrained to certain issues only.

The initial tight fiscal policy measures implemented by the government, among other things, affected some programmes for the poor in parts of the country. However, the big budget cuts were compensated for in some ways by an additional allocation of 3.7 billion ringgit made available as assistance to vulnerable groups adversely affected by the crisis. Government programmes to improve the livelihood of the poorest households were also expanded. Nonetheless, some non-governmental organisations had to reduce their activities significantly, thus affecting their programmes to help the poor and disadvantaged groups.

The fall in the value of the ringgit and the rising cost of overseas education resulted in a reduction in the number of students studying overseas. For example, the number of Malaysian students undertaking tertiary education in Britain dropped by about 44 per cent, from 18,000 in 1997 to 10,000 in 1998. Therefore, the pressure on local institutions of higher learning to accept more students was greater. Given the limited resources available, a significant number of qualified students could not continue their tertiary education. At the same time, local universities increased fees for post-graduate programmes, creating a further disincentive for potential applicants. These developments adversely affected Malaysia's ability to produce the skilled people needed to develop the economy in the future.

Political repercussions

Although the social impact of the crisis in Malaysia was less severe than the economic impact, there was a sea change in the country's political state of affairs. In fact, the political repercussions of the crisis could in the long run adversely affect Malaysia's efforts towards sustainable development. As evidenced by recent developments, although the economic crisis engulfed Malaysians generally, the political crisis appeared to principally affect the Malay community. Before the crisis, the country's leadership has been seen as promulgating wealth-promoting policies, which also benefited the Malays. So ordinary Malaysians, including the Malays, preferred to believe the government's promise of economic progress and the claimed attainment of the social agenda. Since the mid-1980s, in response to the 1985–86 crisis, the Malaysian government had implemented a range of policy measures to induce economic liberalisation and deregulation. These moves served to progressively narrow the role of the public sector to traditional responsibilities such as education and health. The provision of subsidies had been curtailed and streamlined, with a tighter focus on the most disadvantaged in society. These policies were further consolidated in the 1990s with the National Development Policy (2001–10) seeking to maximise economic growth through policies that allow greater freedom of market mechanisms. This change of policy was criticised by some sections of the population, including the Opposition, some NGOs and even some sections of UMNO, for its relative neglect of the need to correct existing socio-economic imbalances in the country. To some, the change of policy was tantamount to the abandonment of the NEP.

Since the early 1990s, concerns have grown among Malaysians, particularly the *bumiputera*, about the uneven distribution of benefits of rapid economic growth among various ethnic groups. These concerns have some foundation. Apart from the increasing inequality between rural and urban areas and between the major ethnic groups mentioned above, the majority of *bumiputera* households still remain in the lower hierarchy of the Malaysian society. For example, *bumiputera* households made up 70.2 per cent of all households in the bottom 40 per cent of the Malaysian society in 1997. Only 12.9 per cent of total *bumiputera* households are included in the top 20 per cent of Malaysian society (Samsudin 1999). This data also indicates the widening income gap within the *bumiputera* community itself.

The adverse impact of the crisis (particularly on the *bumiputera* community), the government's way of dealing with the crisis (which was perceived as bailing out a few of the Malay rich but causing hardship to the majority) and the lack of sensitivity shown by the leaders in handling the *ulama*, further angered the Malays. The opposition to Mahathir gained further momentum when Anwar Ibrahim launched his *reformasi* movement by attacking the country's leadership for 'corruption, cronyism and nepotism'. Further, it was perceived that while the private sector enjoyed more freedom as it was regarded as engine of growth, fundamental liberties were not accorded the citizens of the country. The expulsion of Anwar

Ibrahim as Deputy Prime Minister was the catalyst for increased activism. Momentum in the campaign for greater transparency, more political freedom and the abolition of the Internal Security Act (which permits detention without trial) increased. Among the youth of Malaysia, the Anwar saga has helped to raise political consciousness to a degree not seen since the 1960s and 1970s.

It could be argued that the seeds of the social and political crisis were sown well before the economic crisis. In the few years preceding his dismissal, Anwar Ibrahim was seen to have gone out of his way to promote social justice and develop a liberal philosophy in which human rights and political, religious and racial differences were tolerated. Furthermore, as the country became more affluent and globalisation began to affect the younger generation of urban Malays, people began to question whether the government under the existing leadership was a desirable one. The scepticism then grew with the regional economic downturn; *reformasi*, naturally became the most expedient vehicle for such social expressions. This may explain the voting pattern among the Malay population during the November 1999 election.

Malaysia weathering the storm

The above discussion, which admittedly is based on limited data, seems to suggest that the social impact of the 1997–98 financial and economic crisis in Malaysia was both widespread and potentially long-lasting, despite the rapid recovery of the Malaysian economy since 1999. In fact, if the long-term adverse political impact of the crisis is taken into consideration, it is misleading to argue that the social cost of the crisis was minimal. Furthermore, it is important to remember that the social impact of any financial and economic crisis may take some time to overcome.

Nonetheless, from available information it is evident that the intensity of the social impact of the financial and economic crisis in Malaysia was relatively less severe than that experienced by other countries affected by the crisis in Asia. It is also interesting to note that while the crisis triggered unprecedented political development in Malaysia, it is of a much smaller magnitude compared to that in Indonesia. There were street protests and discontent at the grassroots, especially among the young, after the dramatic dismissal of the Deputy Prime Minister in September 1998. However, unlike in Indonesia, there is relative peace, and inter-ethnic relations were not adversely affected during the crisis period. How is it that the multi-ethnic society in Malaysia was not torn apart during this crisis as was the case in Indonesia? While this question begs further investigation, the different circumstances existing in the two countries may provide some initial explanations.

First, the Malaysian development experience successfully addressed distributional issues, particularly in eradicating poverty and reducing economic disparities between major ethnic groups after the implementation of the NEP in 1971. In addition to its long-term objective of preserving and building on the country's social progress, the Malaysian state was also committed to mitigate the short-term adverse effects of the economic slowdown on vulnerable groups in Malaysian society. For example, the government ensured that budget shares for social services, particularly health and education, in 1998 remained approximately at their 1997 levels and that public expenditure on major anti-poverty programmes was protected in real terms despite the reduction of its total development expenditure. Consequently, the upgrading of rural school facilities, expansion of facilities for skill development, enhancement of the Higher Education Loan Fund to increase accessibility to higher education, construction and equipping of health clinics, particularly in rural areas, and the provision of adequate funds for medicine and other essentials in public health services to cater for the need of the population, all continued despite the crisis.

Second, Malaysia's rapid economic growth during the 27 years before the crisis produced a large and expanding middle class that is multi-ethnic, with the *bumiputera* middle class becoming conspicuous and important. It has been argued that the characteristics of this growing middle class in Malaysia, particularly the attitude of acceptance and acquiescence to the state and political leadership among the significant section of them, has contributed to the maintenance of the status quo (Abdul 2000). This is not to deny that there is an increasing resentment among the middle class, particularly among the *bumiputera* middle class, with the way liberalisation and deregulation measures reversed some of the restructuring achievements of the NEP. Furthermore, the government pursuit of a policy of widespread privatisation of public assets, which created opportunities for the politically-connected corporate leaders to make huge profits while burdening the people, including the middle class (for example, through increased toll charges on privatised roads), created further discontents among the middle class. However, the resentment towards the government, especially after the burst of the 'wealth-creating' bubbles, and opposition to it, has not been along ethnic lines, and thus does not adversely affect inter-ethnic relations in the country.

Third, the rather long period of rapid growth which resulted in labour shortages and the employment of a large number of foreign workers, both legally and illegally, in the economy before this time also played a fairly important role in mitigating the impact of the crisis. With the unemployment rate of 2.6 per cent and the presence of nearly two million foreign workers, the impact of the crisis on employment opportunities was relatively moderate. At the same time, by sending back the retrenched foreign labour, Malaysia was able to export the social cost of the crisis. The restrained attitude of the unions, and workers' willingness to suffer a decline in real wages rather than facing retrenchment, also contributed to this situation.

Fourth, while the medium- and long-term impact of the measures introduced in early September 1998 need further detailed study, the short-term macroeconomic impact of the measures mitigated the adverse impact of the crisis. With the introduction of selective capital control measures on 2 September 1998, the monetary authorities lost no time in sharply reducing the interest rate. The base lending rate (BLR) of commercial banks, which rose from 10.33 per cent at the end of 1997 to 12.27 per cent at the end of June 1998 (thus exacerbating the contraction of economic activities during the first half of 1998) was reduced to a maximum rate of 8.05 per cent on 10 November 1998, which was below the level prevailing before the financial crisis (8.93 per cent at the end of June 1997). This measure helped many firms access cheaper loans and avoid going bankrupt, thus putting a brake on further retrenchment of staff. Thus, although Malaysia's selective capital control measures were described by the IMF Managing Director as 'dangerous and indeed harmful', the short-term macroeconomic impact of the measures helped to lessen the adverse impact of the crisis.

Conclusion

The causes and consequences of the financial and economic crisis in Malaysia and some other East and South-East Asian countries are quite complicated and many of us have yet to understand them in any great depth. Furthermore, available information does not allow a carefully considered assessment of the welfare consequences of the crisis for different socio-economic groups, including the poor and disadvantaged.

However, as the crisis shows, unregulated financial capital will largely end up in short-term and speculative ventures, which will in the long run debilitate growth and efforts to eradicate poverty and reduce income inequality. Consequently, there is now greater appreciation among researchers and the policy makers of nations regarding the dangers of exposing financial systems to fast liberalisation, especially when they lack experience in dealing with the international capital market, and banking regulations and supervision are still insufficient. In addition, governments are now more willing to discipline not only labour but also finance.

The experience of the financial and economic crisis in Malaysia during 1997–98 also challenges the view that, with globalisation, the state is increasingly irrelevant (Ohmae 1991) or that the power of the state is being transcended and increasingly becoming hollow and defective (Strange 1995). The Malaysian experience demonstrates the possibility of different trajectories, despite being increasingly integrated in the globalised world economy, thanks to variation in the role of markets and the state as coordinating mechanisms. In a world in which powerful international organisations and transnational corporations, as well as the states in the advanced industrial countries, are devoted to maximising the freedom of financial capital, and in the absence of any new international financial architecture, the states in developing countries need to assert social control and to continue to pursue redistributive policies that could change the impact of the globalisation process on their people. In this regard, however, a fundamentally different alternative, involving the democratisation of the state and the economy, would have to be considered. This would indeed be a challenge to national and international structures of power.

Furthermore, although the current unexpected sharp recovery in Malaysia may have brought relief to the political leaders and the majority of the population, the social discontent will not be blown away by increasingly favourable economic winds. Also the government's reputation has been damaged, the measures taken to save politically-connected local corporations, and several developments involving the judiciary (including Anwar Ibrahim's trial) have resulted in negative perceptions of the country. These developments, together with the recent highlighting of racial issues by the dominant party in the ruling coalition, are adversely affecting the flow of foreign investment to Malaysia and thus could undermine Malaysia's future growth prospects as well as its political stability. Therefore, the sustainability of the recent recovery is debatable. In fact, the likelihood of the crisis recurring, especially with the increasingly unfavourable external environment, cannot be ruled out. Nonetheless, it must be acknowledged that there have been some positive steps taken since late 2000 to address the problem of negative perceptions of Malaysia. For example, the appointment of a new Chief Justice and Attorney General could be interpreted as a move to restore the integrity of the judiciary. As mentioned above, the future direction of economic and political development in Malaysia will, however, depend largely on the government's ability to reconstruct the institutions characteristic of a modern society.

References

Abdul, Rahman Embong (2000), 'The political dimensions of the economic crisis in Malaysia', in Abdul Rahman and Jurgen Rudolph (eds), *South-East Asia into the Twenty First Century: Crisis and Beyond*, Bangi: Penerbitan Universiti Kebangsaan Malaysia.

Ishak, Shari (1998), 'Income inequalities in Malaysia 1970-1995', paper presented at the workshop on 'Poverty and Income Distribution in Asia and the Pacific', University of New South Wales, Sydney.

Ishak, Shari and Rahman Embong Abdul (1999), 'Rapid participatory assessments of the social impact of the financial crisis in Malaysia', draft final report presented for UNDP Regional Bureau for Asia and the Pacific.

Jomo, K. S. (ed.) (1998), *Tigers in Trouble: Financial Governance, Liberalisation and Crises in East Asia*, London: Zed.

Malaysia (1991), *The Second Outline Perspective Plan 1970–1990*, Kuala Lumpur: Percetakan Nasional Malaysia Berhad.

Malaysia (1998a), *Quarterly Bulletin*, Third Quarter 1998, 13 (3), Kuala Lumpur: Bank Negara Malaysia.

Malaysia (1998b), *Economic Report 1998–99*, Kuala Lumpur: Ministry of Finance.

Malaysia (1999a), *Mid-Term Review of the Seventh Malaysia Plan 1996–2000*, Kuala Lumpur: Percetakan Nasional Malaysia Berhad.

Malaysia (1999b), *Annual Report 1998*, Kuala Lumpur: Bank Negara Malaysia.

Malaysia (1999c), *Monthly Statistical Bulletin, Malaysia*, May, Kuala Lumpur: Department of Statistics.

Malaysia (1999d), *Laporan Pasaran Buruh 1998*, Kuala Lumpur: Ministry of Human Resources.

Montes, Manuel F. (1998), *The Currency Crisis in Southeast Asia*, Singapore: Institute of Southeast Asian Studies.

Ohmae, K. (1991), *The Borderless World: Power and Strategy in the Interlinked Economy*, New York: Harper Perennial.

Rasiah, Rajah and Shari Ishak (1997), 'Malaysia's new economic policy in retrospect', in H. M. Dahlan, J. Hamzah, A. Y. Hing and J. H. Ong (eds), *ASEAN in the Global System*, Bangi: Universiti Kebangsaan Malaysia Press.

Samsudin, Hitam (1999), 'Pencapaian bumiputera dalam bidang ekonomi', working paper at the Fourth Bumiputera Congress, Kuala Lumpur, presented 10–11 September.

Shireen, Mardziah Hashim (1998), *Income Inequality and Poverty in Malaysia*, Lanham: Rowman and Littlefield.

Strange, Susan (1995), 'The defective state', *Daedalus*, 124 (2), 55–74.

15

What determines the long-run movements of the Malaysian ringgit?

Ahmad Zubaidi Baharumshah, Azali Mohamed and
Muzafar Shah Habibullah

Introduction

Lane (1999) explained why the determination of long-run movements in exchange rates should be of interest. First, explaining the long-run behaviour of currencies is illuminating for those interested in tracing the evolution of the global economy. Second, understanding of what determines long-run changes in nominal exchange rate is potentially helpful to investors comparing expected returns on medium- or long-term nominal bonds in different currencies. Third, modelling the long-run behaviour of the exchange rate is the underpinning for useful understanding of the short-run behaviour of exchange rates: it is necessary to know the long run in order to work out whether a given exchange rate movement is a deviation from its long-run path. Finally, long-run movements in exchange rates are less prone to the 'noise' that is present in higher-frequency exchange rate data and hence may more easily be related to the fundamental determinants indicated by theory.

Interest in the determinants of long-run exchange rates is not new and the topic has been revived by the development in the econometric time-series analysis, particularly those relating to co-integration theory. A major puzzle of the empirical exchange rate literature is the poor performance of various exchange rate models. These failures have been documented in Boughton (1988), MacDonald (1988), MacDonald and Taylor (1992), among others. Briefly, these authors argue that problems with endogeneity and simultaneity, single equation approach, complicated dynamics and the possibility of other forms of misspecification are the major reasons that existing exchange rate models give unsatisfactory results.[1]

Malaysia has enjoyed high economic growth in the past two decades and is on the threshold of becoming a newly industrialised economy (NIE). Japan, Singapore and the USA are believed to have strong economic influence on Malaysia. Not only are Japan and the USA Malaysia's two largest trading partners but also its two largest foreign investors. In addition, the dependency of Malaysian trade on both of these countries is increasing. Japan is now the largest foreign investor in Malaysia. Financial liberalisation started in the late 1970s but it was only after the 1985 recession (due to the collapse of commodity prices) that the major reform measures were undertaken. These deregulation processes have led to market determination of interest rates. The liberalisation process has impact on the degree of integration between the domestic and the world financial markets. Several authors found that on the basis of covered and/or uncovered interest rate parity, there is substantial integration between Malaysia and world financial markets (see Faruqee 1992; Phylaktis 1997; Zhou 1996).[2] The relatively stable political and economic environments in the past three decades have allowed a faster pace in the deregulation and liberalisation of financial markets.

A study on the determinants of Malaysian ringgit is of interest for several reasons. First, Malaysia followed a managed-float system after the breakdown of the Bretton Wood System of fixed exchange rate. The Malaysian ringgit is pegged within a margin to a basket of currencies. The central bank, Bank Negara Malaysia (BNM), is responsible for curbing excessive fluctuation in the exchange value of the ringgit. It also has long-standing policies of open capital markets. Malaysia promises to be an interesting case to examine how foreign exchange rates react to macroeconomic fundamentals and see if the monetary model is relevant to small open economy. Second, given the increasing importance of trade and investment in Malaysia within the ASEAN region and its trade dependency on the USA, Japan, Singapore and Europe, it is important to understand the movements of ringgit against these other currencies of major trading partners. Third, because several studies found that Purchasing Power Parity (PPP) does not hold, we seek evidence to examine if the more complete monetary exchange model holds for the Malaysia.[3]

Many researchers have undertaken empirical estimation of the monetary model for exchange rate determination. Although the monetary model is theoretically appealing, its empirical validity is surrounded by controversy. In general, the data up to the end of 1978 for the industrial countries tend to be supportive of the asset market approach to exchange rate determination. In contrast to the earlier work, studies using data beyond 1978 have produced results that are unsupportive of the model.[4] However, empirical studies in the 1990s by MacDonald and Taylor (1991; 1992; 1993; 1994a; 1994b), McNown and Wallace (1994), and Moosa (1994), utilising a variety of econometric methods to deal with non-stationary data, found that a monetary model is a valid framework to analyse movements in major currencies.[5] These key currencies include German mark, Japanese yen, British pound and Canadian dollar. Moreover, studies by Diamandis et al. (1996) and Makrydakis (1998), Diamandis and Kouretas (1996), and Berg and Jayanetti (1993) that focused on the less significant currencies showed that the monetary model works quite well.[6] In other words, the monetary model produces sensible long-run equilibrium relationships and has the ability to track exchange rates even for the smaller economies. These monetary factors are important in explaining the movement of exchange rates.[7]

Malaysia is a small open economy and has received little attention in the exchange rate literature. This chapter attempts to answer the question: Is the monetary model of exchange rates valid in the long run? We employed the monetary framework to analyse the movements of the Malaysian ringgit compared with four other currencies, that is, the US dollar (US), the Japanese yen (JY), Singapore dollar (SD) and the German mark (DM). Following the current tradition, we utilised the Johansen–Juselius multivariate co-integration approach to analyse the long-run movements in exchange rates. The technique fully captures the underlying time series properties of the data, provides estimates of all the co-integrating vectors that exist within a vector of variables and offers a test statistic for the number of co-integrating vectors. An additional advantage of this technique is that it is able to detect several co-integrating vectors, as well as evaluate hypotheses of theoretical interest on the coefficients entering the estimated co-integrating vectors.[8]

We will set out the basic monetary model of exchange rate determination, then describe the data sources and econometric methodology, and report the empirical results.

The monetary model

The monetary model approach relies on two building blocks and may be summarised by the following equations (see Baillie and MacMahon 1989; MacDonald and Taylor 1992 for a more comprehensive discussion):

$$e_t = \alpha + p_t - p_t^* \qquad (15.1)$$

$$m_t - p_t = \alpha y_t - \beta_i \qquad (15.2a)$$

$$m_t^* - p_t^* = \alpha^* y_t^* - \beta_i^* \qquad (15.2b)$$

$$i_t - i_t^* = E_t(e_{t+1}) - e_t, \qquad (15.3)$$

where e_t is the log of the spot exchange rate (units of home currency per unit of foreign currency), p_t is the log of the domestic price level, m_t is the log of the domestic money supply, y_t is domestic real income and i_t is the domestic interest rate. Here, an asterisk denotes the corresponding foreign country variable and in our case the USA, Japan, Singapore or Germany. The term $E_t(e_{t+1})$ denotes the expectation of next period's level of the log of exchange rate, conditional on information available in period t.

Equation (15.1) represent the purchasing power parity (PPP) condition, equations (15.2a) and (15.2b) are the standard home and foreign monetary equilibria respectively and (15.3) is the uncovered interest parity (UIP) condition. The monetary model of exchange rate determination is an extension of the quantity theory of money to the case of an open economy. The model assumes that (i) real income and the nominal money supply are determined exogenously; (ii) capital and goods are perfect substitutes; (iii) goods prices are fully flexible; and (iv) domestic money is demanded only by domestic residents and foreign money only by foreign residents. Under these assumptions a typical monetary model of exchange rate determination may be written by the following unrestricted reduced form equation:[9]

$$e_t = \alpha_0 + \beta_1 m_t + \beta_2 m_t^* + \beta_3 y_t + \beta_4 y_t^* + \beta_5 i + \beta_6 i^* + \mu_t \qquad (15.4)$$

$$\beta_1, \beta_4, \beta_5 > 0, \qquad \beta_2, \beta_3, \beta_6 < 0$$

where all the variables are as defined above and u_t is a residual term, assumed to have zero mean and constant variance. For estimation purposes, all variables, except for interest rates, are expressed in natural logarithms.[10]

Equation (15.4) has been estimated by numerous researchers to test for the validity of the monetary model in a long-run context using the co-integration methodology. The specification given by equation (15.4) considers the fundamental variables (money, real income and the interest rates) as determinants of exchange rates. It is a richer formulation then PPP, because it considers three fundamental variables, whereas PPP consider only one variable—the price differential. As pointed out by Makrydakis (1998) the reduced-form model given by equation (15.4) nests both the flexible version (Frenkel 1976; Bilson 1978) as well as the sticky-price variant of the monetary model (Dornbusch 1976). The former is based on continuous purchasing power parity (PPP) and stable money demand functions for the domestic and foreign economies. The latter relaxes the unrealistic continuous PPP hypothesis, which implies a fixed real exchange rate, and permits instead overshooting of both nominal and real exchange rates relative to their long-run equilibrium (PPP) levels in the short run. MacDonald and Taylor (1992) argued that of the two versions of the theory, the Dornbusch version provides a more useful description of the recent floating exchange rate regime, which is characterised by wide fluctuation of real rates of exchange.

The expected signs on the coefficients in equation (15.4) may be summarised as follows: (a) a rise in domestic (foreign) money supply is expected to cause a depreciation (appreciation) of the ringgit; (b) an increase in domestic (foreign) real income will raise the demand of money leading to an appreciation (depreciation) of the ringgit; and (c) a rise in the domestic (foreign) interest rate reduces money demand and causes the ringgit to depreciate (appreciate). In addition, the monetary model also implies a set of coefficient restrictions on the unrestricted reduced form (equation (15.4)). The most important of these restrictions is the existence of proportionality between exchange rate and relative money ($\beta_1 = -\beta_2 = 1$). Less important for the validity of the monetary model, yet also frequently imposed and tested in the empirical work, are equal and opposite coefficients on relative incomes ($\beta_3 = -\beta_4$) and interest rates ($\beta_5 = -\beta_6$). This implies that the domestic income, interest elasticity of money demand is equal to their foreign counterparts (see Moosa 1994; MacDonald and Taylor 1991; 1994b). The

Johansen–Juselius technique allows us to test these monetary restrictions and these restrictions are displayed in Table 15.1.

Table 15.1: Some commonly imposed monetary restrictions,

$e_t - \beta_1 m_t + \beta_2 m_t^* + \beta_3 y_t + \beta_4 y_t^* + \beta_5 i + \beta_6 i^* + \phi_t$,

H_1: $\beta_1 = -\beta_2 = 1$	H_4: $H_1 \cap H_2$	
H_2: $\beta_3 + \beta_4 = 0$	H_5: $H_1 \cap H_3$	H_7: $H_1 \cap H_2 \cap H_3$
H_3: $\beta_5 + \beta_6 = 0$	H_6: $H_2 \cap H_3$	

Data and methodology

The study uses quarterly frequency data from 1976:1 to 1997:2 to model the long-run bilateral exchange rates of the ringgit (RM) against the US dollar (US), the Japanese yen (JY), German mark (DM) and Singapore dollar (SD). We choose to work with quarterly data since a finer frequency data would preclude the use of macroeconomic data, such as money and income, especially for a developing country where most of the data are available on annual frequency. Exchange rate movements were less volatile and there were no major economic crises in the sample period that might have caused too much noise for the co-integration technique to detect the long-run relationship.[11] Moreover, the choice of time period included an economy emerging from an era of financial regulations. We used three-month treasury bill returns as interest rates, narrow money (M1), and export indices for our measure of output. Exports are positively correlated with output and were used as a proxy for GDP since quarterly figures on GDP were unavailable for this study. The macroeconomic data are all collected from the International Monetary Fund. A recent study on long-run money demand by Arize et al. (1999) has shown that both M1 and M2 can be considered as viable tools for less-developed countries. The financial statistics published by the International Monetary Fund contained series that were all seasonally unadjusted. Seasonality may be captured either through seasonal dummies or through seasonal lags in the set of regressors. In the analysis that follows the 'domestic' country is taken to be Malaysia.

Prior to testing for co-integration, it is necessary to establish the order of integration. Schwert (1987) and DeJong et al. (1992), for instance, have noted that the Augmented Dickey–Fuller (ADF) (Dickey and Fuller 1981) statistics may reject the null hypothesis of a unit root too often in the presence of the first order moving average process. However, Campbell and Perron (1991) have shown that the ADF statistics have better small-sample properties than the Phillips–Perron (PP) statistics (Phillips and Perron 1988; Phillips 1987). To ensure robustness and overcome the criticisms of any individual testing technique, both ADF and Phillips-Perron procedures are considered in the analysis. We carry out the tests on the time series of each variable in levels and differenced forms.

Once we have determined the order of integration of each series, the next step was to test for co-integration relationships among the series. Two common tests for co-integration are the two-step procedure of Engle and Granger (1987) and the Johansen (1988) and Johansen and Juselius (1990) techniques. We employ the maximum likelihood co-integration test because of Johansen (1988), and Johansen and Juselius (1990). The Engle and Granger procedure performs the tests in a univariate set up. The Johansen–Juselius technique is utilised to test for the number of linearly independent co-integrating vectors in the system. The procedure allows not only for testing for the number of co-integrating vectors but also for testing for restrictions suggested by economic theory via a multivariate framework. The procedure provides more robust results than other methods when there are more then two variables (Gonzalo 1994).[12] If a non-zero vector(s) is indicated by these tests, a stationary long-run relationship is implied. A brief discussion on the procedure is provided at the end of the chapter.

Empirical results

The Johansen–Juselius procedure requires that all variables are not I (2). To verify this we relied on two-unit root testing procedures, namely the Augmented Dickey–Fuller (ADF) and Phillips–Perron (PP) tests. In applying these tests, the optimal lag structure is determined using the Akaike Information Criteria (AIC) and Schwartz Criteria (SC). In addition insignificant lags (conventional F-test) were dropped from the regression. If the elimination of lags produced serial correlation then the lags were added back on. To save space, the results of the unit root tests are not reported in this chapter, but generally both the ADF and PP tests suggest that the variables are non-stationary in levels. The same tests were also conducted using first differences, and none of these tests provided evidence against our initial findings. The results overwhelmingly confirm the findings of other studies that both exchange rate and the fundamental macroeconomic variables contain a unit root in level form. Both procedures also show that all variables are stationary after first differencing.[13]

We next proceeded with the co-integration tests using the seven-dimensional vector [e, m, m*, y, y*, i, i*] and for four separate models: RM/US, RM/JY, RM/DM and RM/SD. In the Johansen–Juselius methodology, a lag length must be chosen for the Vector Autoregressive (VAR) model. Our objective was to eliminate serial correlation while avoiding the loss of power due to the presence of too many lags in the VAR model. For this purpose, the lag structure on the seven-vector VAR model is determined using the following strategy. Testing down from six lags, we checked for serial correlation using the Breusch–Godfrey test. The chosen VAR order for each bilateral rate is such that no equations contain serial correlation at 0.05 level. For the RM/DM model, evidence of autocorrelation was detected in some equations with six lags, but no significant autocorrelation was detected from the eight-lag model. The resulting VAR order are: RM/US, two; RM/JY, six; RM/SD, six and RM/DM, eight.

The chosen lag length shows no evidence of auto co-regressive conditional heteroskedasticity error (ARCH) effect. Moreover, there is no evidence of dynamic heteroskedasticity or non-normality. Thus, in general, results of these diagnostic tests suggest that the models appear to be adequately specified. In all cases, a constant term is included in the VAR model used to generate the Johansen results. Indeed, the likelihood ratio statistic indicated that the constant was significant. Thus, the statistics are computed with a constant term in the co-integrating relationship.

The results of using the optimal lag structure for the VAR models are summarised in Table 15.2. Both maximum eigenvalue (λ-max) and trace statistics reject the hypothesis that these are zero co-integrating vectors. In all cases the λ-max test suggests that we can accept one significant co-integrating vector at 5 per cent significance level or better. The results of the trace statistics yield the same conclusion, except for the RM/JY and RM/DM bilateral rates, where four co-integrating vectors are detected. To choose the number of co-integrating vectors, we follow McNown and Wallace (1994), where the vectors revealed to be significant in both tests are considered. It is worth noting that the sample values for both the trace and λ-max are adjusted for degree of freedom. The trace and λ-max value yield many more vectors if the degree of freedom correction were overlooked. For instance, in the case of RM/JY and RM/SD we found three vectors using the uncorrected degree of freedom.

In general, these findings suggest that there are stationary long-run equilibrium relationship between exchange rates and the fundamental variables.[14] For all the bilateral exchange rates we have evidence of stationary relationship between the exchange rate, money supply, income, and interest rates. Our results obtained so far are similar to those of Diamandis and Kouretas (1996), Diamandis et al. (1996) and Berg and Jayanetti (1993), among others who found at least a single co-integrating vector in the system of the monetary variables. However, these results contrast sharply with those of researchers who have been unable to discover even a single long-run relationship for the monetary variables (see Baillie and Pecchenino 1991; Sarantis 1994; McNown and Wallace 1994). Their data failed to capture the effect of macroeconomic variables on the exchange rate for the sample of countries considered in their studies.

In interpreting these results one must bear in mind two important points. First, a co-integrating vector implies a long-run stable relationship among jointly endogenous variables arising from constraints implied by the economic structure on the long-run relationship. Second, the smaller the number of co-integrating vectors, the less stable will be the system of non-stationary co-integrated variables. In our case, we found one significant co-integrating vector (or six stochastic trends) for all bilateral exchange rates.[15] Thus we do not have the problem of identifying the relationship that

Table 15.2: Testing for co-integration using the Johansen and Juselius (1990) method

Tests			RM/US	RM/JY	RM/DM	RM/SD
H_0	H_A	C.V.	(2)	(6)	(8)	(6)
			λ-max			
R = 0	= 1	46.45	63.64*	59.26*	57.65*	47.79*
R ≤ 1	= 2	40.30	27.72	35.38	33.85	24.80
R ≤ 2	= 3	34.40	13.95	32.35	25.91	20.35
R ≤ 3	= 4	28.12	10.11	26.61	21.53	16.90
R ≤ 4	= 5	22.00	8.36	16.60	14.09	13.71
R ≤ 5	= 6	15.67	6.48	8.87	11.70	6.19
R ≤ 6	= 7	9.24	4.75	7.26	8.75	3.08
			Trace			
R = 0	≥ 1	132.70	135.01*	186.33*	173.47*	132.83*
R ≤ 1	≥ 2	102.14	71.36	127.07*	115.82*	85.03
R ≤ 2	≥ 3	76.07	43.64	91.68*	81.97*	60.23
R ≤ 3	≥ 4	53.12	29.69	59.33*	56.07*	39.88
R ≤ 4	≥ 5	34.91	19.58	32.72	34.54	22.98
R ≤ 5	≥ 6	19.96	11.23	16.12	18.45	9.27
R ≤ 6	≥ 7	9.24	4.75	7.26	8.75	3.08

Note: C.V. stands for 5 per cent critical values, from Osterwald–Lenum (1992). The number in parenthesis below the country-pair is the lag length of the VAR. Chosen r: number of co-integrating vectors that are significant under both tests. These statistics are computed with a constant in the unrestricted VAR equation.

represents the process whereby the exchange rate is determined in the long run.

The estimated parameters of the co-integrating vectors (βs) are reported in Table 15.3. Normalising the equations by the exchange rate allows us to directly compare the hypothesised values of the βs in equation (15.4). None of these equations has all the signs that are consistent with theory. For instance, in the RM/US and RM/DM cases, the co-integrating vector has four expected signs. In the RM/SD case, the vector has four wrong signs among the six variables. All signs on y^* have the expected positive sign except in one case (RM/SD). A comparison can be made between the findings in this chapter and those reported in Makrydakis (1998) and Moosa (1994). Makrydakis (1998) found that except for interest rates, the signs of all the other variables are consistent with theory for Korean won-US dollar rate. Moosa (1994), on the other hand, showed that the magnitudes of the coefficients are in many cases excessively high and the signs are inconsistent with those predicted by theory. Pervious studies on demand for money that employed the same methodogy also encountered similar problems. Specifically, the equations obtained by normalising co-integrating vectors on real money demand balances look like money demand functions, money supply functions or some complicated interaction that appears not to make economic sense (see Johansen and Juselius 1990; Dickey et al. 1991; Moosa 1994).

Table 15.3: Estimated co-integrated vectors in Johansen

| | Variable | | | | | | | | |
	e	m	m*	Y	y*	i	i*	Dummy	Constant
RM/US	−1.00	−0.20	0.47	−0.80	1.01	0.05	−0.04	-	−3.51
RM/JY	−1.00	−2.13	0.37	1.94	0.60	−0.07	−0.01	0.22	−10.05
RM/DM	−1.00	1.10	1.14	−1.64	0.37	0.04	0.04	−0.53	−7.48
RM/SD	−1.00	0.22	0.40	0.41	−0.81	0.02	0.01	-	2.49

Note: The estimated coefficients were obtained by normalising the exchange rate variables. For the RM/JY and RM/DM case, we have included a shift dummy to allow for structural break in the long-run relationship.

Table 15.4 presents test results of exclusions restrictions on the exchange rate, money supplies, output, and interest rates in the co-integration relationship. With one co-integrating vector, this LR statistics is asymptotically distributed as $\chi^2_{(1)}$. In each case, the hypothesis that exchange rate does not enter into the co-integrating relationship is easily rejected at least at the 10 per cent significance level. In fact in the RM/US rate, only the domestic money supply variable, m, appears not to enter in the long-run relationship. In the RM/DM case, all the variables enter into the co-integrating relationship. Again this confirms our contention that the bilateral rates of the ringgit are determined by fundamental variables for the 1976–1997 period.

Table 15.4: Test of exclusion restrictions

	RM/US	RM/JY	RM/DM	RM/SD
e	6.32 (0.01)	16.04 (0.00)	46.27 (0.00)	28.63 (0.00)
m	1.14 (0.29)	33.19 (0.00)	46.06 (0.00)	8.62 (0.00)
m*	4.09 (0.04)	0.62 (0.43)	37.23 (0.00)	4.04 (0.04)
y	12.22 (0.00)	43.50 (0.00)	60.55 (0.00)	12.35 (0.00)
y*	14.37 (0.00)	8.41 (0.00)	43.54 (0.00)	22.31 (0.00)
i	8.00 (0.01)	19.63 (0.00)	10.23 (0.00)	16.02 (0.00)
i*	10.01 (0.00)	0.13 (0.72)	17.15 (0.00)	1.63 (0.20)
Dummy	-	5.96 (0.02)	28.64 (0.00)	-
Constant	14.59 (0.00)	12.81 (0.00)	52.58 (0.00)	10.18 (0.00)

Note: For the tests of exclusion restrictions figures are χ^2 statistics with one degree of freedom, and the critical value at the 5 per cent significance level is 3.84. For the RM/JY and RM/DM, we have included a shift dummy to allow for structural break in the long-run relationship. It takes a value of 1 for t = 1984:1 to 1984:4 and zero elsewhere. The dummy variable is found to be insignificant in the other cases.

We also report in Table 15.5 the test results of imposing restrictions on α. The test serves as a test of weak exogeneity. It shows whether the exchange rate or some other variables that adjust clear any deviations from its long-run position. The results of the Wald test show that in all the equations, the exchange rate adjusts to clear any disequilibrium from its long-run PPP (at the 10 per cent significance level). The results also indicate the error-correction term enters significantly in some of the other equations. For instance, in the RM/US model all the variables, except for domestic interest rate (i) adjust to clear any disequilibrium.

Table 15.5: Estimated error correction parameters

	Variable						
	e	m	m*	y	y*	i	i*
RM/US	2.80	23.55	35.39	16.44	5.20	0.00	11.72
	(0.09)	(0.00)	(0.00)	(0.00)	(0.02)	(0.97)	(0.00)
RM/JY	2.90	0.54	0.76	55.44	0.14	1.94	5.17
	(0.09)	(0.46)	(0.38)	(0.00)	(0.71)	(0.16)	(0.02)
RM/DM	3.48	0.08	4.56	8.22	0.93	5.78	7.88
	(0.06)	(0.77)	(0.03)	(0.00)	(0.34)	(0.02)	(0.01)
RM/SD	3.96	2.81	4.91	1.68	1.24	19.14	5.88
	(0.05)	(0.09)	(0.03)	(0.20)	(0.27)	(0.00)	(0.02)

Note: The Wald test is χ^2 distribution with one degree of freedom. The number in parentheses is the marginal significance.

Table 15.6 reports the test results of some of the popular monetary restrictions. Interestingly, the common imposed monetary restrictions (that is, H_1, H_2 and H_3) are not rejected at the 5 per cent significant level for the RM/US case. However, the restrictions are overwhelmingly rejected in all the other cases at the conventional significance level.

Table 15.6: Tests for monetary restrictions

	RM/US	RM/JY	RM/DM	RM/SD
H_1	1.14 (0.29)	16.89 (0.00)	58.73 (0.00)	9.80 (0.00)
H_2	0.87 (0.35)	37.00 (0.00)	53.77 (0.00)	6.82 (0.01)
H_3	0.38 (0.54)	20.13 (0.00)	47.09 (0.00)	6.95 (0.01)
H_4	20.17 (0.00)	37.03 (0.00)	60.19 (0.00)	14.45 (0.00)
H_5	1.14 (0.57)	33.55 (0.00)	65.40 (0.00)	10.27 (0.01)
H_6	3.84 (0.15)	47.56 (0.00)	64.75 (0.00)	7.23 (0.03)
H_7	25.22 (0.00)	53.59 (0.00)	66.59 (0.00)	14.97 (0.00)

Note: H_1 to H_7 denote the hypothesis summarised in Table 15.1. The numbers not in the parenthesis are χ^2 statistics with degree of freedom equal $r \times k$, where r denotes the number of co-integrating vectors and k is the number of restrictions. The number in parentheses is marginal significance level.

The finding that the above hypotheses are generally rejected is in accordance with Moosa (1994), Kanas (1997), MacDonald and Taylor (1991; 1994b). For instance, MacDonald and Taylor (1991) reported that none of the restrictions for Germany could be rejected. For UK and Japan, however, the restrictions are all rejected except for H_2 for Japan. Applying the model for the sterling-dollar exchange rate, MacDonald and Taylor (1994b) found that all the restrictions are rejected at the conventional significance level. In applying the same model to Korea, Makrydakis (1998) found at least three co-integrating vectors for the Korean won–US dollar rate. However, all the parameter restrictions implied by the model are easily rejected by the data. Lane (1991) argued that these restrictions are partly responsible for the failure of the restricted version of the monetary model. Our results may suggest that the restricted version of the monetary model that assumes the equality of coefficients may not be appropriate to model the exchange rate behaviour in Malaysia.

The rejection of the monetary model restrictions may also suggest that the long-run relationship may not be that implied by monetary model. However, Alogoskoufis and Smith (1991; 1992) have argued that the coefficients of a long-run equation, such as the monetary model, could be a combination of adjustment, expectation and structural variables. Since the model used in the analysis did not reflect such variables, the estimated parameters of the co-integrating vectors may not be given structural interpretation (Dickey et al. 1991). This line of argument suggests that rejection of the monetary restrictions does not rule out the possibility that the empirical long-run relationship is consistent with the monetary model (see Kanas 1997). In addition, the results obtained from this study are more promising than those of some of the earlier studies that failed to identify the co-integrating vector.

Conclusion

One characteristic shared by essentially all developing economies is that they must conduct the vast bulk of international commerce and finance in terms of the monies of major industrial countries rather than their domestic monies. Both policy makers and economists would agree, therefore, that exchange rate is an important variable. Yet the empirical work in this area for the less developing countries (LDCs) has remained sparse. In this chapter we examine the monetary models of exchange rate using quarterly data for Malaysia ringgit.

The findings may be summarised as follows. First, we found that all the macroeconomic variables, including exchange rates, are I (1) variables. Second, this study demonstrates that a co-integrating relationship exists between the exchange rate, money, income and the interest rate. Co-integration between the fundamental variables and the exchange rate for all the bilateral exchange rates may be interpreted as evidence of a long-run relationship between the exchange rate and fundamental variables for the country-pairs considered. Third, we tested the commonly imposed monetary restrictions on the coefficients of the model. With perhaps one exception (the RM/US case) the restrictions imposed on the model were easily rejected. Fourth, the estimates of the adjustment parameters show that exchange rates and foreign interest rates most often respond to disequilibrium. In all the models we found that the error correction term enters significantly in the exchange rate equations, implying that the bilateral rates adjust to clear any long-run disequilibrium.

MacDonald and Taylor (1994b) argued that the evidence in favour of the long-run monetary model implies indirect evidence in favour of long-run PPP, since PPP forms the link between stable domestic money demand and the monetary exchange rate equation. Direct empirical evidence on long-run PPP for Malaysia is uncommon except Manzur and Arriff (1995) showed the data on ASEAN economies support the long-run reversion to PPP. MacDonald (1995) demonstrated that PPP as a concept only holds in the very long run (100 years), a period longer than that captured by the data sample used here. Other studies have also shown that PPP holds reasonably well in a more complete system rather than estimating a single equation, which is common in the literature. For instance, MacDonald and Nagayasu (1998) used a version of the real interest differential (RID) model that allows for deviations from PPP to be governed by a real interest rate differential to illustrate this point. They showed that the RID model outperforms the random walk in explaining the yen–US dollar bilateral exchange rate over the float.

The empirical results suggest that monetary variables can account for the long-run movements of the ringgit in relation to the US dollar, the Japanese yen, Singapore dollar and German mark. In other words, the ringgit is largely determined by fundamental factors. Policy makers and business may use these variables to monitor the movements in ringgit in the long term. Some observers argued that the tightening of monetary policy was necessary to stabilise the exchange rate and restore confidence during the Asian financial crisis. Others have argued that rising interest rates will reduce the ability of borrowers to repay loans and thereby weaken the banking sector. This, combined with declining investor confidence, may lead to further weakening of the domestic currency. Unfortunately the results obtained for the long-run parameters of the model do not provide any clear and consistent answers on the impact of monetary policy on the interest rate and the exchange rate. This may be due to the inadequacies in our data set or perhaps in our choice of model for tests. We realised that much more empirical works is required in this area of research.

Before the 1997 financial crisis, Malaysia followed a managed float system and the ringgit was allowed to move in response to market forces in periods of macroeconomic stability. However, the central bank normally intervenes to limit exchange rate volatility, especially when the ringgit is under pressure. For instance, the ringgit was allowed to fluctuate within a band of 2.47–2.57 to the US dollar in the first half of 1997. In this sense, the ringgit is not allowed to float freely. It is sometimes important to allow the ringgit to move by significant amounts even for short periods. Maintaining greater flexibility in exchange rates can persuade private business to recognise and prudently managed the foreign exchange risk. In our view, this is important for an economy with substantial involvement in international trade and global financial markets, given the limited size of its domestic market.

Appendix

The Johansen approach sets up the non-stationary time series (Y) as a vector auto regression (VAR):

$$\Delta Y_t = \mu_0 + \sum_{i=1}^{k-1} \Gamma_i \Delta Y_{t-1} + \Pi Y_{t-k} + \varepsilon_t \tag{15.5}$$

where $\Gamma_i = -(I - \Pi_1 - .... - \Pi_i)$
for $i = 1,..., k - 1 \Pi_i = -(I - \Pi_1 - .... - \Pi_k)$.

Y_t is a vector of p variables, μ_0 is a constant and ε_t is a vector of Gaussian random variables. Γ and Π represent coefficient matrices, Δ is the difference operator, k denotes the lag length.

The matrix Π is called the long-run impact matrix and it contains information about the long-run relationships between variables. The number of co-integrating vectors is determined by the rank (r) of Π, which indicates the number of co-integrating vectors. If Π is of full rank, or r = p, no co-integration is present as all series are themselves stationary. On the other hand, if Π is a null matrix, or r = 0 then no long-run relationship is present as equation (15.5) is the usual VAR model in first differences. In the case when $0 < r < p$, then there exist one or more co-integrating relationships among the variables. The Π matrix can be decomposed as $\Pi = \alpha\beta'$, where the elements of the α matrix are the adjustment coefficients and the β matrix contains the co-integrating vectors. The Johansen procedure uses two likelihood ratio statistics to test for co-integration—the trace and maximum eigenvalue (λ max) statistics.

The trace test for the null of r or fewer co-integrating vectors (versus more than) r is:

$$TR_r = -T \sum_{i=r+1}^{P} \ln(1 - \hat{\lambda}_i) \tag{15.6}$$

where T is the sample size and λ is an estimated eigenvalue. This is a function of the squared canonical correlations ($\hat{\lambda}_i$) between the first difference and the levels of the variables, having factored out the dynamic and deterministic factors. The $\hat{\lambda}_i$ are the solutions to a certain eigenvalue problem. An alternative maximal eigenvalue test statistic of the null that there are r co-integrating vectors against the alternative that there are r + 1 is

$$\lambda \max_r = TR_r\, TR_{r+1} \tag{15.7}$$

Both test statistics may be compared with the appropriate critical values provided by Osterwald-Lenum (1992). The test statistics are non-standard and depend only on the number of degree of freedom, $p - \sigma$. The importance of applying a degree of freedom correction for the Johansen–Juselius technique is now well known. The correction factor is necessary to reduce the excessive tendency of the test to falsely reject the null hypothesis of no co-integration. Several authors have documented the importance of this correction factor (see Reimers 1992; Cheung and Lai 1993; Cushman 1993). To adjust for the finite sample inference problem of the Johansen technique, we used the degree of freedom suggested by Reinsel and Ahn (1992). The correction factor suggested by Reinsel and Ahn is to multiply the test statistics in both (15.6) and (15.7) by $(T - pk)/T$, where p corresponds to the number of variables in the VAR model and k is the number of lags employed.

As mentioned earlier, a further advantage of the Johansen–Juselius approach is that it allows for test of restrictions, which have been widely discussed in the monetary exchange rate model. Based on the outcomes of the Johansen–Juselius co-integration tests, the significance of the estimated coefficients (β and α) in the co-integrating relationship could be tested. Using the notation of Johansen and Juselius, the hypothesis tests that we implement are of the general form:

$$H_3 : \Pi = \alpha\varphi'H' \quad (\text{or } \beta = H\varphi) \tag{15.8}$$

H is a $p \times s$ matrix and φ is a $s \times r$ matrix of unknown parameters. In particular, we test the hypothesis summarised in Table 15.1. For details of the tests of linear restriction on the estimated coefficients see Johansen and Juselius (1990).

Endnotes

[1] Lastrapes (1992) found that much of the variance of exchange rate changes, even at monthly horizons, seems to be due to permanent shocks. Amano and Norden (1995) further support this view. In fact, they argued that existing exchange rate models omit some important sources of shock that alter real exchange rates. Specifically, they showed that the exogenous shift in terms of the Canada–US bilateral exchange rate and the influences of monetary factors play only secondary role.

[2] For instance, Phylaktis (1997) showed that interest rates of the Asia-Pacific countries (including Malaysia) have been moving together since the 1970s in relation to both the USA and Japan.

3 Earlier studies by Gan (1991), Bahmani-Oskooee (1993) and Baharumshah and Ariff (1997) showed that the data reject PPP. However, Manzur and Ariff (1995) showed that the PPP relation holds in the long run for the ASEAN as a whole.

4 The models for the period beyond 1978 produced poor results in terms of the signs and significance of the coefficients as well as the within-sample predictive power, not to mention the poor out-of-sample predicting performance.

5 The Johansen methodology generally provided stronger support for the monetary model, especially when distinction between traded and non-traded goods is introduced. Using the Johansen procedure on three exchange rates (sterling, mark and yen against the dollar), MacDonald and Taylor found evidence in favour of long-run relationship for the three exchange rates. This led them to conclude the monetary model does provide valid explanation of the long-run exchange rate.

6 Diamandis and Kouretas (1996) applied the monetary model to four Greek drachma bilateral rates (drachma–Deutschmark, drachma–US dollar, drachma–sterling and drachma-franc) using data for the recent float.

7 In this chapter the term 'fundamental variables' refers to money, interest rate and income. Both Flood et al. (1991) and Kanas (1997) adopted the same term for these three variables.

8 See Gonzalo (1994) and Campbell and Perron (1991) for more detailed discussion on the advantage of the Johansen–Juselius approach.

9 The restricted version of the model assumes that $\beta_1 = \beta_2$, $\beta_3 = \beta_4$ and $\beta_5 = \beta_6$. In this version of the monetary model the exchange rate equation is given by $e = (m - m^*) - \beta_3(y - y^*) + \beta_5(i - i^*)$. In this case, β_3 expected to be negative and β_5 is expected to be positive.

10 The data were converted into natural logarithms to avoid difficulty presented by Jensen's inequality.

11 We have excluded that data from the recent financial crisis period because of the noise for which the co-integration method cannot detect a stable long-run relationship suggested by the monetary model.

12 Gonzalo (1989) provides evidence that the Johansen and Juselius (1990) method performs better than the single equation methods and alternative multivariate method (for example Stock and Watson 1989).

13 The results are consistent with those reported by Baharumshah and Ariff (1997) and Bahmani-Oskooee (1993). Detailed results from the unit roots test are available for the authors on request.

14 If more than one vector is found, the test may indicate more than one relationship (Johansen and Juselius 1990; Dickey et al. 1991).

15 The finding of more than one co-integrating vector leads to the problem of identifying the single long-run relation of interest. In this case it is the monetary equation that supposedly represents the process whereby the exchange rate is determined in the long run.

References

Alogoskoufis, G. and R. Smith (1991), 'On error correction models: Specification, interpretation and estimation', *Journal of Economic Surveys*, 5, 97–128.

—— (1992), 'Monetary accommodation, exchange rate regimes and inflation persistence', *The Economic Journal*, 102, 461–480.

Amano, R. A. and S. V. Norden (1995), 'Terms of trade and real exchange rates: The Canadian evidence', *Journal of International Money and Finance*, 14, 83–104.

Baharumshah, A. Z. and M. Ariff (1997), 'Purchasing power parity in South East Asian countries economies: A co-integration approach', *Asian Economic Journal*, 11 (2), 141–153.

Bahmani-Oskooee, M. (1993), 'Purchasing power parity based on effective exchange rate and co-integration: 25 LDCs experience with its absolute formulation', *World Development*, 21, 1023–1031.

Baillie, R. T. and P. C. MacMahon (1989), *Foreign Exchange Market: Theory and Econometric Evidence*, Cambridge: Cambridge University Press.

Baillie, R. T. and R. A. Pecchenino (1991), 'The search for equilibrium relationships in international finance: The case of monetary model', *Journal of International Money and Finance*, 10, 582–593.

Berg, H. and S. C. Jayanetti (1993), 'A novel test of the monetary approach using black market exchange rates and the Johansen-Juselius co-integration method', *Economic Letters*, 41, 413–418.

Bilson, J. F. O. (1978), 'Rational expectations and the exchange rate', in J. A. Frenkel and H. G. Johnson (eds), *The Economics of Exchange Rates*, Reading: Addison-Wesley.

Boughton, J. M. (1988), 'The monetary approach to exchange rates: What now remains?', *Essays in International Finance*, 171, International Finance Section, Princeton University.

Campbell, J. Y. and P. Perron (1991), 'Pitfalls and opportunities: What macro-economists should know about unit roots', Working Paper No. 100, Washington: National Bureau of Economic Research.

Cheung, Yin-Wong and S. Lai Kon (1993), 'Finite-samples size of Johansen's likelihood ratio tests for co-integration', *Oxford Bulletin of Economics and Statistics*, 55, 313–328.

Cushman, D. O. (1993), 'Single-equation maximum likelihood estimates of the co-integrating vector in a dollar-lira exchange rate model', *Applied Economic*, 25, 165–171.

DeJong, David N., John C. Nankervis, N. E. Savin and Charles H. Whiteman (1992), 'The power problems of unit root tests in time series with autoregressive errors', *Journal of Econometrics*, 53, 323–344.

Diamandis, P. F. and G. P. Kouretas (1996), 'The monetary approach to the exchange rate: Long-run relationships, coefficient restrictions and temporal stability of the Greek drachma', *Applied Financial Economics*, 6, 351–362.

Diamandis, P. F., D. A. Georgoutsos and G. D. Kouretas (1996), 'Co-integration tests for the monetary exchange rate model: The Canadian–US dollar 1970–1994', *International Economics Journal*, 10, 83–97.

Dickey, D. A. and W. A. Fuller (1981), 'The likelihood ratio statistics for autoregressive time series with a unit root', *Econometrica*, 49, 1057–1072.

Dickey, D. A., D. W. Jansen and D. L. Thornton (1991), 'A primer on co-integration with an application to money and income', *Federal Reserve Bank of St. Louis Review*, 73, 58–78.

Dornbusch, R. (1976), 'Expectations and exchange rate dynamics', *Journal of Political Economy*, 84, 1161–1176.

Engle, R. F. and C. W. J. Granger (1987), 'Co-integration and error-correction: representation, estimation and testing, *Econometrica*, 55, 251–276.

Faruqee, H. (1992), 'Dynamic capital mobility in Pacific-basin developing countries', *International Monetary Fund Staff Papers*, 39, 706–717.

Flood, R. P., A. K. Rose and D. J. Mathieson (1991), 'An empirical exploration of exchange-rate target-zones', *Carnegie Rochester Conference Series on Public Policy*, 35, 7–77.

Frenkel, J. A. (1976), 'A monetary approach to the exchange rate: Doctrinal aspects and empirical evidence', *Scandinavian Journal of Economics*, 78, 200–224.

Gan, W. B. (1991), 'On the deviation from purchasing power parity: The case of the ringgit effective exchange rate', *Applied Economics*, 23, 1461–1471.

Gonzalo, J. (1989), 'Comparison of the five alternative methods of estimating long-run equilibrium relationships', *UCSD Discussion Paper 89-55*.

—— (1994), 'Five alternative methods of estimating long-run equilibrium relationship', *Journal of Econometrics*, 60, 203–233.

Johansen, S. (1988), 'Statistical analysis of co-integration vectors', *Journal of Economic Dynamics and Control*, 231–254.

Johansen, S. and K. Juselius (1990), 'Maximum likelihood estimation and inference on co-integration—with applications to the demand for money', *Oxford Bulletin of Economics and Statistics*, 52, 169–210.

Kanas, A. (1997), 'The monetary exchange rate model within the ERM: Co-integration tests and implication concerning the Germany dominance hypotheses, *Applied Financial Economics*, 7, 587–598.

Lane, T. D. (1991), 'Empirical models of exchange rate determination: Picking up the pieces', *Economia Internazionale*, 44, 210–226.

Lane, P. R. (1999), 'What determines the nominal exchange rate? Some cross-sectional evidence', *Canadian Journal of Economics*, 32, 118–138.

Lastrapes, W. D. (1992), 'Sources of fluctuations in real and nominal exchange rates', *The Review of Economics and Statistics*, 74, 530–539.

MacDonald, R. (1988), '*Floating Exchange Rates: Theories and Evidence*', London: Unwin Hymon.

—— (1995), 'Long-run exchange rate modelling', *International Monetary Fund Staff Papers*, 42, 437–489.

MacDonald, R. and J. Nagayasu (1998), 'On the Japanese yen–US dollar exchange rate: A structural econometric model based on real interest differentials', *Journal of the Japanese and International Economies*, 12, 75–102.

MacDonald, R. and M. P. Taylor (1991), 'The monetary approach to the exchange rate: Long-run relationships and coefficient restrictions', *Economic Letters*, 37, 179–185.

—— (1992), 'Exchange rate economics: A survey', *International Monetary Fund Staff Papers*, 39, 1–57.

—— (1993), 'The monetary approach to the exchange rate: Rational expectations, long-run equilibrium, and forecasting', *International Monetary Fund Staff Papers*, 40, 89–107.

—— (1994a), 'The monetary model of the exchange rate: Long-run relationships, short-run dynamics, and how to beat a random walk', *Journal of International Money and Finance*, 13, 276–290.

—— (1994b), 'Re-examining the monetary approach to the exchange rate: the dollar-franc 1976–90', *Applied Financial Economics*, 12, 167–176.

Makrydakis, S. (1998), 'Testing the long-run validity of the monetary approach to the exchange rate: the won–US dollar case', *Applied Economics Letters*, 5, 507–511.

Manzur, M. and M. Ariff (1995), 'Purchasing power parity: New methods and extensions', *Applied Financial Economics*, 5, 19–26.

McNown, R. and M. S. Wallace (1994), 'Co-integration tests of the monetary exchange rate model for three high inflation economies', *Journal of Money, Credit, and Banking*, 26, 396–411.

Moosa, I. A. (1994), 'The monetary model of exchange rates revisited', *Applied Financial Economics*, 4, 279–287.

Osterwald-Lenum, M. (1992), 'A note with quantiles of the asymptotic distribution of the maximum likelihood co-integration rank test statistics: Four cases', *Oxford Bulletin of Economics and Statistics*, 54, 461–472.

Phillips, P. C. B. (1987), 'Time series regression with unit roots', *Econometrica*, 55, 277–302.

Phillips, P. C. B. and P. Perron (1988), 'Testing for a unit root in time series regression', *Biometrika*, 75, 335–346.

Phylaktis, K. (1997), 'Capital market integration in the Pacific-basin region: An analysis of real interest rate linkages', *Pacific-Basin Finance Journal*, 5, 195–213.

Reimers, H. E. (1992), 'Comparisons of tests for multivariate co-integration', *Statistical Papers*, 33, 335–359.

Reinsel, G. C. and K. Ahn Sung (1992), 'Vector autoregressive models with unit roots and reduced rank structure: Estimation, likelihood ratio tests, and forecasting', *Journal of Time Series Analysis*, 4 (13), 353–375.

Sarantis, N. (1994), 'The monetary exchange rate model in the long-run: An empirical investigation', *Weltwirtschaftliches Archiv*, 130, 698–710.

Schwert, G. W. (1987), 'Effects of model specification on tests for unit roots in macroeconomic data', *Journal of Monetary Economics*, 20, 73–103.

Stock, J. H. and M. W. Watson (1989), 'Interpreting the evidence on money-income causality', *Journal of Econometrics*, 40, 161–182.

Zhou, S. (1996), 'Trade connections and interest rate linkages among ASEAN, Japan, and the USA: An empirical analysis', *Applied Economics*, 28, 617–630.

16

Returns to liquidity on KLOFFE (Kuala Lumpur Options and Financial Futures Exchange)

S. Gulay Avsar and Barry A. Goss

Introduction

Futures contracts provide for the delivery (or settlement) of a specified quantity of a commodity (or financial instrument), of a specified quality, at a specified location at a precisely defined future date. These contracts, therefore, are highly standardised with respect to these four major attributes, and are suitable for trading on organised futures exchanges. In addition to trading standardised instruments, futures markets, unlike spot markets, are impersonal, because a clearing house interposes itself between buyer and seller, and guarantees all transactions.

Futures markets perform three major functions: first, they collect and disseminate information; second, they perform a forward pricing function, and third, they facilitate risk management through hedging. To perform these functions well it is important that futures exchanges are as liquid as possible, so that both buyers and sellers can transact immediately at desired prices. A reduction in liquidity means an increase in transaction costs for both parties.

Telser and Higinbotham (1977) argued that the liquidity of futures markets varies inversely with the standard deviation of market clearing prices, and they found in their sample of 51 commodities on US exchanges that this standard deviation varied negatively with turnover. Telser (1981) argued that there are increasing returns to liquidity, and Goss and Avsar (1998), who defined liquidity in terms of the ask–bid spread, found that for two-thirds of the Sydney Futures Exchange contracts studied, there was a significant negative relationship between volume and the ask–bid spread. If this hypothesis were generally consistent with the evidence, it would help to explain the concentration of futures trading in a few large exchanges around the world, and to explain the concentration of trading in a few key contracts within exchanges, for the cost of liquidity is seen as the dominant cost of transacting (Smith and Whaley 1994). Worldwide the growth and dominance of the major exchanges, such as Chicago Board of Trade, Chicago Mercantile Exchange and London International Financial Futures Exchange, continue, while medium-sized exchanges are merging (such as MATIF (Marche a Terme Internationale de France) and Deutsche

Terminboerse) or are strenuously cutting costs in an endeavour to survive (Sydney Futures Exchange). In the Asia-Pacific area several exchanges are candidates for future dominance of futures markets in the region.

This chapter investigates the hypothesis of increasing returns to liquidity in the Kuala Lumpur Stock Exchange (KLSE) Composite Index (CI) futures contract, the leading contract traded on KLOFFE. The KLSE CI contract, which is based on the prices of shares of 100 leading Malaysian companies, began trading on 15 December 1995; CI futures contracts are traded for the spot month, next month, and next two calendar quarterly months. The contract has a value of the CI multiplied by 100 ringgit, and is closed out by mandatory cash settlement, at final settlement value (which is a form of spot price), as defined by KLOFFE. The behaviour of liquidity costs on KLOFFE, in relation to turnover, is vital in attracting risk management capital to the exchange, and is therefore vital in determining the competitive position of the Malaysian derivatives market, both within Malaysia and externally.

This chapter discusses recent research on liquidity in futures markets and also the specification of the model employed to test the increasing returns hypothesis; then discusses the data, including issues of stationarity as well as estimation procedures, and presents and evaluates the results.

Recent research and model specification

Telser and Higinbotham (1977) argued that liquidity varies inversely with the standard deviation of market clearing prices. Recently, it has been argued that the standard deviation of observed price changes incorporates two factors: first it includes the response of prices to new information, which affects equilibrium prices; and second, it includes the effects of the bid–ask spread, which is the cost of liquidity (Wang et al. 1994). The more relevant spread is regarded as the effective or realised spread, rather than the quoted spread, because the effective spread is taken to be the true cost of transacting. The effective bid–ask spread is defined as the difference between the price at which a market maker buys (sells) a security and the price at which the market maker subsequently sells (buys) it (Smith and Whaley 1994, pp. 438–439). Wang et al. (1994, pp. 837–838) argued that the effective bid-ask spread varies negatively with competition among market makers, and directly with volatility and transaction size.

Unfortunately, without knowledge of dealers' records, the effective bid–ask spread cannot be observed, but must be estimated from price data. No ideal estimator of the effective spread has yet been established: Smith and Whaley (1994, pp. 439–441) review two commonly employed estimators, and introduce one of their own. The estimators reviewed by Smith and Whaley (1994) are first the serial covariance estimator, which has the formula:

$$S_1 = \sqrt{-\text{Cov}(\Delta P_t^0, \Delta P_{t-1}^0)} \qquad (16.1)$$

where S_1 = estimate of the effective bid–ask spread;
    ΔP_t^0 = change in observed price in period t.

If the covariance itself is positive, this estimator results in a complex number, and is impractical. The second estimator reviewed by Smith and Whaley (1994) is the mean absolute price change, which would capture the spread if the expected true price change was zero, and if the variance of true price changes were zero. While the first of these assumptions is reasonable in an efficient market, the second is not. Hence this estimator includes the bid–ask spread and the variance of true price changes, and therefore is biased upward. Smith and Whaley (1994, 441–443) introduce their 'method of moments' estimator, which assumes that observed price changes can be at the bid or at the ask, each with probability 0.5. This estimator is not without difficulty, because it assumes that expected true price changes are normally distributed with mean zero, and variance σ^2. Much evidence has accumulated, however, to suggest that daily price changes in futures markets are not normally distributed, but are leptokurtic (Harris 1987; Hsieh 1988; Hall et al. 1989).

In light of these difficulties it has been decided to employ the standard deviation of market clearing prices, as discussed by Telser and Higinbotham (1977) and used by Goss and Avsar (1999), as a measure of liquidity in this chapter. While this measure includes the effects of both new information and liquidity on prices, the liquidity factor is evidently the dominant component. It has been established (Smith and Whaley 1994, p. 442) that :

$$\sigma_{\Delta P}^2 = \sigma^2 + S^2 \qquad (16.2)$$

where $\sigma_{\Delta P}^2$ = variance of observed price changes;
    σ^2 = variance of true price changes;
    S = bid–ask spread.

In their estimation of bid–ask spreads in the S&P 500 Index futures contract on the Chicago Mercantile Exchange, with intra-day data, Smith and Whaley (1994, pp. 452–453) found that the spread accounts for 79.7 per cent of the variance of observed price changes, when all price data are utilised, and 94.7 per cent of that variance when traded prices only (and not quotations) are used. It seems reasonable, therefore, to proceed upon the assumption that liquidity costs can be well represented by the standard deviation of market clearing prices.

On the assumption that the distribution of market clearing prices is asymptotically normal, Telser and Higinbotham (1977, pp. 970, 976) argue that the standard deviation varies inversely with the square root of the number of transactions. This reasoning led Telser (1981, p. 17) to conclude that there are increasing returns to liquidity. As mentioned above, however, subsequent evidence indicates that the distribution of daily price changes in futures markets is leptokurtic. For this reason, a simple binomial model is used here to predict a direct relationship between the number of transactions and liquidity. If success is defined as buyer and seller each able to transact immediately at desired prices, the probability of success is given by the binomial distribution as

$$f(x) = \frac{n!}{x!(n-x)!} \, p^x q^{n-x} \qquad (16.3)$$

where x =   number of successes;
        n =   number of trials;
        p =   probability of success in a single trial;
        q =   probability of non-success.

It is clear from (16.3) that the probability of zero successes decreases as the number of trials increases; the probability of one or more successes, therefore, increases with n. It is assumed that there is an inverse relationship between the probability of success and the standard deviation of market clearing prices.

The hypothesised negative relationship between volume and standard deviation is given by

$$V_t = \alpha + \beta \, SD_t + e_t \qquad (16.4)$$

where V_t =   volume in period t for a given futures contract for all delivery months;
      SD_t =   standard deviation of daily prices, in period t, for a futures contract with maturity in t (see below: Data);
      α =   constant; $\beta < 0$ on the increasing returns hypothesis;
      e_t =   error term;
      t =   time in months.

For a large part of the sample period volume appears to exhibit near exponential growth, at least until 1998:08, and to take account of this phenomenon, the relationship in (16.4) is expressed in semi-long form as

$$\ln V_t = \alpha + \beta \, SD_t + e_t \qquad (16.4A)$$

Data, stationarity and estimation

In this section the data, tests for unit roots and co-integration and estimation procedures are discussed.

Data

Futures price data, supplied by KLOFFE, are CI last trade, daily prices for the spot month future, that is a futures contract with settlement on the last business day of the current month (the spot month contract is by far the most heavily traded contract). Monthly standard deviations are calculated from these daily prices. Volume data are numbers of contracts traded per month, for all CI futures contracts, and these data were obtained from the KLOFFE website (www.kloffe.com.my). Data were collected from the date of inception (15 December 1995) to the end of December 1999. It can be seen that after the launch period, turnover per month exhibits strong growth until end August 1998, when the effects of the Asian financial crisis evidently were felt. It is suggested, therefore, that the volume data exhibit three distinct sub-periods: the first is the launch period, to the end of April 1997, after which monthly volume first exceeds 20,000 contracts; second, there is the 'mature' period (1997:05 to 1988:08), during which volume continues to grow rapidly; third is the 'crisis' period (1988:09 to 1999:12), which exhibits a large negative shock from the currency crisis, and some recovery afterwards. These sub-periods are one, two and three and they contain 17, 16 and 16 monthly observations respectively. There will be occasion, in what follows, to refer to sub-periods one and two together, and this period will be referred to as sample A.

Stationarity

To avoid spurious regression results, it is necessary that the residuals of the estimating equation (16.4A) are stationary. This condition will be fulfilled if all variables in that equation are stationary (integrated $I(0)$), or if those variables are non-stationary, this condition will be fulfilled only if both variables are integrated of the same order, and are co-integrated. To investigate whether the variables in (16.44A) are stationary, unit root tests were conducted, using both Augmented Dickey–Fuller (ADF) and Phillips–Perron (PP) tests. Both these procedures test the null hypothesis of a single unit root against the alternative hypothesis that the series is stationary. For the variables employed in the model in this chapter, these tests produced essentially similar results, and where there is ambiguity the Phillips–Perron tests are preferred, because of their generally greater power (see Banerjee et al. 1993, p. 113). For reasons of space, the results of the Phillips–Perron tests only are reported, in Table 16.1, for sub-periods one, two, three and sample A. To allow for the low power of these tests (Evans and Savin 1981) and the small sample size, a ten per cent significance level has been employed. It will be seen that for sample A and sub-period one both variables ln V and SD are stationary, while for sub-period two both variables are $I(1)$. For sample A and sub-period one, therefore, estimation can proceed on the relationship in the form of (16.4A). For sub-period two the question is whether the two $I(1)$ variables are co-integrated. The Johansen maximum eigenvalue test (see Johansen 1988; Johansen and Juselius 1990), reported in Table 16.2, suggests that these variables are not co-integrated. (This test addresses the hypothesis that the number of co-integrating vectors m is at most equal to q, against the specific alternative $m \leq q + 1$ (where $q < n$, the number of $I(1)$ variables in the equation).) It can be seen from Table 16.2 that the hypothesis m = 0 is not rejected. Estimation of the relationship for sub-period two, therefore, will proceed with the variables in first difference form:

$$\Delta \ln V_t = \alpha + \beta \, \Delta SD_t + e_t \qquad (16.4B)$$

Table 16.1 shows that the first differences are stationary. For sub-period three Table 16.1 shows that ln V is I(1) while SD is stationary. To avoid spurious results for this sub-period, the relationship is estimated with ln V in first difference form:

$$\Delta \ln V_t = \alpha + \beta \, SD_t + e_t \qquad (16.4C)$$

As Table 16.1 shows, the first difference of ln V, for sub-period three, is stationary.

Table 16.1: Unit root tests: Phillips–Perron

Variable	Calculated test statistic	Ten per cent critical value	Order of integration
Sample A			
ln V	−5.0235	−3.2109	I(0)
SD	−2.8938	−2.6164	I(0)
Sub-period one			
ln V	−5.6443	−3.3086	I(0)
SD	−4.0281	−2.6745	I(0)
Sub-period two			
ln V	−1.7197	−2.6745	I(1)
SD	−1.6132	−2.6745	I(1)
Δ ln V	−4.6789	−2.6745	I(0)
Δ SD	−5.8652	−2.6745	I(0)
Sub-period three			
ln V	−2.2645	−2.6745	I(1)
Δ ln V	−4.4655	−2.6745	I(0)
SD	−3.1090	−2.6745	I(0)

Table 16.2: Johansen co-integration (maximum eigenvalue) test

Equation	Variables	Calculated test statistic	5 per cent critical value	No. of co-integrating vectors: m
Sub-period two (16.4A)	ln V_t, SD$_t$	24.1430 7.1203	25.32 12.25	m = 0 m ≤ 1

Estimation

Estimation of the appropriate form of the relationship for sub-periods one, two and three, in the presence of an endogenous regressor, is by instrumental variables (IV), in order to obtain consistent estimates.[1] For sub-period one, a correction for first order autocorrelation is required. Tests were conducted for the presence of ARCH effects in the residuals of these equations (see Engle 1982; 1983) and there was evidence of ARCH effects in the relationship for sample A only. These effects were represented by an EGARCH (1, 1) process, to capture the asymmetric relationship between innovations and volatility, the lag lengths being determined by general to specific modelling (see Nelson 1991; Maddala and Kim 1998, pp. 78, 191). As a consequence of this representation of volatility clustering, h_t, the conditional variance of e_t in (16.4A), is given by:

$$\ln(h_t) = \alpha_0\alpha_1 \left| \frac{e_{t-1}}{\sqrt{h_{t-1}}} \right| + \beta_1 \ln h_{t-1} + \gamma_1 \frac{e_{t-1}}{\sqrt{h_{t-1}}} \qquad (16.4AA)$$

In addition, an allowance was made for first order autocorrelation in the residuals of (16.4A), and, for sample A, equations (16.4A) and (16.4AA) were estimated by maximum likelihood (ML). The estimations referred to in this section were executed by Lilien et al. (1995).

Results

The results for the various sub-periods are discussed in this section under the headings coefficient estimates and evaluation of results.

Coefficient estimates

Table 16.3 provides the coefficient estimates, asymptotic t values, Durbin–Watson statistics, and number of observations for sub-periods one, two, three and sample A. It will be recalled that support for the hypothesis of increasing returns to liquidity requires that the estimate of β, in the relevant equation, is negative and significant. Table 16.3 shows that in sub-period one, the 'launch' period, and sub-period three, the 'crisis and recovery' period, the estimate of β is negative but insignificant. In these sub-periods, therefore, there is no clear support for the increasing returns hypothesis. In sub-period two, on the contrary, during which contract turnover exhibited strong growth, the estimate of β supports the view that costs of liquidity declined as the market expanded. This result is consistent with, and reinforces the tendency to, financial market concentration. The major policy implications of this outcome are first, that an identical contract traded elsewhere could be expected to fail, unless the promoters of an alternative exchange could persuade major participants on KLOFFE to trade elsewhere, and second, because the tendency of increasing returns to liquidity applies also to multiple contracts within exchanges, any highly substitutable contracts introduced on KLOFFE would not be expected to succeed. Further growth in the turnover of the KLSE CI futures contract, however, could be expected to lead to a further decline in liquidity costs.

Table 16.3: Coefficient estimates: Sub-periods one, two, three and sample A*

Sub-period (equation)	α	β	DW	T
Sub-period one	9.1934	−0.0017	2.3983	16
(16.4A) $\hat{\rho} = 0.5979$ (4.6170)	(26.4164)	(−0.1356)		
Sub-period two	0.0944	−0.0126	2.2711	16
(16.4B)	(1.1037)	(−1.9817)		
Sub-period three	1.5596	−0.0647	2.1487	16
(16.4C)	(0.5313)	(−0.5674)		
Sample A	10.9395	−0.0017	2.0891	32
(16.4A) $\hat{\rho} = 0.9522$ (75.9260)	(43.7859)	(−0.8826)		
(16.4AA)	α_0	α_1	β_1	γ_1
Sample A: Variance equation	0.4103	−0.6288	0.9583	−0.8387
	(2.2040)	(−3.7311)	(20.7966)	(−5.4020)

* Notes: Asymptotic t values are in parentheses.
Estimation is by IV for sub-periods one, two and three and by ML for sample A.
T is the number of observations.
ρ is the first order autocorrelation coefficient.
Sample A comprises sub-periods one and two.

The lack of clear support for the increasing returns hypothesis during the 'launch' period may be due to increasing trade size following inception. Wang et al. (1994, pp. 837–838) explain that liquidity costs increase with trade size, especially as the capacity of individual dealers is reached. The lack of support for the increasing returns hypothesis during the crisis and recovery period may be due to increased uncertainty following the currency crisis, which could lead to increased liquidity costs. These factors would tend to offset the tendency to increasing returns to liquidity during sub-periods one and three respectively.

Evaluation of results

For these results to be valid it is necessary that the residuals of the estimating equations for the various sub-periods are serially uncorrelated, stationary and normally distributed. Table 16.4 presents the results of a range of diagnostic tests on the residuals. The Ljung-Box Q Statistic, which is valid under IV estimation, tests the null hypothesis that all autocorrelation coefficients are zero, up to lag 12. The test statistic is distributed χ^2_{12} and suggests that there is no autocorrelation in the residuals, at 5 per cent level, for any of the sub-periods. The Phillips–Perron test addresses the null hypothesis of a single unit root in the residuals, and suggests, in all cases, that the residuals are stationary. The Jarque–Bera test addresses the null hypothesis that the residuals are normally distributed, and as Table 16.4 shows, in no case can this hypothesis be rejected. The diagnostic tests reported in Table 16.4, therefore, do not create any doubts about the validity of the results discussed above.

Table 16.4: Diagnostic tests on residuals

Test	Sub-period one	Sub-period two	Sub-period three	Sample A
Ljung-Box Q Statistic				
Calculated χ_{12}^2	11.689	8.9145	9.6287	13.807
Critical χ_{12}^2 (0.05)	21.026	21.026	21.026	21.026
Phillips–Perron Test				
Calculated PP Statistic	–4.9808	–4.1569	–4.3044	–7.7680
10 per cent critical value	–2.6829	–2.6829	–2.6829	–2.6181
Jarque–Bera Test				
Calculated test statistic	0.1893	1.5940	0.2107	1.4102
Probability value	0.9098	0.4507	0.9000	0.4941

Conclusion

Transactions costs on organised futures exchanges are dominated by costs of liquidity, which here are represented by the standard deviation of market clearing prices. A simple binomial model is used to derive the hypothesis that liquidity increases directly with the volume of transactions. This hypothesis of increasing returns to liquidity is investigated with daily data for the Kuala Lumpur Options and Financial Futures Exchange Composite Index futures contract for the spot month (most heavily traded), from inception (December 1995) to December 1999. Estimation of the relationship between standard deviation and volume is executed by instrumental variables, in the interests of consistent estimates with an endogenous regressor.

The results indicate that for the period of strong growth in turnover (1997:05 to 1998:08) there is clear support for the increasing returns hypothesis, with a significant negative relationship between standard deviation and volume. In the period from inception to 1997:04, however, and in the currency crisis and recovery period (from 1998:09) there is no clear support for the hypothesis of increasing returns to liquidity. The result for the strong growth period, however, is consistent with the tendency to concentration of world futures market activity.

The main policy implications of these results are: first, that duplicate KLSE CI futures contracts introduced elsewhere can be expected to fail (unless key KLOFFE traders can be attracted to another exchange); second, similar or highly substitutable share index contracts, introduced on KLOFFE or elsewhere, also could be expected to fail; and third, under conditions of continued growth in turnover of CI futures, further reductions in liquidity costs can be expected.

Endnotes

[1] For sub-period one (equation 16.4A) the instruments are $\ln V_{t-1}$, SD_{t-1}; for sub-period two (equation 16.4B) the instruments employed are $\Delta \ln V_{t-1}$, ΔSD_{t-1}, while for sub-period three (equation 16.4C) the instruments $\Delta \ln V_{t-1}$, SD_{t-1} were employed.

References

Banerjee, A., J. J. Dolado, J. W. Galbraith and D. F. Hendry (1993), *Co-Integration, Error Correction, and the Econometric Analysis of Non-Stationary Data*, Oxford: Oxford University Press.

Engle, R. F. (1982), 'Autoregressive conditional heteroskedasticity with estimates of the variance of U.K. inflation', *Econometrica*, 50, 987–1008.

—— (1983), 'Estimates of the variance of U.S. inflation based on the ARCH model', *Journal of Money Credit and Banking*, 15, 286–301.

Evans, G. B. A. and N. E. Savin (1981), 'Testing for unit roots: 1', *Econometrica*, 49, 753–779.

Goss, B. A. and S. G. Avsar (1998), 'Increasing returns to liquidity in futures markets', *Applied Economics Letters*, 5, 105–109.

—— (1999), 'Efficiency and liquidity in the electricity market: A preliminary analysis', in Mustafa Isreb (ed.), *Proceedings of the First International Power and Energy Conference*, Churchill: Monash University.

Hall, J. A., B. W. Brorsen and S. H. Irwin (1989), 'The distribution of futures prices: A test of the stable Paretian and mixture of normals hypotheses', *Journal of Financial and Quantitative Analysis*, 24 (1), 105–116.

Harris, L. (1987), 'Transaction data tests of the mixture of distributions hypothesis', *Journal of Financial and Quantitative Analysis*, 22 (2), 127–141.

Hsieh, D.A. (1988), 'The statistical properties of daily foreign exchange rates: 1974–83', *Journal of International Economics*, 24, 129–145.

Johansen, S. (1988), 'Statistical analysis of co-integration vectors', *Journal of Economic Dynamics and Control*, 12, 231–254.

Johansen, S. and K. Juselius (1990), 'Maximum likelihood estimation and inference on co integration—with applications to the demand for money', *Oxford Bulletin of Economics and Statistics*, 52, 169–210.

Lilien, D. M., R. Startz, S. Ellsworth, J. Noh and R. Engle (1995), *E Views 2.0*, California: Irvine.

Maddala, G. S. and I.-M. Kim (1998), *Unit Roots, Co-integration, and Structural Change*, Cambridge: Cambridge University Press.

Nelson, D. (1991), 'Conditional heteroskedasticity in asset returns: A new approach', *Econometrica*, 59, 347–370.

Smith, T. and R. E. Whaley (1994), 'Estimating the effective bid/ask spread from time and sales data', *Journal of Futures Markets*, 14, 437–455.

Telser, L. G. (1981), 'Why there are organised futures markets', *Journal of Law and Economics*, 24, 1–22.

Telser, L. G. and H. N. Higinbotham (1977), 'Organised futures markets: Costs and benefits', *Journal of Political Economy*, 85 (5), 969–1000.
Wang, G. H. K., R. J. Michalski, J. V. Jordan and E. J. Moriaty (1994), 'An intra-day analysis of bid-spreads and price volatility in the S&P 500 index futures market', *Journal of Futures Markets*, 14, 837–859.

17

'Asian values', moral communities and resistance in contemporary Malaysian politics

A.B. Shamsul

Introduction

In the realm of business management studies there has been a debate on the role of 'Asian values' in the context of the emergence and consolidation of what has been perceived as 'Asian management' models. This debate was conducted in the wake of the rise of the 'Asian tigers' including Malaysia. Malaysia's prime minister, Dr Mahathir Mohamed, and his then deputy, Anwar Ibrahim, made significant contributions to the deepening of this debate by elaborating on the role of 'Asian values' in the context of Malaysian 'business and economic experience'. They did this as an attempt to explain the economic success enjoyed by Malaysia from 1988 to 1997. Their contributions address mainly the non-economic aspects, namely, the social, cultural and political elements that underpinned the Malaysian success story. In short, Mahathir and Anwar argued that Asian values, which were once perceived as negative, were in fact critical in bringing about Malaysia's success in achieving its economic objectives and international competitiveness. Does this argument still hold after the economic crisis? The main aim of this chapter is to provide some answers to this question and to observe the different ways in which the Malaysian version of Asian values has shaped the country's attempt to regain its economic competitiveness in the context of Malaysia's contemporary cultural politics and resistance, and the state's apparent anti-liberalism stance (Henderson 2000).

Since the onset of the economic crisis in mid-1997 and the sacking of Anwar Ibrahim as Deputy Prime Minister, the Asian values debate has almost come to a halt everywhere. In this chapter I wish to have a second look at the Malaysian notion of Asian values and how it came to shape Malaysian 'cultural politics'—one that involves a power struggle for material wealth, ethnic dominance and cultural survival, upon which its past and future economic and business success have come to depend. In other words, Malaysian business is not only about business and commercial activities, but also about the business of politics and culture. The majority of successful business projects and ventures in Malaysia are also about the success of those involved in making sense of the Malaysian 'Asian values' paradigm and its internal non-business dynamics.

Is the 'Asian values' debate dead?

While many want to believe that the Asian values debate is dead, I believe that when the Asian economies recover, the debate will again occupy centre stage. This time it will focus on how Asian values provided Asians with the right ethical and moral basis to withstand suffering and enabled them to weather the crisis commendably. Indeed, I shall not be surprised if the reincarnation of the debate takes place in the USA, the land that has given birth to and popularised such ideas as the 'clash of civilisations', 'Japan as No.1' and 'the spirit of Chinese capitalism'.

However, my interest in the theme of Asian values comes from a slightly different angle than the usual. I'm interested in tracing some universal elements of human cultural practice and habits found in the social life of those embracing Asian values, and in particular, how resistance finds space amongst those who are supposedly community-oriented in their world views and how they then organise themselves to pursue their causes despite real and perceived obstacles. Even though my major works have been on peasant resistance and subaltern movements in Malaysia (Shamsul 1986; Scott 1986), in this chapter I am particularly interested in 'elite resistance', a form of intra-class struggle within the Malaysian elite and intelligentsia.

I sometimes wonder whether the children of the Malaysian peasants of the 1950s would still resort to the 'weapons of the weak' type of resistance, a social phenomenon brilliantly examined and elaborated by Scott (1986), or would simply hide behind the 'weapons of the meek' (my label for those resorting to poison, magic and charms), or if they would devise new devious and deceptive forms of resistance as a result of the availability of technology, such as the internet. I am also interested to discuss how this new form of resistance has given rise to 'moral communities', that is, informal social groups or networks of various kinds formed by a small group of individuals who are motivated by a broad but often idealistic social cause such as social justice. Indeed, from my observations, the formation of moral communities seems to be organisationally indispensable to the cause of elite resistance in Malaysia. Not surprising, parts of the 'moral communities' have, inevitably, become institutionalised in the form of NGOs.

I must mention that though the main empirical focus of the present discussion is the Malay-Muslim in Malaysia, I shall also touch upon the activities of the non-Malay, non-Muslims wherever relevant. However, I would like to begin with a general discussion of Asian values to give a sense of conceptual location for my own presentation on moral communities and 'resistance'.

Revisiting the 'Asian values' debate

It is often argued by commentators considering East Asian patterns of economic growth that the political economies of the territories have been successful because the character of the local societies is particularly appropriate to the pursuit of economic advancement. East Asian society is presented as family- and community-oriented and disciplined. These arguments are available within the general literature of social science and are advanced by European, American and East Asian scholars. The ways in which the arguments are made vary but there is an underlying distinction drawn between the community-oriented East and the individualistic West. It is in this context that the Asian values model emerged with a number of variants, such as the Confucianism variant, the 'Asian renaissance', and 'the spirit of Chinese capitalism'.

The Asian values model of East Asia supposedly consists of three main elements: family, kin and community, non-individualist orientation and discipline and social order. There has been a vibrant debate on the elements of the model, to which we shall now turn and in so doing take note some of the criticisms.

Family, kin and community

In the literature of colonial analysis and post-colonial development theory, the societies of East Asia were conceived as dual, plural and loosely-structured societies whilst the societies falling within the Chinese cultural sphere were characterised in terms of peasant forms of life lodged within strict social hierarchies. The wealth of social forms in East Asia is thus very large. However, the available characterisations have a series of recurrent themes. In all cases, it is suggested that the general nature of the social-institutional system of East Asia centres upon family and kin networks. The focus of the personal life of an individual is the family group, kin network and local community. It is within the family household that the routines of life are pursued, with kin networks as an additional sphere of activity and the community forming the routinely present sphere of collective order.

Some scholars have spoken of the moral resources of the peasant-centred 'little tradition' as a way of gesturing to the self-contained nature of peasant life. Thereafter, the moral schedules of wider authorities—religion or state—present themselves in the materials of the 'great tradition'. It would seem that the pre-contact form of life of the majority of people in the East Asia region was some variant of the model of household-centred peasant life, with more distant authorities making varying claims upon the people and thereby legitimising state intervention.

It is equally evident that these pre-contact patterns of social relationships have been radically remade over the long period of the shift to the modern world. The demands of an expansive industrial capitalism have drawn people into plantations, mines, colonial cities and more recently into the growing internationalised sphere of economic life via the operations of MNCs. In the more highly developed areas within the region the pattern of life is shifting to resemble that of the developed West, with increasing materialism and a diminution of received social forms and beliefs. Nonetheless, it would be wrong to anticipate a convergence upon an atomistic, materialistic individualism, the dystopia of an easily recognisable version of a possible Western future; rather, the development of the countries of East Asia will continue to entail the subtle reworking of received social patterns as the countries continue their shift into the modern world.

Non-individualist orientation

The East Asian model claims that family, kin networks and community are central social-institutional structures in the region. One consequence of this characterisation of social life is that the collectivity is prioritised over the individual. The way in which the matter has been dealt with so far makes this merely a practical report on the nature of the East Asian pattern of life. However, we can add two related lines of possible commentary: social theoretic, in particular the ontology of social life, where the resources of the sociological stream within the classical tradition would point to the social nature of humankind; and ethical, where the resources of the democratic philosophical stream within the classical tradition would point to the appropriateness of lodging practical moral reasoning and activity within the context of the relevant collectivity. In other words, it is possible to argue that the non-individualist form of life affirmed in the East Asian model is appropriate to the fundamental character of human social life.

In contrast, in classical liberal terms there are only individuals and families and the social world is thereafter a realm of contract. It is possible to review classical liberalism in favourable terms as the set of ideas that informed and legitimated the actions of the early English mercantile bourgeoisie in their struggles with feudal absolutism. However, the subsequent development of liberal societies has generated an atomistic expressive individualism that many regard as unsatisfactory, and the liberal tradition itself has come to be regarded as fundamentally misconceived.

The distinction between East Asia and the West can be made positively, in which case the former is lucky to have escaped the trials of Western individualism, or negatively, in which case East Asia is unfortunate to be mired in an anti-individualist traditional culture. It is also clear that this distinction can be read into a series of particular debates ranging from the style of political life, through forms of workplace organisation to patterns of children's behaviour and school performance.

Discipline and social order

A related theme in the literature is the putative continuance of social discipline and order in contrast to the West (again with the image of the USA central). The proponents of the model point to traditions of respect for family, for elders and for those in authority. All this is contrasted often quite explicitly with the individualistic, ill-disciplined and, by implication, declining West. It has been noted by some scholars that Western conservatives and neo-liberals affirm this image in order to propose the adoption of the schedule of practices in the West, a disciplined obedient and deferential population providing an equally obedient workforce. It is clear that these appeals to the East Asian model are exercises in ideological rhetoric, designed to advance domestic political agendas. However, it is also clear that the historical development experience of these territories has generatcd a different way of construing and ordering the relationship of the individual and broader society; one that does, in general, place more weight on the collectivity.

Critics of 'Asian values' model

Responding to the Asian values discourse, David Hitchcock (1997), for one, was motivated to undertake a survey for the Washington-based Center for Strategic and International Studies (CSIS). This survey was conducted in Singapore, Malaysia, Indonesia, Thailand, China, Korea and Japan in 1994. Without seeking to identify the different cultural foundations of the countries he visited, his findings showed a regular collective Asian versus American pattern in terms of personal and societal values and with regard to the 'most important' practices in governance. Typically, the Asians he interviewed scored highest on respect for authority, harmony, consensus, rights of society and orderly society, while the Americans emphasized personal freedom, individual rights, free expression, open debate, self reliance and non-discrimination.

The American component constitutes the usual components of the global-mainstream, liberal-democratic tradition, while the Asian component constitutes the stereotypical features of Asian values democracy. A distinctive feature of Asian values ideology is said to be the principle of duty and discipline on the part of the governed, which in turn is reinforced by 'an organic notion of state and society which is intimately associated with the common "good" of economic development' (Jayasuria 1997, p. 21). This notion appears to have had deep resonance within developing Asian societies, including among Malaysians, which in turn reinforces and further entrenched the governments' developmentalist ideologies.

In the foreword to Hitchcock's survey report, Francis Fukuyama credited Dr Mahathir Mohamed, the Prime Minister of Malaysia, and Lee Kuan Yew, the former Prime Minister of Singapore, for starting the debate on Asian values at the end of the 1980s. However, Fukuyama also noted that such prominent involvement by Asian leaders in the debate also created ambiguities, since it 'was propelled by actors with highly political motives, who were less interested in uncovering the real nature of value differences across societies than in scoring political points or legitimising their own policies' (Hitchcock 1997, p. vii).

Those who do not share the above explanations have suggested that we should begin our analysis of the society and culture in East Asia by pointing to the fact that the region is indeed a diverse one where the more affluent countries enjoy levels of living similar to those of the USA or Europe, whilst the poorer follow patterns of life more associated with the Third World. This has been shown by the 'human development index' constructed by UNDP (United Nations Development Program), which combines economic and social measures relating to human material and social achievement.

The critical analytical issue is that because in the territory of East Asia there are enormous differences in patterns of life, it is important to be able to grasp the detail. This concern for details, or 'the anthropological sense', is absent in the construction of the Asian values model.

'Asian values', 'moral communities' and 'resistance'

Perhaps my proposed presentation would contribute to providing the anthropological sense that seems to be missing in the Asian values debate. Moreover I wish to explore how the so-called collective-community-oriented culture of the Asians could foster the formation of 'moral communities', launching a kind of resistance aiming at bringing about social justice, through whatever means. After all, resistance was never in the Asian values inventory list.

The motivation for this exploratory investigation comes from the realisation that in most of the discussions on Asian values, including those addressing to the discourse in Malaysia, there seems to be no interest at all in how the 'Asians' have responded or organised various forms of responses to repressive governments. There has hardly been any discussion on the massive student and labour protests in Korea and Thailand in the context of Asian values. It seems it is not really part of Asian values to oppose the government, perhaps because government is viewed as a kind of 'Asian collectiveness'. If there has been resistance by anyone, it would then be considered, in the 'individual-collective dichotomy' of the Asian values debate, as an exercise of idiosyncratic self-assertion. This is, of course too simplistic a conclusion on the nature of resistance amongst Asians, fulfilling more the needs of a methodology than explaining the social reality. Perhaps we also need to explore the nature of the resistance and how it leads to the formation of moral communities, particularly amongst the middle class in Asia.

In the following discussion I shall be referring to the Malaysian case as my main empirical source. What I wish to explore is how middle-class

Malaysians, of all ethnic groups but led by a group of relatively open-minded, young and religious Malay Muslims, managed to form cross-ethnic alliances that have primarily taken the form of informal gatherings and social networks and that aim to oppose the state, its rule of law and its public policies they consider unjust and corrupt.

I am also interested to explore how Islamic-Malay values, on the one hand, became the source for solidarity-making amongst the fragmented interest-oriented groups in Malaysia, and, on the other hand, motivated the formation of a nationwide resistance movement. This is not to deny the influence of the universal democratic, civil society and human rights concerns that have been critical in the formation of many Malaysian NGOs, organisations that have now become part of the resistance movement. It is the role of a local influence (read 'Asian values') that fostered the movement that attracts my attention more.

What is more significant in this context is the fact that the state, against which the resistance has been mounted, has also claimed that it is promoting Asian values. It is the contestation of meanings and practical articulations of Asian values that is of great interest and significance to this chapter. Of course, it could also be framed in the wider context of the 'anti-liberalism' that seems to dominate the thinking amongst the elite and intelligentsia in both developed and developing economies.

'Asian values' and resistance in Malaysia

The competing perspectives and contestation

Analytically, and in a popular sense, there are at least two major perspectives, or interpretations, on the practical articulation of Asian values in Malaysia. The first, I would call the 'authority-defined' perspective and the second the 'everyday-defined' one (Shamsul 1996, pp. 2–6). The former is based on observation and interpretation, an approach usually adopted by those in the position of authority. In this chapter we shall highlight the role the state and state leaders who, using existing institutional structures, have formulated and implemented policies claimed to be informed by the Asian values concept. The everyday-defined perspective has been adopted mainly by those at the grassroots, popularly described as 'ordinary people', informed or motivated mainly by experience, both collective and personal. The experience, good or bad, happy or unhappy, has often motivated individuals to create formal and informal networks or collectives, such as the NGOs, in order to make themselves heard and their requests attended to, by the state and others.

Authority-defined perspective

Internationally, the government is anxious to represent Malaysia as the 'friendly face of Islam'. It also wishes Malaysia to be regarded as a stable country, profitably engaged in the global economy, industrialized, information technology savvy, and with a forward looking agenda, namely, 'Vision 2020' outlined by Mahathir in 1991. Mahathir envisions that by 2020 Malaysia will be a fully 'united Malaysian nation', or *Bangsa Malaysia*. However, it is also a fact that Mahathir is the leader of UMNO (United Malays National Organization), and that UMNO has remained the dominant political force in Malaysia since its formation in 1946. It follows that UMNO, the dominant political party in the present ruling National Front coalition, would be the main influence in charting the nation's course and identity.

Additionally, by virtue of its dominant position in the Malaysian political system, UMNO is responsible for maintaining ethnic harmony and the general good of this multi-ethnic, multi-cultural, multi-ideology and multi-religious nation. It is therefore critical that UMNO strives, at all times, for *muhibbah* (goodwill), or cultural and religious tolerance and accommodation. It is only then that UMNO can achieve its notion of good governance. Nonetheless, the UMNO leadership has continued to call upon the Malays, as 'the definitive people' of the nation, to maintain their traditional and legitimate political leadership through educational achievements and by embracing technological advances. Malays are also exhorted to reform their culture and society towards greater conformity with Islamic teachings, particularly those aspects that are progressive in terms of economic and intellectual achievements (Hussin Mutalib 1993).

From the early 1980s, Mahathir's government initiated a gradual Islamisation policy, initially through the programme 'Assimilation of Islamic Values into Administration'. The policy stresses the universal values of good character, fair and accountable leadership, and enlightened attitudes that are the hallmarks of Islam, as well as being recognised universally. This was followed by the establishment of Islamic institutions and the implementation of Islamic-oriented policies in the education, media, welfare, banking and financial spheres. Soon it permeated all areas of state-sponsored activity.

For the then Deputy Prime Minister, Anwar Ibrahim, these policies were essentially 'guided by moral precepts and faith reawakened'. In other words, the intention was to create an ethical political system with an Islamic thrust that would facilitate the emergence of a responsible and accountable civil society that also would be responsive to the government's agenda. Specifically, it meant the creation of a *masyarakat madani* (civil society) that promises not only greater governmental accountability but also greater scope for fundamental liberties, and so a greater role for responsible participation by the citizens. Otherwise, the intention appeared to be a continuation of the original democratic polity with no change to its overall secularist structure and orientation.

On the surface Anwar's notion seems to be in tune with Mahathir's agenda for Malay intellectual and economic development via progressive Islamic values. In his book *The Challenge* (1986) and in his 1997 speech at the 40th UMNO General Assembly entitled *Menebus Maruah Bangsa* To Reaffirm Malay Dignity, Mahathir clearly outlined his political philosophy that the Malays can only progress if they live out the true Islamic spirit of resilience, high achievement, self-confidence and humbleness before God. This has been echoed and amplified by other government and UMNO leaders at all levels. In the 1980s and for most of the 1990s this new Islamic thrust by UMNO was bolstered by the entry of members of the Islamic revivalist youth movement called ABIM (*Angkatan Belia Islam Malaysia* or Malaysian Islamic Youth Movement) into UMNO, following the move by ABIM's leader, Anwar Ibrahim, who joined UMNO in 1982.

These new UMNO members were imbued with the spirit of modernist, progressive and development-oriented Islam that Anwar's leadership had inculcated. They were also committed to *dakwah*, or calling others towards the appreciation of Islam, in the moderate but firm and incremental approach. They have been generally credited for transforming UMNO from a 'secular Malay-nationalist political party' to a moderate, progressive, modernist and developmentalist Islamic Malay national movement. It would seem that UMNO has more or less embraced the spirit of the 1970s' and early 1980s' Islamic revivalism but stops short of propagating an Islamic state (Chandra Muzaffar 1987; Zainah Anwar 1997). This is directly related to the concept of 'moderate and friendly' Islam that it upholds and from which it hopes to ensure continuous Malay majority support for it, as well as create favourable impressions of Malaysia internationally.

However, there is the other side of Malaysian society to take into account, the non-Malay and non-Muslim ethnic groups that constitute approximately 45 per cent of the population. Their Asian values are based mainly on the religious and cultural traditions of Confucianism, Hinduism, Buddhism and other indigenous sub-cultures and belief systems. Traditionally, they have refrained from participating, at least publicly, in discourses that relate to the role of Islam in the Malaysian political, social and economic spheres. One view is that 'they are hesitant to speak out about the process of incremental Islamisation, because as they are unqualified, it would be presumptuous and even sacreligious ... to criticize or show concern about Islam' (Hussin Mutalib 1993, p. 121). In addition Malays are deemed to be sensitive to discussion of their religion by others. The non-Muslims therefore adopt the culture of public silence on the subject.

However, the government has sponsored a series of academic civilizational dialogues mainly between Islam and Confucianism. The fact that Islam and Confucianism have no history of direct clashes and share some universal values and that Confucianist teachings continue to have a hold over a majority of Chinese Malaysians made it a politically pertinent dialogue. Serious consideration appears to have been given toward expanding and institutionalising this dialogue. The Centre for Civilisational Dialogue was set up in the country's oldest university, Universiti Malaya, with Dr Chandra Muzaffar, a well-known academic, social analyst and human rights activist, as its director. The motivation behind institutionalising this dialogue was, perhaps, as observed by Anwar that 'the Asian at heart is persona religious. Faith and religious practice, not confined to the individual, permeate the life of the community' (Anwar Ibrahim 1997, pp. 4–5).

At any rate, the Asian values that prevail in Malaysia arguably are those which have been promoted by UMNO. They are in essence Islamicist in orientation and resonate with Malay political principles. They are largely inspired and guided by the political thinking of Mahathir Mohamad and Anwar Ibrahim. In turn, these values determine important salient features of 'democracy according to our own mould' (Mahathir Mohamad 1991, p. 12). Considering that the majority of Malaysians are Malays and Muslims, these values are widely accepted by Malaysians and may be considered as the basis of the regime's legitimacy to a certain degree. Moreover, their realisation in the form of state policies are carefully moderated in order to safeguard the intricate pluralism that exists in Malaysia.

Everyday-defined perspective

However, this top-down definition of Malaysian democracy and civil society based on the Malaysian mould (read Malaysian Asian values) has not gone unchallenged. There are Malaysians, including those in the NGOs, who are critical of this state project and its delimiting of democratic participation for all.

It is worth examining the cycle of opposition and cooperation between the various NGOs and the Malaysian government since the 1970s and in particular the central role of ABIM and its leader Anwar Ibrahim, not only before and after he joined the ruling party but also after he was sacked in September 1998. This will also give us some sense of the nature of intra-elite and elite-grassroots resistance within the Malaysian society and the kind of cross-ethnic alliances and moral communities that can be formed to resist and adapt to the strong state.

Indeed, in the end it leads to the formation of what I would call the 'new politics' movement in Malaysia, one that is not concerned simply with winning votes and general elections but more with openly articulating differences, plurality, and dissent. It was a nationwide 'politics of resistance', a struggle for social justice, and therefore an attempt to transform 'civil society' to 'democratic civility'. The movement is based on a variety of interests, largely non-communal and non-class in nature. Indeed, its survival in the last three decades has been dependent on maintaining the continuous formation of 'moral communities', mostly across ethnicities and cultures.

ABIM, since its inception in 1969, has been a powerful and well-organised group consisting mainly of modernist Malay-Muslim ex-student leaders led by Anwar Ibrahim (Monutty 1990). It demonstrated its powerful influence amongst students and youths during the December 1974 student uprising, when the streets of Kuala Lumpur turned into a 'sea of demonstrators', many times bigger and more violent than what we have seen live on CNN recently. In fact, thousands of them were arrested and charged in court for illegal gathering. Anwar Ibrahim, along with other student leaders and some academics, was arrested and detained without trial under the Internal Security Act (ISA).

Many analysts and politicians, including Mahathir, who was then the Minister of Education, saw this development and concluded that it was simply student politics. It may have been so at the surface and in its outward articulation, but it was certainly more than just that. It was the early beginnings of the 'new politics' in Malaysia, a nascent one, which has survived through the formation of cross-ethnic alliances and moral communities, some of which became institutionalised or formalised, while others remained as informal groupings or social networks and became the microsites of resistance, in this case of an intra-elite kind.

Outside the Malay political realm, but in a quieter mode, NGOs began to mushroom in Malaysia in the 1970s, representing a variety of interests, ranging from the protection of consumers, the environment, urban squatters, the Orang Asli, abused wives and children, to those advocating human rights, social justice, academic freedom, peace issues, legal issues and social welfare concerns (Eldridge 1991; Lim Teck Ghee 1995; Gurmit Singh 1987).

Around thirty of these different interest groups, consisting of Malays and non-Malays, men and women of different classes, writers, artists and professionals, formed an informal alliance in 1981, the Action Committee Against the Societies Act, with Anwar Ibrahim as the chairperson (Monutty 1990, p. 252). The Action Committee was to launch campaigns, locally and internationally, to oppose the amendments to the Societies Act, as a result of which registered formal societies and organisations are regrouped into 'social' and 'political' societies. Such legislation has been introduced under the emergency situation that Malaysia is supposed to be experiencing (Rais Yatim 1995). A few people from this group eventually established the Centre for Peace Initiatives (CENPEACE), with Fan Yew Teng, an ex-Democratic Action Party's Member of Parliament and human rights activist, as its founding executive director. CENPEACE has since been involved in activities related to civil society concerns.

Even though Anwar Ibrahim entered 'old' mainstream politics when he joined UMNO in 1982, his relationship with the groups within the new politics remained strong. The ABIM-led social network continues to maintain various forms of cross-ethnic alliances and conduct numerous informal activities of a capacity-building type aimed at resisting or opposing any state policies perceived as corrupt or unjust.

In fact, in the new position he was able to assist these groups, so that the new politics was able to survive and flourish at the fringe of mainstream politics. Anwar, as a finance minister, was able to contribute indirectly to the strengthening of the financial position of the groups through various means, including tax relief for writers and artists on the royalties they received, allocating funds from the government budget for NGOs, and getting international funding agencies (such as the Konrad Adeneur Foundation and Friedrich Ebert Stiftung) and Malaysian-based multinational organisations and financial institutions, and successful Malay entrepreneurs in the corporate world to make generous donations.

He introduced and promoted at the national level the concept of *masyarakat madani* (a Muslim version of civil society), arguing that Muslims, as individuals, not unlike the individual in the Western notion of civil society, have rights in the eyes of Allah, as documented clearly in the *Qur'an*, which must be respected and protected at all costs. He also repeatedly emphasised that the concept and practice of *masyarakat madani* is deeply rooted in the nation of *keadilan sosial*, or social justice. Through CENPEACE and, especially, through an ABIM think-tank called Institut Kajian Dasar (IKD), or the Institute of Policy Studies, the concepts of *masyarakat madani* and *keadilan sosial* were promoted nationwide in numerous workshops in order to reach a wider audience of all ethnic groups, classes and interests. Anwar also initiated a Malaysian version of the Peace Corps, called SALAM, with the major aim of sending young Malaysians abroad as volunteers. At the intellectual level, he encouraged what he called 'inter-civilisational' dialogue, both at the national and international level, such as at the Islam–Confucianism Conference in 1994. In fact, the Centre for Civilisational Dialogue was intended to serve this intellectual interest. Anwar, too, published his speeches and writings (Anwar 1996; 1997).

So between 1970 and 1997, we saw the rise of the 'new politics' in Malaysia, one that is interest-oriented, largely non-communal and non-class-based. It articulated itself and survived mostly through a political culture that spawned the formation of a series of moral communities. It is no surprise, therefore, that it was initiated in the form of a fragmented movement, if it could be characterised as a movement, struggling and pushing to create a political space. It was fragmented because of its 'now-you-see-now-you-don't' character, because it existed at the fringe, because each of the different groups appeared publicly representing a different cause and voicing different issues, because we got it mixed up with the opposition political parties, and because analytically observers like us were trapped in the 'old politics' mode, looking for ethnicity and class elements, which of course were present but not central to the movement.

Resistance as an Asian Value

On 2 September 1998, the informal 'new politics' movement came alive again when its leader Anwar Ibrahim left the bandwagon of the old politics. The old politics had been dominated by powerful institutional bureaucratic and state structures (political parties, the parliament, the police, and so on) and issues related to the modernisation project (expensive mega-projects, cronyism and nepotism, bailouts and many more), could not care less about environmental issues, gender issues and abused wives (since 1970, none of these issues has been listed on the agenda of UMNO General Assembly, nor mentioned in Mahathir's speeches), and was motivated by unbridled entrepreneurship greed.

The leaders of the various fragmented groups gathered around their dethroned leader, Anwar Ibrahim, every day and every night at every opportunity. They occupied numerous web pages. They rallied and received transnational support, almost from anyone who had a grudge against Mahathir or Malaysia. The voices that were heard through the CNN, the internet and various other sources, were not simply pro-Anwar or anti-Mahathir, they were the voice of the makers of the new politics in Malaysia, a mass politics of dissent, perhaps populist, more interested in creating space to express discontent of all kinds than winning votes. They are not on the fringe any more they are in the middle, together with the mainstream, old politics, trying to carve out a permanent niche.

Indeed, *reformasi* is the slogan that united the fragments, from near and afar, in the Malaysian new politics movement. This movement is simultaneously local and global; local in initiatives and ideas but global in terms of support and ideas too. It survived and was sustained through what I would term as political culture of moral communities that helped the movement to shape and reshape itself according to the intensity of state coercion, in a kind of political tango.

Since April 1999, a large component of the *reformasi* movement members have worked to set up a political party called Parti Keadilan National, or the National Justice Party. The party performed credibly in the Malaysian general elections of 29 November 1999. We shall be watching where it is heading from here on.

What is significant in the success of the *reformasi* movement thus far, viewed from the everyday-defined approach, is the fact that it has emerged not from a revolutionary tradition of Marx, Lenin, Mao Ze Dong or Ho Chi Minh, but from within the sphere of Islam and Islamic values, which in Malaysia has been the basis of Malay 'Asian values'. This is contrary to the kind of 'Asian values' discussed by academics, or those promoted by the Japanese management system or advanced by Lee Kuan Yew or indeed favoured by Mahathir himself, because there is space for resistance and difference. Whether one would like to call it 'civil society' or 'social justice' movement, even a pro-liberal or anti-liberal one, the fact remains that the values that the Malaysian *reformasi* movement espouses have emerged from within, and have a strong Islamic influence.

The state of play: In lieu of a conclusion

Politics similar to the new politics in Malaysia have also developed in the developed countries that have enjoyed economic success and social benefits. Such politics have been called, by the German sociologist Ulrich Beck, 'subpolitics' (Beck 1997), where personality and politics fuse and develop into multiple trajectories but unite in opposition to the existing dominating state. Although its methods and agendas are contemporary, almost existentialist, and its appeal is popular, it is increasingly attracting and drawing mass support from the same political constituency that the old politics depended upon.

This emerging form of movement or social organisation, found not only in the developed but also in the developing and underdeveloped economies, has been called by Henderson (2000, p. 3) 'new millennium collectivism'. Interestingly, he also noted that there is a common presumption within this collectivism that 'the existence of large disparities (within the society) provides proof, or at least evidence, of remediable injustice. In combination with the alarmist consensus, this forms the main doctrinal basis for anti-liberalism 2000'. In most cases the 'market' has always been the bogeyman. Thus, to this new movement, interventionist measures and programmes have been perceived as solutions to control the 'unfettered markets'. Ironically, these recommendations are no different, at least in principle, to those already put in place by the state.

In the Malaysian context the new politics have emerged and survived, for the last three decades, based on the political culture of moral communities formation described earlier, conducted through a series of cross-ethnic alliances, combining as it were the various Asian values orientations and subsequently launching nationwide resistance that culminated in the formation of a *reformasi* movement in Malaysia. Part of this movement has been become a political party, Parti Keadilan Nasional (National Justice Party), but other components continue as NGOs or informal social collectives, or moral communities.

Since the new movement seemed more interested in seeing a 'more transparent and accountable as well as a less corrupt government' and less interested in initiating any major structural changes, it is by default promoting an approach not dissimilar to that of the government it opposes. To what extent this new movement will remain the inverse of the state will be interesting to observe.

Bibliography

Anwar Ibrahim (1996), *The Asian Renaissance*, Singapore: Times Books International.

—— (1997), 'Islamic Renaissance', *Islamic Herald*, 18 (1), 4–5.

Beck, Ulrich (1997), *Reinvention of Politics*, Cambridge: Polity Press.

Chandra Muzaffar (1987), *Islamic Resurgence in Malaysia*, Petaling Jaya: Fajar Bakti.

Crouch, Harold (1996), *Government and Society in Malaysia*, London and Ithaca: Cornell University Press.

Eldridge, Philip (1991), 'Reflections on non-governmental organisations and social movements in Malaysia', paper presented at the 7th Malaysia Society Colloquium, University of Melbourne, 4–6 October.

Gurmit Singh, K. S. (1987), *Malaysians Know Your Rights*, Petaling Jaya: Fajar Bakti.

Henderson, David (2000), 'Anti-liberalism 2000', IEA website: www.iea.org.uk/

Hitchcock, David (1997), *Factors Affecting East Asian Views of the United States: In Search for Common Ground*, Washington DC: CSIS.

Hussin Mutalib (1993), *Islam in Malaysia: From Revivalism to Islamic State*, Singapore: Singapore University Press.

Jayasuria, Kanishka (1997), 'Asian values as reactionary modernisation', *NIASnytt*, 4, 19 27.

Lim Teck Ghee (1995), 'Nongovernmental organisations in Malaysia and regional networking', in Tadashi Yamamoto (ed.), *Emerging Civil Society in the Asia Pacific Community*, Singapore: ISEAS.

Mahathir Mohamad (1986), *The Challenge*, Petaling Jaya: Pelanduk.

—— (1991), 'Malaysia: The way forward', paper presented at the Inaugural Meeting of the Malaysian Business Council, Kuala Lumpur, 28 February.

—— (1997), 'Menebus Maruah Bangsa', speech at the official opening of the UMNO's 40th Assembly, Kuala Lumpur, September.

Mahathir Mohamad and Shintaro Ishihara (1995), *The Voice of Asia: Two Leaders Discuss the Coming Century*, translated by Frank Baldwin, Tokyo: Kodansha and Kinokuniya.

Milne, R. S. and D. K. Mauzy (1999), *Malaysian Politics under Mahathir*, London: Routledge.

Monutty, Mohammad Nor (1990), 'Perception of Social Change in Contemporary Malaysia: A Critical Analysis of ABIM's Role and its Impact among Muslim Youth', PhD thesis, Temple University, USA.

Rais Yatim (1995), *Executive Power in Malaysia: A Study of Executive Supremacy*, Kuala Lumpur: Endowment.

Scott, James (1986), *Weapons of the Weak: Everyday Forms of Peasant Resistance*, New Haven: Yale University Press.

Shamsul A. B. (1986), *From British to Bumiputera Rule: Local Politics and Rural Development in Peninsular Malaysia*, Singapore: Institute of Southeast Asian Studies.

—— (1996), 'Debating about identity in Malaysia: A discourse analysis', *Tonan Ajia Kenkyu (Southeast Asian Studies)*, 34 (3), 476–499.

—— (2000a), 'Development and democracy in Malaysia: A comment on its socio-historical roots', in Hans Antlov and Tak-Wing Mo (eds), *The Cultural Construction of Politics in Asia*, Copenhagen: NIAS and Curzon.

—— (2000b), 'Redefining cultural nationalism in multiethnic Malaysia: A recent observation', *Inter-Asia Cultural Studies*, 1 (1), 169–171.

—— (2000c), 'Making sense of politics in contemporary Malaysia: Resisting popular interpretation', in Ng Chee Yuen and Charla Griffy-Brown (eds), *Trends and Issues in East Asia 2000*, Tokyo: IDRI and FASID.

Zainah Anwar (1987), *Islamic Revivalism in Malaysia: Dakwah among the Students*, Petaling Jaya: Pelanduk.

Index

Printed and bound by CPI Group (UK) Ltd, Croydon, CR0 4YY

23/04/2025

14660984-0003